MIGRANT WORKERS IN JAPAN

Japanese Studies
General Editor: Yoshio Sugimoto

Images of Japanese Society: *Ross E. Mouer and Yoshio Sugimoto*
An Intellectual History of Wartime Japan: *Shunsuke Tsurumi*
A Cultural History of Postwar Japan: *Shunsuke Tsurumi*
Beyond Computopia: *Tessa Morris-Suzuki*
Constructs for Understanding Japan: *Yoshio Sugimoto and Ross E. Mouer*
Japanese Models of Conflict Resolution: *S. N. Eisenstadt and Eyal Ben-Ari*
Changing Japanese Suburbia: *Eyal Ben-Ari*
The Rise of the Japanese Corporate System: *Koji Matsumoto*
Science, Technology and Society in Postwar Japan: *Shigeru Nakayama*
Group Psychology of the Japanese in Wartime: *Toshio Iritani*
Enterprise Unionism in Japan: *Hirosuke Kawanishi*
Social Psychology in Modern Japan: *Munesuke Mita*
The Origin of Ethnography in Japan: *Minoru Kawada*
Social Stratification in Contemporary Japan: *Kenji Kosaka*
Sociology and Society of Japan: *Nozomu Kawamura*
Diversity in Japanese Culture and Language: *John C. Maher and Gaynor Macdonald*
Difference and Modernity: Social Theory and Contemporary Japanese Society: *John Clammer*
Migrant Workers in Japan: *Hiroshi Komai*

MIGRANT WORKERS IN JAPAN

Hiroshi Komai

Translated by
Jens Wilkinson

Routledge
Taylor & Francis Group
LONDON AND NEW YORK

First published 1993 by
Kegan Paul International

2 Park Square, Milton Park, Abingdon, Oxon OX14 4RN
711 Third Avenue, New York, NY 10017, USA

*Routledge is an imprint of the Taylor & Francis Group,
an informa business*

First issued in paperback 2016

British Library Cataloguing in Publication Data
A catalogue record for this book is available from the British Library

ISBN 978-1-138-98106-5 (pbk)
ISBN 978-0-7103-0499-5 (hbk)

Contents

Tables and Figures

Maps

Preface to the English Edition

I am delighted that this English edition will be able to appear, exactly five years after I began writing the original Japanese manuscript. The issue of foreign workers in Japan has already reached a turning point, as they are quickly changing from a flow into a group of settled residents. This change has been accompanied by a great deal of research in Japan, but there have been precious few attempts to grasp the problem in a unified manner, and this book represents such an attempt.

A significant amount of the data which appears in this book comes from my own intensive field research. Doing on-the-spot research on foreign workers is made very difficult by the fact that many have been placed into a position of illegality. In particular, it has been almost impossible to conduct surveys on actual numbers. I am certain, however, that the results of in-depth interviews presented in this book make up for those deficiencies.

In addition, one of my goals was to gather a comprehensive list of information on the issue of foreign workers which appeared in research, from government agencies, and from newspaper and magazine articles. At the end of the book I have made a list of these sources. Much of the material is in Japanese, and I hope it can be of assistance to researchers with Japanese ability.

I should note that in the Japanese edition I included a chapter on the situation of foreign workers in the United States and Western Europe, but it has been left out of this edition since much of the material is available in other languages.

I have strong expectations that this book will be of use in providing the world with a view of the situation foreign workers face in Japan. In addition to that, however, I have a deep desire for this book to become a contribution to debates within the global community on the shared concern over international responses to the movements of immigrants. I believe that the main focus of this international movement must be to form a network of NGOs, which includes the immigrant workers themselves, which can straddle the source and accepting countries, and that the main goal must be to protect the human rights of immigrants and of undocumented persons.

Because I am Japanese, arranging for an English edition of this book presented me with great difficulties. Japanese social science and sociology have a history going back more than 100 years to the Meiji Restoration, and there have been important achievements. In spite of this long history, however, precious few works have been translated into English or other foreign languages, and the import of ideas has long overshadowed their export.

One of the major reasons behind this state of affairs is the lack of motivation for Japanese scholars to publish their research results abroad, and another is the closed and self-sufficient nature of the Japanese publishing market. To get to the bottom of the matter, we can point to the fact that, for most Japanese, writing a manuscript in English is next to impossible. To Japanese, for whom English is a difficult foreign language, expressing ourselves in that language is a difficult task. In spite of this, there is very little social support given to the task of translating Japanese materials in English, and scholars are often left with no choice but to bear this burden themselves.

This situation has also been aggravated by the lack of native English speakers who are able to fully understand Japanese. In view of this, it was a great good fortune for me to have been able to meet Jens Wilkinson, who translated this book. A graduate of the State University of New York, he is fond enough of Japan to have decided to settle here permanently. His comprehension of Japanese is impeccable, and I must admit there are even sections of the book which are clearer in English than in the original Japanese. He seems at the forefront of a young generation of foreigners who have broken through the wall presented by the Japanese language. I am certain that the future will see an increasing number of such people, and that as a result we will see increasing exports of the results of the work of Japanese scholars.

I would like, in addition, to use this space to thank the following persons who provided invaluable assistance in this project: Junko Yamaka, from Lingua Guild, Inc., a translation company, for checking the manuscript; my research assistant Tae Michiue, who took on the tedious task of checking the English names of organizations and sources as well as performing general editorial work; Akio Ishii, the president of Akashi Shoten, which published the Japanese edition, for his enthusiastic consent for the project; and above all Yoshio Sugimoto, professor at La Trobe University in Australia, for presenting me with the opportunity for this English edition and for the valuable assistance that he gave so generously.

Hiroshi Komai
June 1994

Preface

In my early childhood I had the experience of becoming a repatriated citizen, or a stranger in my own land. At the age of just three months I was taken by my mother to Dalian, China (present-day Lu-ta, Liaoning Province, which was at that time a part of Manchukuo, Japan's puppet kingdom in northern China), where I found myself at the end of the war. We went there to join my father, who had been drafted into the Japanese Army. He was captured by the Soviets, interned in Siberia as a prisoner of war, and was only later repatriated. It is not the intention in this book, however, to speak of the suffering that my family experienced in the former Japanese colony at the end of the war, and particularly what we experienced in the immediate postwar period. I should say, however, that what impressed me most about that period of my life was the unbelievable cruelty with which Japanese society welcomed us back – my mother, my brother and sisters, and six-year-old me, who had come back with such difficulty, and how they tried to reject us as 'foreign elements.'

Dalian was a cosmopolitan port city with an exuberant atmosphere of culture. Undoubtedly the fact that I grew up there habituated me to that cultural fragrance. To my Japanese contemporaries, who had grown up in a society where conformity and the rejection of difference were cardinal virtues, I could only be an object of ridicule and attack. To make things worse, my family, who had lost everything with the end of the war, was forced to live a precarious existence. As a repatriate, I continued to live as an alien in my own country. In other words, I had crossed over to China as an immigrant, and had then come back to Japan, again as an immigrant.

The surveys I've done on the labor and living conditions of foreign workers have brought back vivid images of my own early childhood. Most of these people find their way into Japan as unwelcome foreigners, offer what they can, their cheap labor, and are forced into a daily encounter with a perverse society that seems to pride itself on being monoracial. One of the major motives that drove me to write this book was the feeling of sympathy that I, as one 'foreigner,' feel toward other foreigners who have been forced to come and live in this society.

This book is based on a series of 25 essays that began running in the August 22, 1989 issue of the Japanese monthly magazine *Economist* (published by Mainichi Shimbunsha), and ended in the March 20, 1990 issue. However, in the period following the publication of that series there have been many rapid changes in the situation of foreign workers in Japan – the 1990 revision of the Immigration Control Act, the influx of Nikkeijin (Latin Americans of Japanese descent), and the first hints of an acceptance of foreign labor under the 'trainee' system. As I absorbed this new information, I began to feel that it was necessary to rewrite the manuscript completely. In addition, the contents have been updated to cover events up until August, 1992. I should also note that I have given false names to all the foreign workers who appear in the book, and have dispensed with all honorific titles, (i.e. Mr. or Ms.). [Translator's note: As is the convention in many English writings on Japan, the order of Japanese names has been rearranged to fit English standards, i.e. the personal name appears first, followed by the family name.]

I think it is necessary to give a brief explanation of how it is that I came to write the series of essays for the *Economist*. In the past I have conducted several surveys on the situation of immigrant groups throughout the world, including Chinese in Thailand, Samoans in Hawaii, Sikhs in Toronto, Canada, and Japanese in Brazil, and as an extension of this project I wrote an essay in my university's academic bulletin on the subject. Tatsuyuki Kitamura, a member of the *Economist*'s editorial staff, saw the piece and asked me to write a serial for his magazine. Thus I owe him a deep debt of gratitude for having encouraged me to begin this book. I must also thank the many readers of the magazine who gave me encouragement.

I have been given credit as the author of this book, but in fact it is the result of a joint project carried out by students majoring in sociology at the University of Tsukuba, where I teach. None of the chapters would have been possible without their dedicated work in gathering data, conducting various kinds of interviews, and travelling to different parts of the world to collect information.

I would like to thank the following students, who worked on the following sections: 1–1, Futaya Sakaida, Hitoshi Yoshida; 1–2: Masaki Takahashi; 1–3: M:akiko Harada, Tatsuyuki Tayama; 2–1:

Yumiko Koga; 2–2: Hiroyuki Toda, Ken'ichi Ito, Shin'ichi Kura; 2–3: Izumi Moriyama, Masaru Horinouchi, Shin'ichi Kura; 2–4: Hisashi Oiji; 3: Hiroshi Oki, Kaori Oike; and 4–2-c: Shin'ichi Kura. The interviews on workers of the following nationalities were conducted by: Bangladeshis: Izumi Moriyama, Ken'ichi Ito; Thais: Masaki Takahashi; Filipinos: Masaru Horinouchi; Brazilians: Shin'ichi Kura; Koreans: Yumiko Koga, Shin'ichi Kura, Hiroyuki Toda; and Chinese: Kaori Oike, Makiko Harada. The country interviews were conducted by: Pakistan: Takahiro Ono; Philippines: Masaru Horinouchi; Korea: Hiroyuki Toda; China: Tatsuyuki Tayama, Makiko Harada; Thailand: Masaki Takahashi; and Brazil: Shin'ichi Kura.

Furthermore, I must note that the joint research owes much to a 1988–1989 Education Ministry Special Grant, and to a 1990 Science Research Subsidy.

In addition, this research project could not have proceeded without the generous cooperation of the many foreign workers who agreed to be interviewed. I am deeply grateful to them. I also offer my deep gratitude to the many organizations who generously let us access data. The names of these institutions are listed in the References. I am also very thankful to Atsuko Ishi and Tae Michiue, two staff members of my laboratory, who contributed on many levels to the completion of this book.

Additionally, this project could never have come to fruition without Akio Ishii, the president of Akashi Shoten, who has long been a publisher of books concerning respect for human rights. I would like to thank him and Hajime Miyasho of the editorial department.

Lastly, I would like to dedicate this book, with deep love, to my late father, who was driven to death by this society because of his ideals, by coincidence, at the same age that I have reached as I write these words.

The problem of foreign workers that we witness in Japan today can only be a prelude to what will come later, and it is bound to become a much bigger issue and to have effects on Japanese society that are difficult to grasp at present. It will be of great pleasure to me if this book can be of some use to the work of those both in Japan and in the Third World who are trying to devise responses to this issue.

Hiroshi Komai
September 5, 1992

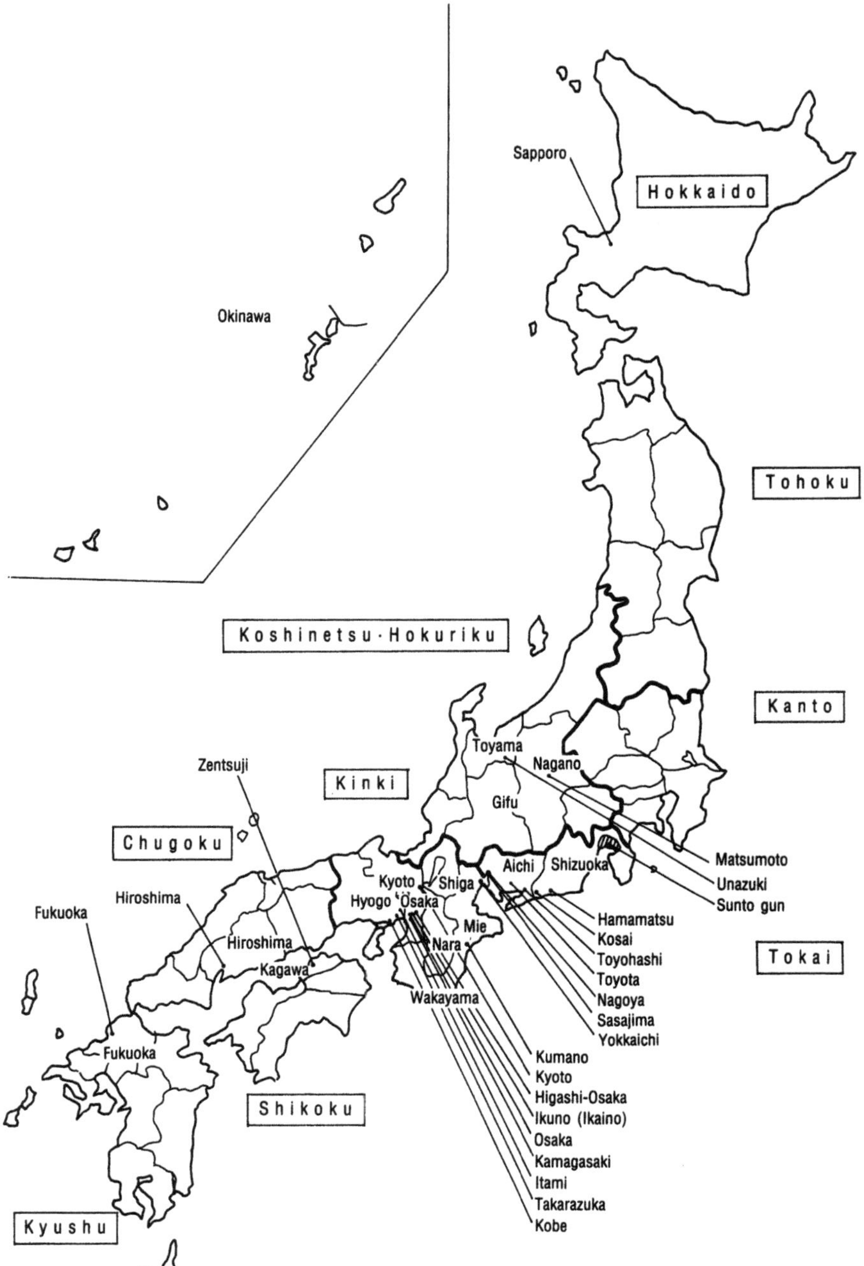

Okinawa
Sapporo
Hokkaido
Tohoku
Koshinetsu·Hokuriku
Kanto
Toyama
Nagano
Zentsuji
Kinki
Gifu
Chugoku
Matsumoto
Unazuki
Sunto gun
Aichi
Shizuoka
Kyoto
Shiga
Hiroshima
Fukuoka
Hyogo
Osaka
Hamamatsu
Mie
Kosai
Hiroshima
Nara
Toyohashi
Tokai
Kagawa
Toyota
Wakayama
Nagoya
Sasajima
Yokkaichi
Fukuoka
Kumano
Kyoto
Higashi-Osaka
Ikuno (Ikaino)
Shikoku
Osaka
Kamagasaki
Itami
Takarazuka
Kobe
Kyushu

Map 1 Japan

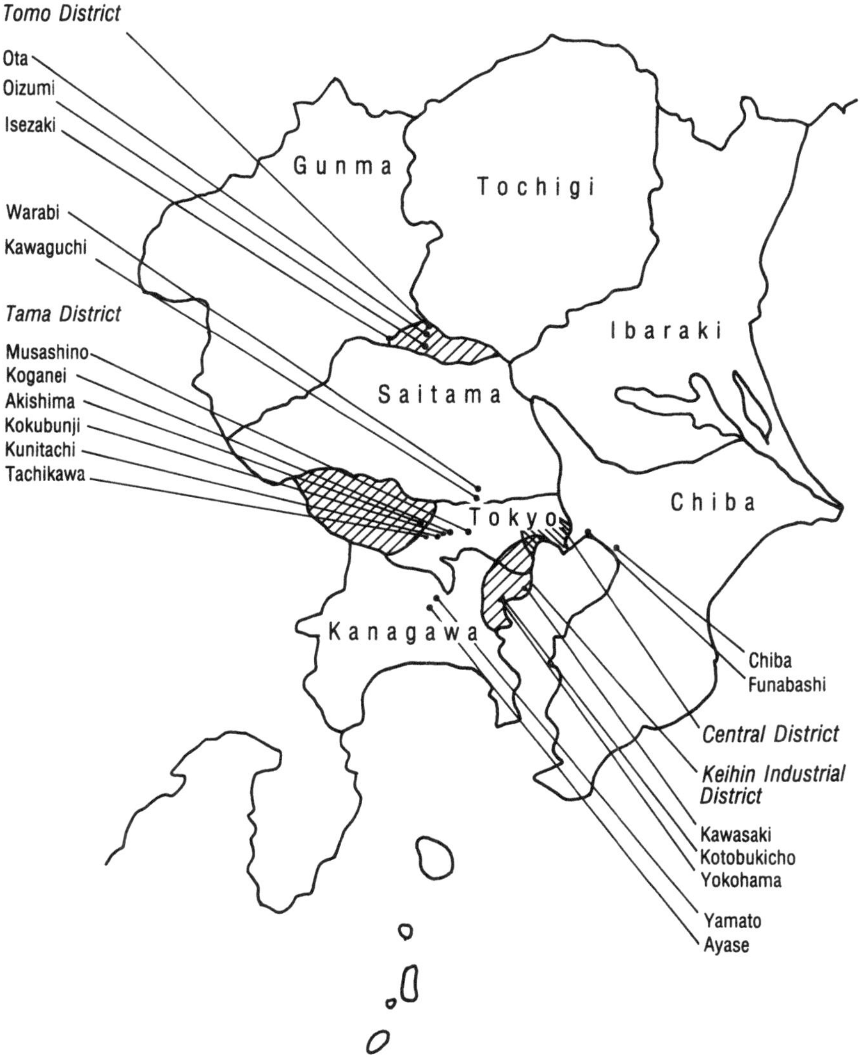

Map 2 The Kanto region

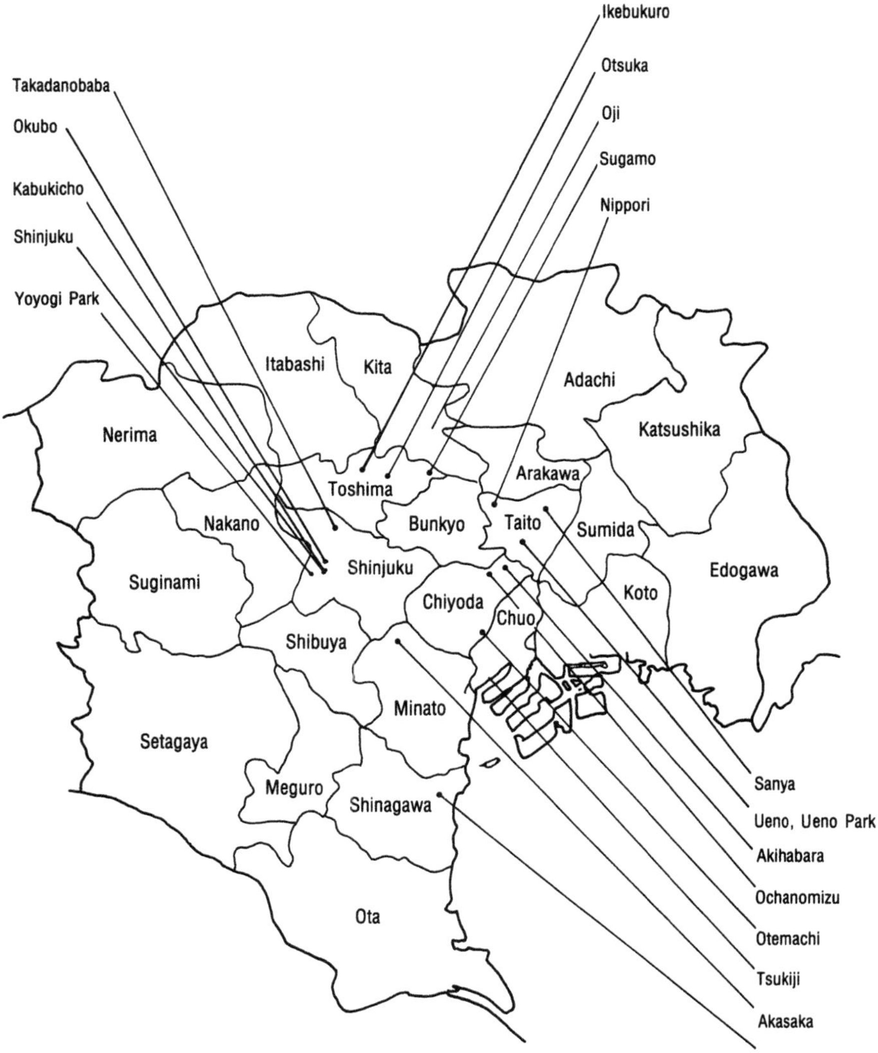

Map 3 Tokyo's central wards

Introduction: The Revision of the Immigration Act and the Situation of Foreign Workers

1 The Revision of the Immigration Act

It is a certainty that we will soon witness a great flood of foreign workers flowing into Japan. In recent years it has become commonplace to see Asian women in the red light districts, but foreign faces have also become increasingly conspicuous on our streets and in our trains. It is no longer difficult, either, to find foreigners working in coffee shops, restaurants and bars.

The question of 'foreign workers' does not really deal with skilled specialists from Western Europe and the United States, nor does it address the issue of foreign language teachers. It deals with the question of the people who have been lumped into the category of so-called 'unskilled' workers, including women working in the sex industry, who are now coming into Japan in large numbers.

As I will show later, it is believed that there are currently a total of nearly 600,000 of these 'unskilled' laborers living and working in Japan. They greatly outnumber the legally recognized workers who come with high skills or qualifications.

It is very difficult, however, to come to an accurate count of these numbers. One way to approach the problem is to look at the flow of laborers. In 1991, the following numbers of people were given new work permits to enter Japan for periods of more than three months (excluding those admitted as diplomats and government officials, as well as those working in the entertainment industry, for which people often work outside of their given status): 6,416 as 'specialists in humanities/international service'; 3,780 as 'intra-company transferees'; 3,166 as 'engineers,' which means those with specialized knowledge or skills in their fields; 2,651 as 'instructors,' which for the main part means foreign language teachers; 2,381 as 'skilled laborers' such as cooks; 2,073 for 'religious activities'; 1,523 as 'investors/business managers'; and 2,037 for an assortment of other statuses – professors, artists, journalists, researchers, and specialists in such fields as 'legal/ accounting' or 'medical' services. This adds up to a total of 24,027 people (Ministry of Justice C).

If we look at stock rather than flow, we see that as of the end of 1990 a total of 46,845 working people held alien registration cards (excluding Korean and Chinese residents of Japan as well as the categories which were excluded above). The largest categories within this number were international specialists (14,426), instructors (7,569), investment/business managers (7,334), engineers (3,398), and skilled workers (2,972) (Ministry of Justice w).

Thus, the number of workers with specialized knowledge and skills doesn't even amount to one tenth of the number of the so-called unskilled workers. Therefore, the use of the word 'foreign workers' in this book will refer exclusively to those who are 'unskilled.'

The issue of foreign workers in Japan is not new. Before World War II, Japan brought foreign workers from the Korean Peninsula, which it had colonized, as forced laborers. Many of them stayed on in Japan, and were forced to walk a tortuous path as they were eventually incorporated into the bottom strata of society as 'Zainichi' Koreans and Chinese. The current question of foreign workers, however, concerns a different phenomenon from that of these long-term residents.

The harbinger of the current situation was the flow of trainees into Japan during the late 1960's and early 1970's, although the first significant flow started only fairly recently, in the late 1970's, with the large-scale influx of women into the sex and entertainment industry. In the late 1980's males began to make their appearance, coming to work as manual laborers in the manufacturing and construction industries.

More recently, students at Japanese language schools have also joined the ranks of foreign laborers by engaging in the service industry in the broad sense of the term. Beginning in 1990, the issue of foreign workers in Japan reached a new stage as Nikkeijin (Latin Americans of Japanese descent, mainly from Brazil) came into Japan in rapidly increasing numbers, and as the trainee system became institutionalized.

The history of foreign workers in Japan is thus recent, and the most surprising aspect of the phenomenon is the speed with which it has occurred. Foreign workers can basically be placed in four categories: first, those who entered the country illegally or with false passports;* second, so-called overstayers, who came into the country with short-term visas and then stayed on past the expiration dates; third, those who are performing 'unauthorized labor,' meaning that they have a valid visa but are employed in unskilled labor, which falls outside of the activities for which they were granted their visa; and fourth, people of Japanese descent from Latin America who have been given the legal right to work as unskilled laborers.

The best known category of illegal entrants is that of Chinese coming in as fraudulent refugees (pretending to be Vietnamese) of which we will have more to say in Chapter 4–2, but recently there has also been an increase in incidents of foreign ship crew members jumping ship and entering the country illegally. In 1991, 353 people entered the country in this manner, most of them from Southeast or South Asia (*Nikkei Shimbun*, 30 April 1992).

In this book, when referring to the 'illegal' workers in the first three categories (i.e. illegal entrants, overstayers, and those working outside of status), we will use the term 'undocumented' rather than 'illegal.' The reason for this is that the term 'illegal workers' carries with it a strong nuance of criminality, and hence serves to encourage prejudice and discrimination against these people. Furthermore, the term 'undocumented' is widely used in the Western nations where much importance is attached to human rights (Okabe, p. 251; Yoko Kojima).

When estimating the number of undocumented workers in Japan, it is useful to examine the data compiled by the Ministry of Justice. According to the Ministry's Immigration Bureau, there were 32,000 overstayers as of June 1986. Its figures indicate that this number rose to 42,000 by June 1987, increased 1.3 times in the following year to 57,000 in June 1988, and a further 1.8 times to 101,000 by June 1989 (Tanaka b, p.204). However, the institution of measures to deter overstayers later halted this growth, and the number remained stable at roughly 100,000 at

* This includes those who have 'landed' illegally. The two terms will be considered to be equivalent. The distinction only hinges on the difference between entering the 'country,' indicating the territorial waters and sky, and entering the 'land,' which indicates the territory.

the end of 1989. In addition, the revision* of the Immigration Control Act in June 1990 led many workers to leave Japan, but their numbers still remained above the 100,000 mark, with an estimate of 106,497 in July of that year.

The increase in overstayers continued despite the revision of the law. By May 1991, ten months after the new law went into force, there were an estimated 159,828 overstayers, up 1.5 times from the previous period. By November of the same year, the number had reached 216,399, and by May of 1992 had climbed to 278,892, nearly reaching the 300,000 mark (Ministry of Justice B). This indicates that the revision of the Immigration Control Act had almost no effect on the number of overstayers.

There are two major means that can be used to prevent the presence of undocumented workers. The first is to stop them from entering the country, and the second, which occurs when they are already inside the country, is to apprehend and deport them. According to the Ministry of Justice, a record number of 27,137 people were refused entry in 1991, a 94.8% increase over the previous year. A record number of 32,908 undocumented workers were caught inside Japan, a 10.1% increase over the previous year, and roughly 2.9 times the number caught in 1987. Of this total, 1,518 were apprehended for illegal entry, 30,405 for overstaying, 882 for working outside of their given status, and 103 on other charges (Ministry of Justice C).

It is difficult, because of the nature of the circumstances, to grasp the exact number of people working outside of status, but as we will see in Chapters 1 and 2, it is generally believed that a stock of approximately 70,000 people have entered the country on entertainment, student, and trainee visas, but are engaged in unskilled labor.

In regards to the numbers of Nikkeijin, who are legally permitted to perform unskilled labor, the Ministry of Foreign Affairs has conjectured that as of June 1991 there were 148,700 people in the country, made up of mostly Brazilians (80.7%), followed by Peruvians (12.1%), Argentineans (5.7%), Bolivians (1.0%),

* In the book the author uses the Japanese term '*kaitei*' rather than the usual '*kaisei*.' This is because '*kaisei*' carries the generally positive nuance of 'improved,' which is difficult to apply given that the changes in the legislation were intended to drive undocumented workers out of the country, instituting, for instance, criminal charges against employers hiring these workers. *Kaitei* is a more neutral term.

and Paraguayans (0.5%). The same estimate for 1990 was 76,150, meaning that their numbers roughly doubled in the space of just one year (JICA, p. 69). It is therefore certain that as of August 1992 their numbers exceeded the 200,000 mark. Furthermore, in 1991, the Overseas Japanese Association (*Kaigai Nikkeijin Kyokai*) carried out a survey (no sampling) on Nikkeijin in Japan, with 1,027 valid responses, and found that approximately 20% held Japanese citizenship (see Chapter 2–2).

If we look at the overall results of these figures, we can conjecture that there are nearly 600,000 foreigners who are either overstayers, working without authorization, or working as legal unskilled laborers. In addition, it appears that there is a sizable flow of people who enter the country with tourist visas, work during the period of the visa's validity, and then exit the country.

How are these numbers divided by sex? In 1991, 25,350 males were apprehended as non-registered workers, compared to 7,558 females. An increasing trend has continued among males since their numbers first surpassed those of females in 1988. In terms of age, the most common group for both males and females was those between 25 and 30 years of age (Ministry of Justice C).

In response to these growing numbers, the Japanese government introduced an amended Immigration Control Act to the National Diet at the end of 1989 in an attempt to both preserve the existing spirit of the law and at the same time to expel undocumented workers. The bill became law, and went into effect on June 1, 1991. The major change in the new act was the introduction of a system of penalties for employers, setting punishments of up to three years imprisonment and/or fines of up to ¥2 million for anyone either knowingly hiring undocumented workers or working as a broker to secure employment for them.

However, after much meandering in the Diet, a supplementary resolution was added to the bill stipulating that 'This bill was intended to prosecute wicked brokers and employers, and care must be taken that it not be misused.' Let us now look at how the new law has been implemented. In 1990, there were 41 cases of exposure involving 54 individuals, and in 1991, 242 cases involving 306 people. And what about the industries that were most affected? If we look at the total number of employers apprehended in 1991 under the Man-Power Dispatching Business Act, Employment Security Act, Labor Standards Act, or employer section of the Immigration Control Act, we see that of the 338 cases involving 440 people, 57.1% of cases, and 71.4% of people, were in the construction and manufacturing sectors, and the remainder were involved either in prostitution or in the entertainment trade (National Police Agency e, p. 221).

The new Immigration Law, the intent of which was to expel undocumented workers by punishing employers, was patterned after the United States' Immigration Law, which went into force in 1986, but it should be noted that the penalties are significantly more severe.

Provisions for the punishment of overstayers existed in the previous law. However, because of technical difficulties these provisions were rarely enforced, and most offenders were simply deported without any fine being levied. Just before the new law was instituted, however, some Japanese English-language newspapers printed a series of stories giving the misleading idea that new and severe penalties had been instituted against overstayers (*Daily Yomiuri*, 19 March 1990, 13 April 1990, and 1 May 1990; *Japan Times*, 4 May 1990). A 'repatriation panic' ensued among overstayers in the wake of these articles, and during that period approximately 1,000 people a day surrendered to the Immigration Bureau. A significant number of people ended up returning to their home countries.

A similar fear spread among employers as well, against whom new legal sanctions had been instituted, because foreign workers were already working in large numbers, especially in the capital area.

There is, however, a supplementary provision to the law (no. 11) which exempts employers from penalties if they hire workers who were already in Japan as of 1 June 1990 or if they believed that the worker had been in Japan before that date (*Official Gazette*, 15 December 1989). If this piece of information had been made known earlier, a great deal of confusion could have been avoided.

In reference to this incident, then Justice Minister Shin Hasegawa was questioned on 1 June 1990 in the National Diet Upper House Justice Committee, and explained that, 'There were some deficiencies in our public relations, and I apologize for the fact that there was some panic' (*Yomiuri Shimbun*, 2 June 1990).

As we will see in Chapter 2, most foreign workers are employed by small and medium-sized enterprises, and we can get a realistic glimpse of the conditions they face from a survey conducted by KSD (*Chusho Kigyo Keieisha Saigai Hosho Jigyodan*), a damage compensation corporation for small and medium enterprise employers, on its members in the metropolitan region (Tokyo, Kanagawa, Chiba, and Saitama).

The survey was conducted in March-April 1990, just before the new Immigration Act went into effect, with questionnaires mailed to 10,000 firms selected by random sampling. Out of these, 2,218 responded (a response rate of 22.2%). More than 90% of the responses came from companies with fewer than 50 employees. A larger number of the firms, 13.9% (or almost one in seven), admitted that they had hired foreign workers at some time during the two previous years. Moreover, 23.5% of the workers they had hired were staying in Japan on tourist visas, meaning that they fell into the category of 'undocumented workers' (KSD). We can thus see that the hiring of foreign workers has become commonplace.

The fact that many enterprises have become so dependent on foreign laborers that they cannot survive without them can be gleaned from a 1991 survey carried out by the People's Finance Corporation (*Kokumin Kinyu Koko*) on 8,000 firms from the city of Tokyo, and from Gunma, Nagano, and Shizuoka Prefectures, in the manufacturing, service, and construction sectors. The survey achieved a 21.9% response rate. Of the respondents, 172, or 11.5% were employing foreigners at the time.

The firms which gave an affirmative answer to the question of whether they were hiring foreign workers were asked what measures they would take if they couldn' t hire such workers. A total of 27.0% said either 'We would have to cut back or suspend our operations,' or 'We wouldn't know what to do.' A further 11.5% responded that 'There is a possibility we might have to cut back or suspend operations.' Only 12.2% answered that 'It would have no relation to our business' (Inakami, Kuwabara et al., p. 106).

We can get some picture of the situation in the Kansai region (Western Japan) by looking at a survey conducted in March 1991 by the Joho Center. Questionnaires were sent out to 8,000 firms in the Kyoto-Osaka-Kobe region which had placed ads in help-wanted information magazines seeking part-time workers, and the survey received 879 responses. A total of 30.4% of respondents had hired foreigners as non-regular employees in the previous year. Most of the hirees had visas, either as foreign students, Japanese language students, or trainees, but 16.9% did not fall into any of these categories, and the Joho Center surmised that they were most likely overstayers (Joho Center). We can thus see that the use of foreign workers is widespread in the Kansai region as well.

The revised Immigration Act differs from the previous law in several aspects other than the imposition of new fines for employers. They are as follows:

(1) In response to the current situation, finer subdivisions were instituted in entrance and residency status categories. In particular, a new status, 'trainees,' was created.
(2) The new regulations stipulated that Immigration Bureau permission was necessary before anyone on a student visa could become employed. However, such permission was only granted in 9,610 cases between June and December of 1990 (Management and Coordination Agency (the central government agency in charge of overall administrative coordination), p. 76). Furthermore, a Justice Ministry administrative order issued simultaneously with the new Immigration Act's enforcement limited the number of hours a student could work to 4 hours on any day on which he or she attended classes.
(3) The new law set up a system to institute a 'Work Certificate' for foreigners which would show the range of work permitted to the holder. By giving employers an easy way to find out whether a foreigner had such qualification, this aimed to exclude workers without such permission.

It is also important not to overlook the fact that, as mentioned above, the exclusionary policies toward undocumented workers have been accompanied by a gradual increase in legal ways of working in Japan. As we have already seen, Nikkeijin have, without any indication that there was any real debate, become a main force among foreign workers. As we will see in Chapter 1–2, the Japan International Training Cooperation Organization (*Kokusai Kenshu Kyoryoku Kiko*), or JITCO, was set up, mainly by the traditionally isolationist Justice and Labor Ministries, and starting in about 1993 a system was set up to allow special trainees who have completed their period of training to seek (though with limited terms) jobs in Japan. So despite the existence of the revised Immigration Act, Japan has gradually become more open to foreign workers.

2 Human Rights Violations

Undocumented workers (or people hoping to become undocumented workers) are placed into a difficult situation if they are refused entry into the country, but even when they enter the country successfully they must still avoid being deported within a certain period of time. The reason for this is that even before they come to Japan they must bear the expenses of an airline ticket, temporary living expenses, and must often pay a sum of money to a broker or to a contact in Japan. In addition, they often come with money borrowed from family, relatives or acquaintances.

This total debt load is often enormous, and for all practical purposes impossible to repay in their home countries. Being turned away at entry or being caught and deported before having the chance to save a certain sum of money means enormous financial loss. In passing, it is important to note that when foreigners are forcibly repatriated (deported) to their home countries, it is they who must pay for the airfare, and if they are unable to afford this sum they find themselves confined in a detention center.

In consequence, undocumented workers must expend a great deal of energy avoiding apprehension by Immigration Bureau and police officials. The major concern of their life becomes the avoidance of the public eye. Going outside implies danger, so the best policy is, whenever possible, not to venture out of their small rooms.

In connection to this, the Tokyo Immigration Bureau and National Police Agency have shown a really outrageous meanness in their efforts to catch undocumented workers. In November 1991 they conducted a 'survey' of foreign workers at Yoyogi Park, where Iranians from the metropolitan region and nearby regions gather on Sundays to exchange employment information.

The officials began by asking seemingly innocuous questions, 'Do you know how to use a telephone?' 'Do you have any difficulties living in Japan?' and then as soon as the workers were at ease went on to ask to see the respondents' passports. They arrested 40 individuals for not carrying these documents, and after investigations sent 15 of them to the Immigration Bureau on charges that they were in Japan illegally. Similarly, in December 1991 authorities carried out a mass crackdown, again disguised as a 'survey,' at Nippori Station in Tokyo, and ended up deporting 15 Iranian workers (Forum on Asian Migrant Workers b, pp. 21–). Apart from the ethical question of whether such counterfeit measures should be allowed, one grave problem is that these actions have resulted in increasing fears among foreign workers about surveys in general.

As a result of these kinds of activities, the stigma of 'illegality' has been branded on a great part of the undocumented foreign workers in Japan. If we take a careful look at this activity, however, we cannot escape the conclusion that it is very different from what we think of as regular crime. Undocumented workers are not injuring other people or stealing property. Rather they are seriously and diligently performing work that Japanese people don't want to do, and they are doing it for low wages and in places hidden from the eyes of society. In consequence, despite the fact that they have been branded as 'illegal,' they are not aware of being involved in any evil deeds.

The background for this consciousness is that, first of all, in the countries from which they come, working overseas is generally not prohibited, and in fact in many cases is encouraged. This will be discussed in further detail in Chapter 4, but one of the major reasons behind this is the severity of unemployment in their countries of origin, as well as the worsening of international financial flow conditions for these countries. There is even some consciousness that migrant workers are heroes involved in a project of national salvation.

A second reason is that the families of many of these undocumented workers anxiously await the income of their fathers, husbands and daughters who are working in Japan. There are precious few job opportunities in the home countries, but families there still need to eat, and have to send their children to school. In addition, commercials broadcast on television encourage consumption. It is because of this that the labor of migrant workers is given a positive meaning – it is often a matter of life and death for the families back home.

It is of course a major problem that these workers are considered criminals under Japanese law despite the fact that they have no awareness that they are committing any crime, but it is also important to realize that the criminalization of foreign workers makes them susceptible to human rights violations and oppression.

In principle, undocumented workers cannot appeal to government agencies or local government bodies for help when their human rights are violated. The reason for this is that all civil servants are required, under one of the provisions of the Immigration Act, to report any foreigner they know to be living in Japan illegally to immigration authorities. For an undocumented worker, being reported to the Immigration Bureau leads directly to deportation. What this means is that the protection of the law has been withdrawn from this group of people.

We cannot simply ignore human rights violations in the workplace. Despite the fact that Japan's various labor laws are supposed to apply indiscriminately to all situations inside Japan, regardless of the nationality of the people involved, and regardless of whether foreign residents are documented or not, the working conditions faced by foreign workers have continuously deteriorated.

The problem of workplace accidents demands our attention more than anything else. Injuries and accidents are a constant threat to foreign workers, since they work mostly in areas which are called the '3D' jobs – deriving from the words dirty, difficult, and dangerous. The Work Accident Compensation Insurance Law applies to foreigners who are injured at work in Japan, but it is nearly impossible for undocumented workers to register such claims.

The reason for this situation is that Labor Standards Inspection Offices receiving such claims may report the person's status to the Immigration Bureau, and the claimant may face deportation. In reality, however, since 1988 there have only been 116 cases (spread out among 16 regional administrative regions) of Labor Ministry-related organizations filing such reports, and such notification is not carried out at all in five prefectures (Management and Coordination Agency, pp. 24–25). A further barrier to compensation claims is that companies employing undocumented workers fear that they will face prosecution for abetting illegal workers as well as other troubles they might run into with immigration authorities or with the police, and they try their best to conceal even serious accidents. For these reasons, it is unusual, except in the case of extremely serious cases, for claims to be filed.

A second area where the label of criminality affects foreign workers in the workplace is in the problem of wages. Foreign workers generally have a weak position vis-à-vis their employers, but in the case of undocumented workers the inequality is extreme. The result is that low wages are an everyday state of affairs, and incidents involving non-payment of wages are frequent.

In the earlier cited survey by KSD, 79.2% of companies reported that they paid the same wages to foreigners as to their Japanese staff, 12.8% said they paid roughly two-thirds of the normal wages, and 1.9% said they paid their foreign staff just one half the Japanese wages, with 6.4% of the firms either answering 'none of the above' or not responding. This survey, in which nearly 80% of companies said they paid the same wages to Japanese and non-Japanese alike, does not support the claim of low wages (KSD).

Similar results appeared in a survey carried out in October 1990 by the Study Committee on the Effects of Foreign Workers on the Labor Market, a private group organized by the chief of the Labor Ministry's Employment Security Bureau. This survey, done with the cooperation of several industry associations, carried out research on 348 companies in Tokyo and in five prefectures which were members of these associations and which were hiring foreign workers. Of the firms, 20.1% said they were employing foreigners on short-term visas, and a further 27.3% were workers of whose visa status they were unsure. Judging from these numbers, it appears that the percentage of undocumented workers was quite high.

According to this survey, the pay (per hour) of foreigners performing the same job (or a similar job) as Japanese nationals was as follows: in 54.3% of the firms, there was no differential; in 15.5% of the cases, the pay for foreigners was higher; in 22.7% of the cases the pay for foreigners was between 70% and 100% of their counterparts; in 4.6% the foreigners received less than 70% of what Japanese received; and 2.6% of the firms gave no response. In other words, in roughly 70% of the cases foreigners' wages were either on par or higher than those of their Japanese counterparts (Ministry of Labor k, Supplement p. 46).

However, one problem with these surveys is the question of whom among Japanese workers one compares foreign workers to, and this problem is demonstrated by a survey carried out in July 1989 by the Tokyo Metropolitan Institute for Labor. Its questionnaire was mailed randomly to 5,200 small or middle size (more than 10 employees) firms in Tokyo, with 2,080 responses received (a response rate of 40.0%) (Tokyo Metropolitan Government k).

The results showed that 78.6% of the firms hiring foreigners as store clerks, 50.0% of those hiring them as factory workers, 62.5% of those employing them as waiters, waitresses or dishwashers, and 81.8% of those using foreigners as cleaning staff said they paid them 'the same wages as part-time Japanese staff in the same work category.' In many cases, then, what firms mean when they say they pay foreigners 'the same as Japanese' is that they pay foreigners who work full-time the same as part-time Japanese workers.

However, I should add that before the onset of the economic recession there were cases in which Nikkeijin workers, who are legally permitted to do unskilled labor in Japan, received higher wages than regular Japanese employees performing the same jobs.

On the question of non-payment of wages, we can make use of data gathered from undocumented workers who were arrested in 1987 (Machida). When asked, 492 or 4.4% of the total number said that they had been victims of wage non-payment in the past. This figure was higher for women (5.6%) than for men (2.3%), and it is said that there has been a rise in such occurrences since the enactment of the new Immigration Law, which employers have used as a weapon against their employees, threatening to report them to the authorities (CALL Network, p. 14).

Living conditions are an important issue too, as illegal entrants and overstayers cannot get either health or livelihood assistance. They are not covered by health insurance, and therefore the costs accruing to them if they fall ill are extremely high. Even when they fall into destitution, there is nowhere for them to turn for assistance.

We should add, in passing, that tax offices take a uniform 20% levy on the incomes of foreign workers, including overstayers, under the reasoning that they are short-term stayers or, in other words, non-residents. What this means is that they are obliged to pay taxes but do not receive the privileges that should rightfully accompany the taxation.

The problems of human rights violations against foreign workers was shown vividly by a telephone hot-line operated in December 1990 by the Lawyers for Foreign Laborers' Rights (LAFLR), a group of mostly young lawyers in the Tokyo metropolitan region. Of the 240 calls they received, 88 concerned immigration matters such as visa status changes and repatriation, 72 dealt with unpaid wages, workplace accidents and other labor-related matters, and 41 involved living conditions – problems such as marriage, divorce and taxes (*Asahi Shimbun*, 12 December 1990).

It must also be remembered that brokers are always lurking in the shadows as foreign workers enter Japan and begin to work. For foreigners, successfully crossing over the thick wall that the Immigration Bureau has set up in their path and finding work is a formidable challenge. Because of this, a class of organized 'professionals' who take unreasonable fees for their services has emerged. This phenomenon will be discussed again in Chapter 1–1, but we should mention here that there has been an increase in incidents involving unpaid wages, rake-offs (brokers taking a cut of workers wages) and people being held against their will.

From the viewpoint of human rights, it is also impossible to ignore the high-handedness with which the Immigration Bureau has tried to crack down on foreign workers. In immigration screenings, the attitude of the officials is typically extremely overbearing, and during apprehensions their actions betray any pretension of respect for human rights.

To raise just one example, the following incident is said to have occurred in May 1988 at an apartment in Saitama Prefecture renting specially to foreigners:

1) An official shouted the words '*Konoyaro-!*' (an extremely strong expletive in Japanese, perhaps equivalent to 'you bastard!' in English) over and over; 2) officials walked over people's beds with their shoes on (an act considered to be extremely rude in Japan); 3) they kicked the inhabitants without any reason; 4) they shouted 'Go back to Bangladesh!' to one resident who had a valid student visa; and 5) they hauled the residents to the Immigration Bureau and hung placards around their necks

inscribed with their names and nationalities (Group Akakabu, p. 217).

In another incident, a Myanmarese (Burmese) citizen was discovered smoking a cigarette in the toilet at the Regional Immigration Office in Otemachi, Tokyo, and was taken into a room. Then, 1) five or six officers surrounded him and one of them began verbally abusing him; 2) another ten employees appeared, slapped him repeatedly, and then twisted his right arm; and 3) he was beaten and kicked repeatedly. He finally sought assistance from the Human Rights Protection Committee of the Japan Federation of Bar Associations, and was given a medical examination. The doctor estimated that he would require two weeks of medical treatment (*Japan Times*, 31 May 1990).

Another incident at the same office, experienced by a Japanese women who was married to a Bangladeshi overstayer, shows the lack of respect for human rights of Immigration Bureau officials. The officer in charge of their case suddenly started shouting angrily, a guard called them using the term, 'omae!' (an extremely impolite summons), repeatedly and deliberately blew smoke in their direction, and spoke to them in a very loud voice (Shahedo and Sekiguchi, p. 118).

Between March 12–14, 1990, four support groups in the Tokyo region set up phone lines to listen to foreigners' complaints concerning their treatment by immigration officials, and received 221 calls from citizens of 22 countries, mostly from Asia. Of these calls, 96 concerned the poor behavior of immigration officers, and 40 involved screenings for visa status changes (*Nikkei Shimbun*, 25 March 1990). These figures also help to demonstrate the high-handed behavior of immigration officials.

3 The Beginnings of a Gradual Opening

In the past, the Japanese government has maintained a policy of forbidding so-called 'unskilled' laborers from working in Japan. Because of this, the relationship between government measures and the mushrooming population of foreign workers can be compared to a game of 'Whack a Moley' (a popular game in which the player tries to hit, with a hammer, an ever-increasing number of plastic mole dolls sticking their heads out of holes in a board). In other words, the workers took advantage of whatever loopholes they could find in existing laws and administrative measures as they flowed into Japan; in response, the government instituted new policies to close up these holes; and foreigners found new blind spots in the new regulations. The government faced a situation in which no matter how hard it hit, new holes would open up, and an ever-increasing number of moles would pop up through the holes. I should add, however, that the use of 'moles' is simply meant as an analogy for foreigners, and is not meant to be discriminatory.

However, as we have seen earlier, the government has, because of the severity of Japan's labor shortage, finally begun a gradual and partial opening of the door to foreign workers. If we continue with the analogy of the mole-whacking game, what has happened is that not only has the government stopped whacking certain holes, but it has also allowed these holes to grow bigger. The issue of foreign workers in Japan has thus reached a major turning point.

Changes in the countries of origin of foreign workers provide a good illustration of this process. Table Intro–1 shows the change over time of the nationality of undocumented workers apprehended by officials. Interestingly, according to 1986 data, 83.7% of people apprehended surrendered of their own volition (Tanaka b, p. 182). It is believed that most of these cases occurred when the foreign workers wanted to return home.

According to Table Intro–1, the largest number of apprehended workers came from South Korea, making up 29.7% of the total figure. This number jumped three times between 1988 and 1989, and has kept rising since then, due to a great extent to the existence of the support network of permanent Korean residents in Japan, as well as to the South Korean government's relaxation of travel restrictions in January 1989, and to the additional fact that the construction boom which accompanied the 1988 Summer Olympics was just coming to a close.

The reason for the sudden increase in Iranians, who came to occupy second place, at 23.4%, in 1991, is the existence of a mutual agreement between Japan and Iran allowing travel without visa. In April 1992 this agreement was suspended, however, and the numbers have stopped growing. In the case of the third-place Malaysians, whose number reached 14.8% of the total, a

Table Intro-1 Changes in numbers of apprehended undocumented workers

	1987	1988	1989	1990	1991
South Korea	208	1,033	3,129	5,534	9,782
	(109)	(796)	(2,209)	(4,417)	(8,283)
Iran	0	0	15	652	7,700
			(13)	(648)	(7,611)
Malaysia	18	279	1,865	4,465	4,855
	(15)	(265)	(1,691)	(3,856)	(3,892)
Thailand	1,067	1,388	1,144	1,450	3,249
	(290)	(369)	(369)	(661)	(926)
Philippines	8,027	5,386	3,740	4,042	2,983
	(2,253)	(1,688)	(1,289)	(1,593)	(1,079)
Mainland China	494	7	39	481	1,162
	(210)	(5)	(26)	(428)	(981)
Pakistan	905	2,497	3,170	3,886	793
	(905)	(2,495)	(3,168)	(3,880)	(793)
Sri Lanka	0	20	90	831	307
		(20)	(87)	(821)	(295)
Bangladesh	438	2,942	2,277	5,925	293
	(437)	(2,939)	(2,275)	(5,915)	(292)
Others	150	762	1,139	2,618	1,784
	(70)	(379)	(664)	(1,957)	(1,198)
Total	11,307	14,314	16,608	29,884	32,908
	(4,289)	(8,929)	(11,791)	(24,176)	(25,350)

Notes:
1 Figures in parentheses are for males.
2 For 1987–1988, figures for Iran and Sri Lanka are included in the category 'Others'.
3 The 1987 figure for 'Mainland China' includes both Taiwan and Hong Kong.

Source: Ministry of Justice C.

similar agreement was in place. Their numbers jumped in 1990, made up mostly of people of Chinese descent. If we look at Thais, who held fourth place with 9.9% of the total, we see that most were women, and that their numbers doubled in 1991 along with the development of a broker network. Most of these women are working in the entertainment trade.

Filipinos, who held the top position up until 1989, formed the fifth largest group, with a relatively small share of 9.1%. The reason for this drop is said to be the increasing severity of visa screenings. The high percentage of females among those apprehended has remained consistently high. Many of those from mainland China, which held the sixth highest number at 3.5%, are

Table Intro-2 Changes in numbers of overstayers according to nationality/place of origin

	1 Jul 1990	1 May 1991	1 Nov 1991	1 May 1992	Perc. of total as of May 1992
Thailand	11,523	19,093	32,751	44,354	15.9%
Iran	764	10,915	21,719	40,001	14.3%
Malaysia	7,550	14,413	25,379	38,529	13.8%
South Korea	13,876	25,848	30,976	35,687	12.8%
Philippines	23,805	27,228	29,620	31,974	11.5%
China	10,039	17,535	21,649	25,737	9.2%
Bangladesh	7,195	7,498	7,807	8,103	2.9%
Pakistan	7,989	7,864	7,923	8,001	2.9%
Taiwan	4,775	5,241	5,897	6,729	2.4%
Myanmar	1,234	2,061	3,425	4,704	1.7%
Sri Lanka	1,668	2,281	2,837	3,217	1.2%
Others	16,079	19,851	26,416	31,856	11.4%
Total	106,497	159,828	216,399	278,892	100.0%

Source: Ministry of Justice B.

believed to be people who arrived on student visas and then overstayed their visas. Visa exemption agreements were causes behind the large numbers of Pakistanis (7th place) and Bangladeshis (9th place) up to 1990, but the suspension of these agreements in January of 1989 led to a significant decrease in 1991.

One remarkable feature of the 1991 figures is the internationalization of apprehendees. A total of 75 countries were represented in the rolls. This growing diversity has come particularly from Africa (21 countries in the 1991 survey compared to just 14 the year before) and Latin America (14 countries, compared to 12 the year before), showing that the phenomenon has taken on a truly global dimension (Ministry of Justice C).

The Ministry of Justice also compiles calculations on its estimates of the stock of overstayers. According to Table Intro–2, Thais form the largest group with 15.9% of the total, with Iranians coming in second, followed by Malaysians, South Koreans, and Filipinos (each with at least 10% of the total), and then by Chinese, Bangladeshis, Pakistanis, and Taiwanese.

The data in this table refers only to overstayers, but there is also a significant number of people working outside of their given status, and also, as mentioned above, the group of Nikkeijin who are legally permitted to do unskilled labor in Japan.

We have thus seen that significant changes have occurred in the past in terms of countries of origin. What is the likely future scenario? Because the Nikkeijin are able to work legally, their numbers are bound to increase for some time, but there is only a limited population of people of Japanese descent in Latin America, so the number will surely level off at some point in the future.

It is also easier for undocumented workers with physical features resembling those of the Japanese to avoid detection when compared to people with more distinct characteristics, so it is likely in the future that there will be greater numbers of people with Japanese-like faces. This fact is already seen today in the increases of both South Koreans and Chinese Malaysians.

In terms of the standards for accepting foreign workers, we will probably soon witness changes reflecting a similar reasoning. As was mentioned earlier, the striking increase in Latin Americans brought about by the legalization of Nikkeijin labor has taken place simultaneously with a change in the composition of people performing unauthorized labor, where the tendency has been for the numbers of students to stagnate and those of trainees to increase.

Under the old Immigration Act there were no clear regulations on the status of students attending Japanese language or other technical schools, and people were given a status on the basis of a miscellaneous category 'others who are given special permission by the Ministry of Justice.' With the increasing acceptance of students conducting studies in Japan, their numbers, and in particular the number of people studying Japanese language, has increased.

Under the old law, these students were given permission to hold part-time jobs for up to 20 hours per week as long as they reported their work, but in fact there were only haphazard checks on their work situation, and this opened the possibility of people carrying out unauthorized labor. The number of students continued to rise dramatically until 1988, with 35,107 entering the country that year, many of them Chinese. In 1989, however, because of increasingly severe screenings, the number fell sharply to 18,183, and then stabilized at 20,851 in 1990 and 20,654 in 1991.

During this period, trainees began to replace students as the main source of unauthorized labor. In many cases, the authorities have not screened the organizations accepting trainees except on paper, and the system has become a convenient blind for the hiring of foreign workers. Typically this has been accomplished by calling the work 'on the job training.' In many cases, however, the 'trainees' have been forced to perform actual labor, and because of their status as trainees the companies have been under no obligation to pay them proper wages, getting away instead with granting them a small allowance. The number of trainee entrants has risen steadily, from 23,432 in 1988, to 29,489 in 1989, 37,566 in 1990, and finally to 43,649 in 1991.

There is also an increasing trend for people to enter Japan on a tourist visa, work during the period of validity, and then leave Japan when the visa expires. This seems to be very common among South Koreans, and cases have been reported of employment agents in Japan asking Japanese brokers in Korea to recruit laborers there (Shinano Mainichi Shimbun b, p. 47). In one case that occurred during a period of 'increased vigilance' in November 1991, four middle-aged men from Korea who had multiple visit visas (valid for 15 days each time) underwent a screening at Osaka Airport and as a result were refused permission to enter the country because they were unable to explain their sightseeing plans, and because they had work clothes in their luggage (Ministry of Justice y).

4 Striking Roots and the Effect of the Recession

Some foreign workers have begun to show signs of striking roots in Japan. In the above-mentioned survey on Nikkeijin, 74.3% of the respondents said they hoped to return to their home countries, but a relatively high number (25.7%, or roughly one in four) said they hoped to remain in Japan. However, only 18.7% of those who said they wanted to return home said this desire was unconditional, with the rest saying they wanted to go back 'when the economic situation improves there' or 'when I have saved money,' and in these cases the prospects of them returning in the near future cannot be said to be very bright (JICA, p. 134).

If we look at a similar survey carried out in 1990 by the Okinawa International Foundation (limited to people of Okinawan descent who were living abroad), with 208 valid responses (no sampling), we see that 71.4% of those who wanted to return to their home countries said they planned to come back to Japan some day. In other words, many of those who said they wished to return to their homelands also intended to leave again and come back to Japan (Okinawa International Foundation, p. 31). In passing, in the previously mentioned survey on Latin Americans of Japanese descent, 30.5% of respondents said their fathers had come from Okinawa, with a similar figure of 32.2% for mothers (JICA, p. 84). It is also said that more than 80% of people who come to Japan as migrant workers end up coming back again (Watanabe, Yuge, et al., p. 81). Among people traveling from Brazil to Japan it is increasingly common to find families coming to join their fathers or husbands working here (*Asahi Shimbun*, 16 April 1992).

The tendency for Nikkeijin to settle in Japan seems to be somewhat different from other groups of foreign workers in that the trend is being strengthened by the many families coming to live here. Of the 438 respondents to the survey on Nikkeijin who reported having dependent families, 25.9% had brought their entire families to Japan with them, 9.5% had brought some members with them, and 64.6% had left their families behind. This means that one third were living with at least some part of their family. Of the 153 respondents whose families were also in Japan, 77, or roughly half, had school-age children (JICA, p. 105).

Women, and in particular Filipinas, have also shown a tendency to settle in Japan. For example, if we look at the data on people apprehended as overstayers in 1991, 37.9% of the women had overstayed their visas for at least one year, compared to a similar figure of only 26.9% for men. For Filipinas the figure was even higher, at 59.3%.

It cannot be said, however, that the length of time overstayers remain in Japan is getting longer. Of those caught in 1987, for instance, 38.5% had been working for less than six months, 34.2% had been working between six months and one year, and 27.3% for more than one year (Machida). The similar figures for 1991 were 38.7% for less than six months, 31.9% for between six months and one year, 16.5% for between one and two years, and 12.7% for over two years (Ministry of Justice C).

A striking phenomenon that has accompanied this taking of

Table Intro-3 Monthly income according to country of origin (yen)

	Less than 200,000	200,000 299,999	300,000 399,999	More than 400,000	Unknown	Total
Pakistan	6	5	1		3	15
Philippines	1	10	4	4	1	20
South Korea	4	5	8	3	1	21
Latin America	3		12		3	18
China	5	1			11	17
Total	19	21	25	7	19	91

Source: Tezuka, Komai, et al., p. 288.

roots has been the emergence of various gaps between people of different national origin. We conducted interviews (without sampling) on 74 foreigners either living or working in Kanagawa Prefecture, and the results are displayed in Table Intro–3. In the case of Pakistanis, 6 out of the 12 respondents said they received wages under ¥200,000 per month, whereas for Filipinos 10 out of the 19 were getting wages in the ¥200,000–300,000 range. For South Koreans, 8 out of 20 people received wages in the ¥300,000–400,000 range, and for Latin Americans of Japanese descent 12 out of 15 respondents fell into this range. In other words, there is a pyramid-like structure, with Pakistanis at the bottom and Nikkeijin at the top.

Ironically, this gap seems to be inversely proportional to the level of education of the workers. Many of the Pakistanis and Filipinos are university graduates, the percentage of high school graduates is high among South Koreans, and in the case of Latin Americans, many have graduated from either high school or only elementary school. The wages are low among the Pakistanis and Filipinos, who have high educational attainments, and are high among the South Koreans and Latin Americans whose educational levels are low (Tezuka, Komai, et al., p. 287).

Incidentally, one notable phenomenon is the tendency for Nikkeijin to improve their wages by changing jobs. The Ministry of Labor conducted a survey in January 1991 of 795 workers focused on people visiting their Nikkeijin Employment Service Center, and found that among the respondents 290 had changed jobs at least once in the past. What stood out about these job switches is that they accounted not only for wage raises, but also for workers advancing from manufacturing positions to jobs as technical specialists, salespeople or office staff. Moreover, people who had changed jobs had higher Japanese language ability than those who had not (Ministry of Labor n).

Gaps have also begun to appear within the ranks of the Nikkeijin themselves. As we will discuss later in Chapter 4–4, the activities of unscrupulous local brokers have led to a large influx of 'fake Nikkeijin' from Peru. For example, between October 1991 and February 1992, 854 Nikkeijin were refused applications to have their short-term visas changed to long-term residency, and 91.9% of these cases involved Peruvians (*Nikkei Shimbun*, 4 May 1992). Many Peruvians do not even ask for a change in their visa status, and this coupled with the fact that Peruvians are said to be poor speakers of Japanese has contributed to a drop in their status.

In regards to the Iranians, whose numbers increased in a relatively short period of time, one survey was conducted on 17 Iranians in Oota City, Gunma Prefecture, by Kitagawa and others. The monthly wage received by these workers was found to average ¥184,000, lower than a similar figure of ¥208,000 for Pakistanis and Bangladeshis working in the same city. However, before coming to Japan four had been technicians who had graduated from university or technical schools, three had been university students, three had worked as civil servants, one was an ex-military draftee, and one had been a hospital staff member (Yamashita, pp. 232–). However, as can be seen by the data provided above, Iranians have been placed at the lowest position among all foreign workers in Japan.

The Japanese economy began to slip into recession around 1991, and this is now beginning to have a major effect on foreign workers. According to Ministry of Labor statistics, the ratio of effective labor demand to supply dropped consecutively during the 16 months between March 1991 and June 1992, and reached a ratio of 1.04, the lowest level since September 1988 (*Nikkei Shimbun*, 28 August 1988). The downturn first became serious in the manufacturing sector, and particularly in the automobile and electrical industries. As a result, unemployment problems are becoming particularly striking among Nikkeijin, who have tended to work in this sector.

When the Labor Ministry became aware of many cases of Nikkeijin and temporary workers being dismissed from companies in the Northern Kanto, Tokai and Chubu regions, it issued a circular to local governments instructing them to prevent companies who had Nikkeijin workers from dismissing them in an easygoing way with no greater excuse than 'deteriorating business conditions.' Roughly 70% of the workers who have come to visit the Nikkeijin Employment Service Center in Ueno, Tokyo, have been unemployed (*Nikkei Shimbun*, 22 April, 16 May, 5 August 1992). In March 1992 the Center received 182 help-wanted requests, but there were 535 applications for jobs (*Asahi Shimbun*, 9 April 1992).

To look at one concrete example, Isuzu Motors made the decision to cut 40%, or roughly 1,300 people, from its temporary workforce, and approximately 800 of these were Brazilians of Japanese descent (*Nikkei Shimbun*, 5 February 1992). There have been many cases of Nikkeijin who had once worked in other regions flowing into the Tokai area to find jobs, but in Hamamatsu City, for example, mass layoffs have also been commonplace. One major temporary staff placement company has failed to make wage payments to 530 of its Nikkeijin Brazilians because it has received no work orders from companies (*Yomiuri Shimbun*, 16 July 1992).

Because of personnel cuts, the wages of Nikkeijin, which at one time were better than those of native Japanese, have also shown a decreasing trend. Hourly wages in Toyota City, which once stood at ¥1,700-¥1,800, have fallen to ¥1,300 in 1992 (*Nikkei Shimbun*, 22 March 1992). At the Nikkeijin Employment Service Center, the salaries offered by companies posting help wanted ads have dropped to somewhere in the ¥200,000/month range (*Asahi Shimbun*, 9 April 1992).

Among the Nikkeijin, Peruvians have received the greatest shock, and it is among them that one finds the most unemployment and homelessness (*Chunichi Shimbun*, 14, 27 May, 1992). In Hamamatsu City, in particular, there have been many cases of Peruvians being dismissed as their visas expired (*Asahi Shimbun*, 15 May 1992).

The economic downturn has also been a blow to undocumented workers. There have been many cases of small and mid-sized companies dismissing foreign workers because of a lack of orders and then justifying their actions by the fact that the workers are illegal (*Nikkei Shimbun*, 22 March 1992). This has been a particularly serious problem for Iranians. As the latest arrivals, their job-seeking channels are not well developed, and this is compounded by communication problems. Because of this it has become increasingly difficult for them to secure jobs.

The number of Iranians gathering on Sundays at Yoyogi Park in Tokyo, a major meeting place for the workers to exchange information, increased from roughly 1,500 at the end of 1991 to 6,000 or 7,000 in July 1992 (*Asahi Shimbun*, 20 July 1992). In Tokyo's Ueno Park, another such location, their number on any given day has increased to 100–300 people. As with Peruvians, many Iranians have found themselves unemployed and have fallen into homelessness.

According to direct interviews conducted on 88 Iranians in Yoyogi Park in March 1992 by a citizen's group, 'Association to Regain Life and Human Rights,' (*Inoken*) 29 of the respondents said they were unemployed or searching for a job at the time. Moreover, 27 said they had experienced unpaid wages, and 8 people had been injured on the job without receiving any compensation for their medical fees (Forum on Asian Migrant Workers b, p. 34).

Another survey, carried out by Yoshihiko Yamazaki and others in June 1992 at Ueno Station and in nearby Ueno Park, with 143 Iranian respondents (who participated voluntarily in the interviews), gives crucial information on the effects of the economic downturn. Of the respondents, 78 said they had worked during the previous month, whereas 50 had not, meaning that the group had an unemployment rate of 39%. Even among those who had found jobs, 23 had worked for less than 10 days, 26 had worked between 11 and 20 days, and just 22 had worked for more than 21 days. Fully two-thirds had worked for less than 20 days.

As a result of this, significant numbers of workers have become homeless. When the respondents were asked where they were sleeping (with multiple answers permitted), 45 answered 'a friend's apartment,' 31 'my own apartment,' 28 'in a company dormitory,' 14 'in a park,' 8 'in a hotel,' 3 'in a sauna or movie theater,' and 3 'none of the above,' meaning that a total of 13% were sleeping in either parks, saunas or movie theaters (Yamazaki, Wakabayashi, et al.).

The downturn has also begun to have effects on other non-Nikkeijin documented workers. A group of 27 computer technicians who were brought to Japan from Shenyang City, China by a dispatching company, were not able to find proper work, and their unpaid wages have reached a total sum of ¥25 million

(*Asahi Shimbun*, 24 August 1992). In passing, it should be noted that the employment situation of long-term refugees from Indochina is also very serious. Because of the lack of help-wanted requests, seven families with a total of 18 members have been unable to leave the Yamato Resettlement Promotion Center Refugee Assistance Headquarters Foundation for Welfare and Education of Asian People (*Teiju Sokushin Center*) in Yamato City, Kanagawa Prefecture (*Asahi Shimbun*, 8 July 1992).

Some attempts at self-organizing and at social movements have accompanied the lengthening experience of foreign workers in Japan. A union formed in February 1990 by Filipino computer operators who had come to work at Atras Japan (under the National Union of General Workers (*Zenkoku Ippan*), Tokyo Southern District Branch), and the formation of a council of foreign language teachers unions, are two examples of this (CALL Network, p. 5).

In addition, there is the case, for instance, of the Edogawa Workers' Union in Tokyo, a local union which accepts members on an individual basis. The union has 70 foreign members from 10 countries throughout the world, who make up 20 percent of its total membership (*Mainichi Shimbun*, 7 February 1992). Also, just before May Day, 1992, 200 foreign workers gathered in Tokyo's Itabashi Ward to adopt a 'Declaration on the Rights of Foreign Workers' which called for an end to discrimination and prejudice (*Asahi Shimbun*, 30 April 1992). If one recognizes the idea that changes in social conditions must ultimately be based on subjective movements, the sprouting of these types of movements acquires great significance.

Thus, the flow of foreign workers into Japan and their striking of roots in this country is increasing inexorably. It is thus obvious that the work of protecting the human rights of the foreigners working and living inside Japanese society is a current issue of utmost importance. This is, however, a completely different issue from that of whether Japan should accept the inflow of foreign workers. In this book, I would like to label this idea the 'theory of the unavoidability of the presence of foreign workers.' The following chapters will be an analysis given from this position of 'unavoidability.'

1 How do Foreign Workers Enter Japan?

1 The Role of Brokers

This chapter examines the methods by which foreign workers enter Japan. The first section takes a general look at the important role played by job brokers, and the second discusses the trainee system, which is certain to grow in the future. The third briefly examines the situation of *shugakusei* (an immigration category of foreign students in language and technical schools) and Japanese language schools. The role of brokers who work exclusively in the entertainment industry will not be treated here, but will be dealt with later, in Chapter 2–1.

Throughout this chapter we have used the term broker to indicate more specifically job brokers, and have applied the term indiscriminately to all those who make profits by assisting foreign workers in finding work, regardless of whether the work is legal or not.

First, we will consider the question of how deeply brokers are involved in foreign labor. In 1991, 12.5% of all foreign workers apprehended as undocumented workers said they had received some assistance from brokers, either in their countries of origin or in third countries. This assistance took the form of solicitations, recruiting, and preparing passports and visas (including forged documents). The brokers were of the following nationalities: Thai (33.1%), Korean (22.8%), Filipino (17.9%), Chinese (6.8%), Japanese (6.2%), with the remaining 13.2% made up of other nationalities.

In addition, 13.2% of those apprehended had experienced some contact with brokers inside Japan, including, for instance, being met upon arrival at the airport. The nationalities of these brokers were Japanese (30.6%), Koreans (17.0%), Thai (15.9%), Chinese (8.5%), Filipinos (6.4%), with the remaining 21.6% made up of other nationalities (Ministry of Justice C).

A similar situation can be seen in the 1990 survey by the Labor Ministry which we mentioned in the Introduction.

Among companies that hired foreign workers (with multiple answers permissible), 29.4% said they had been directly approached by the workers, 28.5% had met them through the introduction of friends, 17.0% through the introduction of another foreigner, 16.1% through the introduction of a business colleague, 10.1% through help wanted advertisements, 5.8% through the services of job brokers, 4.9% through the introduction of a labor dispatch company, 3.5% through intercompany transfers or transfers between affiliated companies, 2.9% through schools, with 7.8% 'through other means,' and with the remaining 0.3% not responding. The intervention of brokers and labor dispatch companies was apparent in only roughly 10% of the cases (see Ministry of Labor k, Appendix, p. 45).

According to a 1987 Ministry of Justice document (Ministry of Justice b), in the early stages of the phenomenon foreign workers often received information by word of mouth, from friends who were already living in Japan, or from job magazines, and there was no need for brokers. Starting in the fall of 1985, however, broker intervention began spontaneously, accompanying the increase in numbers of undocumented workers. In 1987, immigration official Tetsuo Yamazaki reported that in 30.9% of the cases (involving either male or female workers) the broker was Japanese, and that in a much larger 69.1% of cases the broker was of the same nationality as the worker (Yamazaki).

The same Ministry of Justice document set up a four-category system to characterize the division of labor between Japanese and foreign brokers. In the first type, the 'work-sharing case,' the foreign broker sends the recruits to Japan, and they are met at the airport by the Japanese broker who then assists them in finding employment and controls them. The second pattern is the 'complicity case,' where both the Japanese and foreign broker participate in the recruitment, accompany the recruits, assist them in finding employment, and manage them. In the third pattern, the 'Japanese case,' a Japanese national recruits the workers either personally or through a local broker, takes them to Japan, and personally finds jobs or manages them. In the last pattern, the 'foreigner case,' a foreign broker recruits the workers, brings them to Japan, and personally finds jobs and conducts supervision.

The same 1987 document also reported that the commission brokers typically received a ¥50,000 to ¥100,000 commission from employers, and that in many cases this fee was paid in advance.

In Thailand, private employment offices geared toward overseas labor have sprung up in large numbers, acting like a kind of network of private employment security offices, and in Bangkok there are said to be over 500 such companies (Hinako a).

The Ministry of Justice Document also introduced the following example involving Thai brokers in the section on the so-called 'foreigner case':

Case 1: G, a Thai male (29) worked with H, a Thai female (31) to recruit 13 Thai males and find them jobs working in a civil engineering firm in Nagano Prefecture. The division of labor was as follows: G brought the workers from Thailand to Japan, and H negotiated with the company in Japan, taking a broker's fee as well as a cut from the workers' wages.

The specific activities carried out by brokers seem to differ from country to country. In the Philippines and Thailand, travel agencies act as brokers for the travel outside the country, getting false passports and visas, and preparing 'show money,' a large sum of cash that the workers can present to Immigration authorities to demonstrate that they are 'real tourists,' and not entering the country in order to work.

According to the document, the fee for acquiring the false passports and visas ranged between ¥100,000 and ¥200,000, with the total sum starting with the passage between the host country and Japan and ending with successfully finding a job reaching anywhere from ¥250,000 to ¥300,000. These fees, however, are currently showing an upward trend because the revised Immigration Law has made it more difficult to enter Japan. Furthermore, brokers often assist Filipino overstayers who want to leave Japan under a false name. In this case, the fee for preparing the necessary photographs for the false passport is approximately ¥100,000.

In 1989, 483 people were caught trying to enter Japan with forged passports and/or with documents belonging to other people, with 455 of these people being either Thais (281) or Filipinos (170) (Ministry of Justice q, Table 17). What these figures demonstrate is the level of activity of brokers in those countries. In the case of Bangladeshis and Pakistanis, there were once many cases of people coming to Japan on *shugakusei* visas, then using those visas as cloaks to work for extended periods. This will be examined again in the section on students.

Current information indicates that in Pakistan the brokers have formed regionally based networks. It is believed that the Pakistani brokers have been using this system to procure recruits from their own regions and then send them to work in Japan. Apparently a melee that broke out in March 1988 between two groups of Pakistanis in Kawaguchi City had its origins in disputes between groups from different regions (*Asahi Shimbun*, 23 March, 13 April 1988).

Of the 17 Iranians interviewed in the survey held in Oota City, Gunma Prefecture which was mentioned in the Introduction, four said they had found their jobs through friends, one through family, and a similar number, four, said they had gone through brokers. Many of the brokers were Pakistanis, whose commissions have recently climbed into the vicinity of ¥100,000 to ¥200,000 (Yamashita, p. 235).

The following example involves Bangladeshis:

Case 2: In October 1988, police apprehended a group of undocumented workers including 53 Bangladeshis and three Indians, and found that they had come through the mediation of a personnel dispatch firm located in Hamamatsu City. Between March 1887 and October 1988, the company had employed a total of 176 workers (164 Bangladeshis, 10 Indians, and 2 Filipinos) and sent them to work in 31 area companies, including automobile and motorcycle parts factories, and painting shops. In exchange, the dispatch firm received a net commission of ¥1,300 to ¥1,400 per man hour.

The workers who were apprehended in this incident were receiving salaries of ¥100,000 to ¥120,000 per month, although a Bangladeshi national was apparently deducting ¥60,000 from this sum as an introduction fee. The workers had answered a help-wanted advertisement in Bangladesh, with the understanding that they would go to Japan. They were taken to Bangkok by a fellow Bangladeshi, and waited there until they were finally led into Japan and introduced to the dispatch firm (Ministry of Justice f).

This example points to the collusion that exists between Japanese and Bangladeshi brokers, and is thus an example of the 'complicity case.'

There have also been cases of Bangladeshis being swindled by brokers from their home country.

Case 3: On one Sunday, we were able to interview three Bangladeshis who had come to Akihabara in Tokyo to shop for electrical appliances. All three were attending Japanese language school but simultaneously working in a plastics factory. The man who seemed to be the leader, whose nickname was Babu, said he had come to Japan a year and a half earlier. When he left Bangladesh, a broker took ¥300,000 from him (¥100,000 for the airplane ticket), falsely saying that he would find a job for him in Japan. When Babu arrived, he was left to find a job himself, and finally was introduced to work by friends in Japan to whom he had written. A second man named Masoom said he had been unemployed for his first month and a half in Japan. He had paid ¥50,000 to a fraudulent Bangladeshi broker in Japan. The third, named Farooq, said he had found his job through Babu's introduction.

Case 4: In an example involving Korean workers, a construction company in Fukuoka Prefecture that was prosecuted was found to have diversified its business into labor dispatch, and was currently doing this as its main line of business. The owner, a Korean resident of Japan, had been recruiting laborers in Korea and hiring them out to companies in Japan (Ministry of Justice f).

Case 5: One large-scale incident of this kind involved a civil engineering and construction firm in Shinjuku Ward, Tokyo. Starting in about 1986, the firm began hiring Malaysians, Filipinos and other workers after bringing them into Japan on tourist visas. The company had hired a total of 1,000 workers, dispatching them to a dozen firms in the metropolitan area as construction workers. Each worker received an average of ¥13,000 per day, but the dispatch company skimmed 40% off of the wages, achieving a profit of some ¥300 million. The recruiting in the home countries had been carried out by former employees who had returned to their home country. The company had also been providing accommodation for foreign workers (*Yomiuri Shimbun*, 22 January 1990).

These were all cases where the workers came into Japan illegally or worked on tourist visas, and it is clear that they were in fact undocumented workers. We will now look at some examples where, for instance, trainees entered Japan using training visas, or students entered on study visas, and took advantage of these apparently legal categories to perform actual labor.

First, let us look at a situation where brokers made use of trainees.

Case 6: A Japanese national who held a position as director of a dormant (non-active) auxiliary organization of the Ministry of Foreign Affairs used the trainee system to bring 250 Chinese citizens into Japan in the space of nine months and subsequently sent them to work in 25 companies and factories. The workers, who had been employed in factories in various parts of China, had applied to their bosses to be sent to Japan for training. After being screened by regional Science and Technology Committees, a selected group of workers were given over to the Japanese man and sent to Japan. All of the companies and factories were 'members' of the dormant organization, and were paying a 'membership fee' of ¥10,000 per month for each Chinese worker they employed. At times, brokers working in specific regions had acted as mediators between the man and the factories.

When the Chinese workers entered Japan, their applications stated that they would receive Japanese language instruction and technical training, but no such programs were ever carried out. The Chinese were simply made to do strenuous unskilled labor from morning to evening, and were forced to work long overtime hours. As compensation, they received a meager ¥70,000-¥80,000 in living expenses which was paid from the factory, occasionally via a broker, to the Japanese national, and then finally to the workers (*Mainichi Shimbun* a, pp. 140–146).

Case 7: We were able to interview two Thai men, one 26 years old and the other 35, who were working in a metal processing plant in the northern Kanto region. We will call the younger man Sompong and the older one Paitoon. Neither could speak any Japanese at all, though Sompong was carrying a Japanese language text designed for Thais.

Both men were farmers from a place about two hours north of Bangkok by bus. Six months earlier they had come to Japan on a two-year contract. However, they had not signed the contract directly with the factory, meaning that the management was not aware of how long they would be in Japan. Paitoon had been introduced to the job by a cousin, while Sompong had been sent after applying to a Thai company specializing in dispatching trainees to Japan.

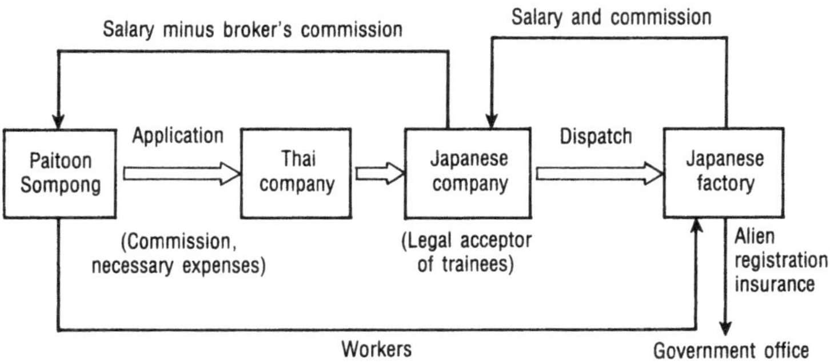

Chart 1–1 Framework for work under the trainee system

The company charged Sompong a total fee of ¥275,000 including the passport and visa charges. In addition, he had to pay roughly ¥100,000 as a registration fee, which was provided as a loan. The company in Thailand had a connection with a Japanese brokering company to which it sent trainees (see Chart 1–1).

In Thailand, a full day's work was probably only worth ¥360, so this was a substantial amount of money.

At the time we conducted the interview, nine other trainees in the same position as Sompong were working in the factory. Their salaries were paid by the factory to the Japanese broker, which then passed it to them, deducting in the process a portion to pay back the trainees' debts as well as some cut off the top.

Sompong and Paitoon received daily wages of ¥3,500, plus ¥500 per hour of overtime, with an ¥800 daily allowance for meals. They didn't know how much their Japanese co-workers received. Although they were nominally trainees, not only had neither Sompong nor Paitoon ever received any Japanese language instruction, but they had not even been given any technical instruction. It is certain that when they return to Thailand they will not have anything to show for the experience other than the probably useless experience of having been forced to perform unskilled labor in Japan. The factory admitted this reality, but justified its actions by saying that 'we have to consider business first, and so this is unavoidable.'

The case of these two Thai men, like the following example, is believed to be a classic case of how brokers use the trainee system for their own purposes.

Case 8: P Company, a construction firm in Tokyo, was employing 200 trainees as of March 1986, and was hiring them out to 12 other firms called 'cooperating companies.' The firm began this operation in 1982, when it brought 10 Bangladeshis to Japan as trainees. The agreement was that the 'cooperating companies' would pay P Co. ¥128,700 a month per worker. P Co. in turn paid the Thai trainees ¥50,000 per month and the Bangladeshis ¥45,000. The company did, however, pay the trainees' travel and insurance costs. It was supposed to have in its service specialists who would conduct technical and Japanese language training, but the courses were never carried out (*Shimotsuke Shimbun*, 14, 16 March 1986).

Next, we will look at another status which is often abused as a cover for unauthorized labor, namely that of *shugakusei*. Japanese language schools have been seen as fertile ground for brokers. The previously mentioned Ministry of Justice document reported that brokers hiring Pakistanis and Bangladeshis often took advantage of this. The fees they charged for bringing one 'student' into the country ranged from ¥250,000 to ¥300,000. In cases of people coming from these two countries, Japanese brokers were almost never involved, and it was usually done according to the 'foreigner case.' We will now consider two examples taken from the aforementioned document.

Case 9: One Pakistani male (34) was dismissed due to poor attendance from the Japanese language school he had supposedly come to study at. He was found to be using the cover of a job at a rug importing and sales company to bring other Pakistani 'students' to work in Japan.

Case 10: A group of four Bangladeshis including L (male, 23) were found to be recruiting people from their own country. They told their victims that for a fee of ¥300,000 they would get them into Japan to work while attending a Japanese language school. In reality, however, they did no more than buy them an airplane ticket and get them into the country without visas. They did nothing about the language school.

There have also been examples of brokers engaging in malicious activities in the lobby of Narita Airport.

Case 11: A Pakistani broker was arrested in November 1990 for finding work in a construction company for three Iranians who had entered the country on tourist visas. It is common to see foreign brokers like this waiting in the arrival lobby at Narita

Airport and accosting new arrivals (*Asahi Shimbun*, 28 February 1991).

In addition, many of the labor dispatch companies that deal with Latin Americans of Japanese descent are involved in malicious brokering activities.

The way these brokerages usually operate is by recruiting Nikkeijin workers, telling them that they are filling orders for Japanese companies. The services these companies usually offer range from giving advances for airplane tickets to meeting workers at the airports, providing apartments or dormitories and lending out daily necessities, renewing visas, taking care of alien registration procedures, caring for the workers' daily lives, transporting them to and from their workplaces, and taking care of the money they send back home (Watanabe and Mitsuyama, p. 26).

According to the Overseas Japanese Association (*Kaigai Nikkeijin Kyokai*) survey of Nikkeijin that we presented in the Introduction, 62.9% of the respondents said they were working under contract with a labor dispatch company or mediator, 34.7% said they had a direct contract with the company they were working for, and 2.3% were free agents (JICA, p. 108). Similarly, the survey of people of Okinawan descent which was also cited in the Introduction showed that 22.9% of the respondents had started working directly for their factories, 72.1% had found the job through a dispatch company, and 5.0% had found their jobs through a public employment security office (Okinawa International Foundation, p. 20). These two surveys seem to indicate that labor dispatch companies have a large involvement, approximately 60–70%, in the employment of Nikkeijin.

Not only do these dealers take a large cut from the wages of the Nikkeijin workers, but they also make them virtual prisoners by confiscating their passports, levying large fines against them if they leave their job before the contract expires, and expropriating money to pay for airfares and registration fees for passports and visas (*Migrant*, 25 February 1991). In particular, illegal labor contract clauses such as 'a fine of ¥300,000 shall be levied if the worker quits his or her job before one year has passed' have led to many complaints among Nikkei workers (*Asahi Shimbun*, 7 March 1992).

Incidentally, the Man-Power Dispatching Business Act of 1985 forbids the dispatch of unskilled workers. In consequence, these companies are acting in violation of that law. In addition, actions such as 'skimming,' where a portion of wages is appropriated by a mediating agent, infringes on the Labor Standards Act. Charging workers for assistance in finding jobs is a violation of the Employment Security Act.

The first major case of Brazilian recruiters sending workers to Japan occurred in 1985, when a group of laborers were brought to work at S Industries, a company based in Yokohama. In subsequent years there was a rapid increase in this type of business, and by 1988 there were more than 20 such recruiting agents in Sao Paolo (Maeyama a). However, at the end of 1989 the most prominent firm, S Industries, as well as N Machines, a company in Chiba Prefecture, were prosecuted under the Man-Power Dispatching Business Act.

Case 12: S Industries employed between 500 and 2,200 workers, mostly Nikkeijin, housed them in company dormitories and apartments, and used company minibuses to transport them to and from over one hundred firms, including automobile parts manufacturers, in the Kanto and Tokai regions. The company took a 40% cut from the workers' wages, and accumulated a profit of ¥680 million in a three-year span (*Asahi Shimbun*, 13 October 1989, *Nikkei Shimbun*, 13 October 1989). Similarly, N Machines employed a total of 2,300 workers, including 1,200 Nikkeijin, dispatching them to factories throughout Kanto, and taking a cut of approximately 30% from their wages. The company earned roughly ¥500 million in profits (*Asahi Shimbun, Nikkei Shimbun*, 1 November 1989).

When employers became aware of these profits they began to hire workers directly, but labor dispatch companies, as mentioned above, remain the major route for companies recruiting workers. In both of the cases mentioned above, for example, the recruitment was done through ads placed in Japanese-language newspapers in the host countries or through local Nikkei brokers. In the Sao Paolo region there are approximately 180 local brokers, with most of their work focusing on getting airline tickets. They charge a fee of approximately ¥100,000 per person (*Chunichi Shimbun*, 17 December 1991). Thus the problems originating from these companies involved in the dispatch of Latin American labor have only intensified, and yet nothing is being done in spite of the fact that their activities are illegal.

To summarize what we have seen above, brokers exert a strong degree of control over the employment of foreign workers, and their activities, which include intermediary exploitation and fraud, contain a significant element of evil. Furthermore, the behavior of brokers differs greatly according to nationality, and their activities include the use of supposedly legal and often overlooked categories such as trainees, students, and Latin Americans of Japanese descent.

2 Unauthorized Labor in the Guise of Trainees

In order to find a resolution to Japan's serious labor shortage, both the business world and government agencies have begun considering permitting the use of foreign unskilled labor, and the trainee system is one breach that has opened up in the traditional barriers. The use of the 'trainee' adopts the pretext that these are not unskilled workers, and thus avoids infringing on the wall. Moreover, when the system was introduced it was believed that the fact that trainees would only come to Japan for a limited stay would prevent the occurrence of many of the social problems that have plagued other Western nations. In this section, we will examine this trainee system, which in the future is bound to become a critical issue.

In August 1989, the Ministry of Justice released the findings of a survey conducted on training programs initiated since April 1988, compiling a list of 40 companies (and 547 persons) which it suspected were carrying on such programs in a problematic way. Specifically, it pointed to many situations where the category of trainee was being used illegitimately to guarantee a supply of cheap labor.

In other words, the survey showed that many companies are in fact using the training system to accept trainees whom they really plan to use as laborers. It admitted to some of the problems that exist in the system, finding that there were cases where companies never carried out the academic courses or lectures they promised Immigration Bureau officials they would provide, others in which trainees were sent right onto assembly lines, without any distinction being made between 'employees' and 'trainees,' where the border between labor and training was blurred, and still others where the training periods were scheduled late into the night hours. In principle, the Ministry of Justice does not permit on-the-job training to be conducted late at night. It recognized the fact that in some cases it was doubtful that the training would have any positive effect when the trainees returned to their home countries (Ministry of Justice k).

We have thus seen that the labor carried out by trainees is being legitimized under the pretext of 'on-the-job training,' or OJT. The original meaning of OJT was, of course, the use of actual work to impart technical skills.

Out of the forty companies that appeared in the survey, eight were subjected to on-the-spot inspections in June of 1989, in the first such action involving trainees. The inspections found that not a single one of the eight companies had conducted any academic training at all – they had simply sent the trainees to job sites. Nor was any time allotted to Japanese language study. According to one of the inspectors, 'The air was dirty, and it was hot. The labor conditions were very bad. The work was close to unskilled labor, far from anything one could call training. This seems to reflect the problem of the labor shortage – there was no room at all for any classes.'

Despite the fact that the 'training' is in reality plain labor, the compensation given to trainees is extremely low. For instance, two Chinese working in a cast metal factory in Kawaguchi City were paid just ¥50,000 per month; a group of 20 Thai women working in a lunch box shop within the jurisdiction of Sapporo City were given ¥40,000 a month; and seven South Koreans working in a rubber manufacturing plant in Osaka received ¥50,000 a month. There are, however, cases where the wages are slightly higher, such as one automobile parts factory in Nagoya City which was paying a salary of ¥120,000 to three Filipinos. Furthermore, although regulations on trainees forbid overtime work, the Osaka rubber factory was forcing its trainees to do 1.5 hours of overtime work a day (*Asahi Shimbun*, 20 June 1989).

One well-known incident, which occurred in Nagano Prefecture in 1987, involved a group of Sri Lankan women. They were working in an electronics parts factory, doing the same jobs as the regular workers, working overtime and even on holidays, and the only compensation they received besides meals and housing was a meager ¥5,000 per month. It turns out that the women had been hired by a factory which had set up shop in Sri Lanka, and in exchange agreed to receive training without pay for one year in Japan. The agreement even stipulated that if they broke their promise they would have to pay a fine. A broker who worked finding Asian brides for Japanese men was reportedly involved in the deal (*Mainichi Shimbun*, 13 February 1988).

The examples we have seen so far have been of small- and mid-sized companies, but there has been widespread use of this pretext to hire unauthorized workers even among large firms. In March 1990, a major tire manufacturer brought eight Filipinos from a company in Manila with which it was carrying out technical cooperation, and had them work in its plant in Itami, Hyogo Prefecture. In April, however, the trainees fled the plant and took refuge in a Catholic church in the city. They complained that, 'What was supposed to be training turned out unskilled labor – cleaning floors and carrying boxes around. We couldn't stand it. For an allowance which was much lower than what the Japanese received we had to work late into the night.' They had been placed into the same two-shift system as their Japanese colleagues, working a 12-hour late night shift which began at 8:30 p.m. and ended at 8:30 the next morning. Their allowance was ¥63,000 per month (*Mainichi Shimbun*, 17 April 1990).

We have seen in this section that the trainee system had become a hotbed for the exploitation of foreign workers. One of the biggest problems is that this has betrayed the expectations of people who have come to Japan expecting to be given training. Any hopes they have had of being able to return to their countries with high technical skills have been cruelly dashed as they found themselves treated as nothing more than cheap labor power.

Those who are in reality performing unauthorized labor face more severe problems than others – they receive lower wages, despite the fact that they are in practice kept imprisoned by their employers, and are not given any protection under labor laws – making this category the most problematic at the present time. Moreover, when they are apprehended by authorities, the company which ordered and executed the 'training' receives, at the most, 'administrative guidance,' and escapes without any penalty at all.

One of the major reasons why unauthorized work began to emerge behind the cloak of 'training' is that the Ministry of Justice's screening system has been insufficient. It is said that the inspection system involved no more than paperwork, without any on-the-spot inspection, meaning that in general the visas were granted if the firm was able to prepare the proper forms. Many companies which had no organization in the host country allegedly said, as an excuse to get the trainees, that they had 'future plans' to set up such an organization.

In order to deal with this problem of the training system being used as a cover to bring in unskilled labor, the Ministry of Justice issued a ministerial circular at the time the new Immigration Law came into effect. The new directive set out the following rules:

1) The techniques, skills or knowledge (hereafter abbreviated as 'techniques') in which the trainees will receive training must not be attainable by the simple repetition of one task.
2) Trainees must be at least 18 years of age, and there must be arrangements for them to be employed in work that makes use of the techniques they have acquired after their return to their country of origin.
3) The techniques trainees plan to acquire must be impossible or very difficult to acquire in their home countries.
4) The training must be conducted by full-time employees of the accepting institution who have had at least five years of experience with the techniques to be trained.
5) In cases where the training will involve actual work, the accepting institution must fulfill the following requirements: a) It must possess living facilities for the trainees; b) It must possess training facilities; c) The number of trainees must not exceed one-twentieth of the number of the institution's regular employees; d) It must have staff responsible for guidance of the trainee's day-to-day living; e) It must obtain insurance for cases in which trainees die, are injured, or become ill; and f) The training facilities must be equipped in accordance with the Labor Safety and Sanitation Act.
6) In cases where the training will involve actual work, the trainees must be full-time members of at least one of the following organizations in their home country: a) a national or local public organization, or an equivalent; b) a joint venture or local branch of the accepting

organization (this may include cases in which the joint venture or local branch is being planned and as been granted approval); or c) an organization which has carried out transactions with the accepting organization for at least one year, or an organization that has conducted at least ¥1 billion of trade with the accepting institution in the previous year.

7) The period of time devoted to on-the-job training must not occupy more than two thirds of the total training time.
8) Neither the accepting organization nor any person associated with it may have, in the previous three years, carried out any illegal actions related to a training program.
9) The organization mediating the training must not be seeking profits (Ministry of Justice p).

This directive assumes two different kinds of relationships between dispatching and accepting organizations. The first involves those between national and local public organizations, or similar bodies, and the second those between Japanese companies and overseas joint ventures, local branches or companies cooperating in their business, and is mainly aimed at business enterprises capable of international activities. In any case, it is fairly clear that the Ministry was not considering the case of very small-scale companies accepting trainees.

Because of this, the directive was amended soon after its release because of persistent demands by small- and medium-size companies that wanted to accept trainees. In order to accommodate this possibility, the provisions of (5)-c which set the number of trainees as not more than one twentieth of the number of the accepting organization's regular employees, were relaxed as follows: 15 trainees would be permitted for an organization with between 201 and 300 regular employees; 10 for an organization with between 101 and 200 employees, 6 for one with between 51 and 100 employees, and 3 for an organization with 50 or fewer employees (*Ministry of Justice Bulletin*, 17 August 1990).

It also became possible for small- and mid-sized companies to jointly organize Japanese-language and technical training classes at the level of small business cooperative or commercial associ-

Table 1–1 Number of foreigners entering Japan as trainees (by country/place of origin)

	1987	1988	1989	1990	1991
China	2,688	3,840	3,496	7,624	10,688
Thailand	2,428	4,708	4,502	5,075	6,290
Philippines	1,207	2,314	3,974	3,460	4,476
South Korea	2,800	3,343	4,125	4,485	4,439
Malaysia	757	1,329	2,175	3,564	4,307
Indonesia	1,310	1,378	1,748	2,891	3,883
Taiwan	375	444	539	1,239	1,312
Brazil	576	628	851	1,027	640
Others	4,940	5,448	8,079	8,201	7,634
Total	17,081	23,432	29,489	37,566	43,649

Source: 1987–88 (Yamagami b), 1989 (Ministry of Justice r), 1990 (Ministry of Justice u), 1991 (Ministry of Justice c).

ations, with on-the-job training being entrusted to members of these associations (*Nikkei Shimbun*, 30 July 1990).

Table 1–1 shows the population of trainees entering Japan by year and country. The numbers began to rise steeply starting in 1987, and crossed well over the 40,000 mark, at 43,649, in 1991. Since 1990, China has stood in first place among countries of origin, with its rapidly growing number of trainees crossing the 10,000 mark. Thailand was next, with somewhere in the 6,000 range, followed by the Philippines, South Korea, and Malaysia, all in the 4,000 range, and finally by Indonesia, whose numbers stood in the 3,000 range. All of these countries are nations in which Japanese companies have established a strong presence.

How many foreign workers, then, are masquerading as trainees? It is extremely difficult to come to an exact figure, but as we have said previously, the organizations that accept the trainees must receive official recognition, and the characteristics of these organizations can therefore give us some clues.

The institutions can be divided into three broad categories. The first consists of government agencies such as JICA and the Asian Productivity Organization, which do not entrust any on-the-job training to private corporations, and which are totally funded by the Japanese government. In 1991, these two organizations accepted 6,470 and 1,711 trainees respectively, adding to a total of 8,181 people. In these cases it is inconceivable that the system is being used as a conduit for unskilled labor.

The second category is where a foundation or other body

working under the jurisdiction of a government ministry or agency carries out the training, receiving financial assistance from the government, and then entrusts the trainees to member corporations for in-service training. This implies that in many cases the companies bear a significant burden in training expenses. If we consider that many programs are initiated by the member companies, there is significant room to believe that this system is often being used to hire unskilled labor disguised as trainees, and there is a large gray area where it is difficult to distinguish this from the rightful training program.

Of the foundations belonging in this category, the largest seems to be the Association for Overseas Technical Scholarship, or AOTS (*Kaigai Gijutsusha Kenshu Kyokai*), which falls under the jurisdiction of the Ministry of International Trade and Industry (MITI), and which is 75% subsidized by the government. AOTS accepted 3,370 trainees in 1991. Other major organizations that belong in this category include the Association for International Cooperation (*Koryu Kyokai*) (under the Foreign Ministry and MITI), the ILO Association of Japan (*Nihon ILO Kyokai*) (under the Ministry of Labor), the OISCA International Development Body (OISCA *Sangyo Kaihatsu Kyoryokudan*) (under the Foreign Ministry), and the Overseas Fishery Cooperation Foundation (*Kaigai Gyogyo Kyoryoku Zaidan*) (under the Ministry of Agriculture, Forestry and Fisheries). Incidentally, most companies accepting AOTS trainees are in the automobile, electrica and construction industries, and those accepting ILO Association of Japan trainees are mostly in the automobile, machinery and construction industries.

The International Youth Vocational Training (*Kaigai Seinen Gino Kenshu*) scheme, which was initiated in February 1990 by the Ministry of Labor, also fits into this category. It is operated by the Japan Vocational Competency Ability Development Association, or JAVADA (*Chuo Shokugyo Noryoku Kaihatsu Kyokai*). In this program, which forms part of Japan's official development assistance (ODA), 204 trainees were brought from three countries, Malaysia, Thailand and Indonesia in fiscal 1989, and underwent a program for a maximum period of one year and nine months. The twenty private firms, mainly in the automobile, machine processing, and spinning industries, that are currently participating in the program, bear the food and lodging costs of the trainees. In addition, the trainees receive a monthly allowance of ¥40,000. Of the people who came to Japan in February, 60% had come from the ranks of the unemployed (*Nikkei Shimbun*, 11 December 1989, *Asahi Shimbun*, 4 February 1990).

MITI also has accepted trainees, in the area of computer software, and has used a pre-existing foundation as its accepting institution. As in the previous case, this program uses ODA money for the training, and private sector firms are given responsibility for the in-service training. The training period can be two years or more (Kanto Federation of Bar Associations, pp. 133–134).

In the same way, the Ministry of Construction set up its own Construction Industry Education Center (*Kensetu Sangyo Kyoiku Center*) in 1991. The trainees receive classroom training for a period of four months, undergo a two-month technical training period at a private firm, and then finally carry out in-service training for a private company for a period of up to one year (Construction Industry Study Group on the Problem of Foreigners). The Center began by accepting 200–300 trainees a year (*Nikkei Shimbun*, 10 January 1991).

We should also mention that in May 1990 Saitama Prefecture signed an agreement with sister-region Shanxi Province in China to accept trainees. This agreement attracted attention as the first example of a local government acting as an accepting organization for trainees. A group of 23 trainees came for a period of ten months to one year, and were given in-service training at eight prefecture-based companies, in the bread-making, machining and metal working, and automobile parts industries. The cost for the training was ¥135,000 a month, including an ¥80,000 allowance, and the prefectural government subsidized ¥50,000 of the cost (*Nikkei Shimbun*, 25 June 1990).

Starting in 1990, the Tokyo Metropolitan Government has also accepted 30 trainees each from sister cities Beijing and Jakarta (*Nikkei Shimbun*, 23 February 1992). The training period of one year and nine months has involved in-service training in companies within the metropolis (*Nikkei Shimbun*, 15 June 1990). Starting in 1992, Kanagawa Prefecture has also accepted some 100 trainees from Liaoning Province in China, and the training has been entrusted to companies belonging to the Chamber of Commerce and Industry and smaller business associations (*Nikkei Shimbun*, 11 February 1992).

In the third category, private sector companies accept trainees and carry out the training themselves. In principle the firms are expected to bear the cost of the training. This category includes cases where organizations such as smaller business associations accept trainees and then assign them to member companies. It is believed that this category holds the greatest possibility for the use of the trainee system as a cover for non-authorized labor.

We conducted a survey on the situation relating to categories two and three in September 1990, with the cooperation of the Ministry of Justice. Our survey was conducted on a sample of 597 firms selected from among companies that had accepted trainees within the period of May 1989 to March 1990, or roughly one in five of the firms. The survey was conducted by mail, and we received 261 responses (a response rate of 43.7%).

In terms of the routes by which the trainees were accepted, the answers can be roughly divided into the following categories: the government route, local subsidiary venture route, business partner route, Japanese private sector route, and others. The government route corresponds to the second category above, and all the others fall into the third category. The local subsidiary route applies to cases where employees of a Japanese firm's local subsidiary or joint venture (or of a planned local firm) are brought to the parent company for training. The business partner route applies to cases where employees of a company that either does business with the Japanese firm or conducts technical cooperation with it are brought to Japan. Finally, the Japanese private sector route applies to cases where trainees are brought through the mediation of a private employment agency or job broker in Japan.

The routes can be divided into simple and complex paths, and 192, or 74.4% of the respondents, said that they had used a simple route. The number of trainees fitting into this category was 879, divided into the following routes: government, 16.8%; local subsidiary, 28.8%; business partner, 37.8%, Japanese private sector, 3.9%, and others, 12.7%. This means that more than two-thirds of the trainees came through either the local subsidiary or business partner route, and were mainly dispatched by Japanese corporations that have developed foreign activities.

To what extent are these trainees forced to carry out unauthorized labor? Our survey tried to judge this by using the five following standards: (1) whether the intention of the accepting company was to acquire labor; (2) the level of the training; 3) (the period of training; (4) whether or not there was training outside of regular working hours; and (5) how the training classes were conducted. However, we determined that (5) was not statistically correlated to (1), and decided that it was inappropriate as a standard.

In the four remaining categories, the companies were distributed into the following dichotomies:

In category (1), 56.3% of the companies had such intention, 20.7% did not, and in 23.0% of the cases the results were unclear (total: 261 companies). On point (2), in 28.7% of the cases the training was equivalent to or lower than what was sufficient to produce an assistant, in 72.4% it was sufficient to produce a full-fledged technician or higher, and the results were unclear in 2.3% of cases (total: 270 firms, with multiple answers). On point (3), in 64.3% of cases the period of training was either shorter or longer than an optimum level required for independence, and in 35.7% it was an appropriate period, (total: 185 firms). On point (4) in 45.6% of cases training occurred after working hours, in 51.0% it did not, and in 3.4% of cases it was unclear (total: 261 firms).

It is also possible to divide the firms participating in the survey into groups ranging from those that did not have any problems with any of the four standards of non-authorized labor above to those that had problems under all four. We divided the companies into the following groups: those that did not violate any of the standards: 'no problems,' those who violated one of the standards: 'slight problems,' those with two violations: 'considerable problems,' those with three violations; 'extreme problems,' and companies found insufficient in all four standards: 'cannot be called training.' The distribution of these groups was as follows:

For 3.0% of companies there was 'no problem,' 24.8% had 'slight problems,' 28.3% had 'considerable problems,' 24.8% had 'extreme problems,' and in 9.0% of cases it 'could not be called training (total: 133 firms). This means that an incredible 72.2% of the surveyed firms had at least 'considerable problems,' and there was a high probability that they were using unauthorized labor. Moreover, a full 57.1% of the trainees were working for firms whose intention was to acquire cheap labor.

What are the characteristics of firms that accept foreign trainees? In terms of size, 14.6% of trainees were accepted by firms with 100 or fewer employees, 15.2% by firms with between 101 and 500 employees, 17.7% by firms with between 501 and 1,000 employees, 25.1% by firms with between 1,001 and 10,000 employees, and 27.4% by firms with over 10,000 employees. This means that just over half of the trainees were accepted by companies with at least 1,000 employees (total: 1,815 firms).

Looking from another point of view, 49.6% of companies that accepted trainees had 100 or fewer employees, 29.5% had between 101 and 500, and 20.9% had more than 500 employees, meaning that more than half of the firms had fewer than 100 employees (total: 254 firms). In other words, most of the firms accepting trainees were small- and medium-sized companies, but because each one had just a small number of trainees, the trainees ended up being equally distributed between smaller and large companies.

In addition, we cannot overlook the fact that the accepting companies are largely concentrated in specific manufacturing industries. Our results indicated that 32.1% of the trainees were accepted by companies in the automobile or auto parts industry, and 20.6% by firms in the metal working and machining industry, meaning that over half of all trainees were in these two sectors. Both of these industries are known to suffer from particularly serious labor shortages. In addition, 13.6% were accepted in the electric appliance and electronic parts industry, 16.9% in other manufacturing areas, 5.5% in the construction and civil engineering industry, 2.4% in the primary sector, and 8.8% in the tertiary sector (total: 1,817 firms).

In other words, it is possible to conclude that a large portion of foreign trainees are in fact non-authorized laborers. It is believed that there are generally two categories of firms accepting foreign trainees. The first consists of companies with a foreign presence, and in these cases the necessity of training key local personnel is combined with a desire to deal with labor shortages in the parent company. The firms involved in this type of training are usually of relatively large scale. The second category is composed of firms principally trying to mitigate a labor shortage, and consists mostly of smaller firms (Komai c, Komai d).

As we will see more clearly in the next chapter, foreign workers in the past were principally employed in minor/small- and middle-sized companies. The introduction of the trainee system, however, was epoch-making in that it opened the road for major corporations to begin the large-scale employment of foreign workers.

Trainees have been accepted on a very wide scale. A September 1988 survey carried out by the Employment Advance Research Center (*Koyo Kaihatsu Center*) on 4,500 Japanese multinational companies and foreign affiliates in Japan (with 1,240 respondents, or a response rate of 27.6%), found that 19.1% of these firms had accepted trainees in the preceding three years (Employment Advance Research Center). In another survey carried out by the Shinagawa Ward Labor Administration Office on 2,000 offices in Tokyo's 23 wards with at least ten employees (by mail, with a response rate of 42.9%), 14.8% of the 827 respondents said they had trainees at the time (October, 1988), and 12.6% said they had accepted trainees in the past. These two figures add up to 27.4% (Tokyo Metropolitan Government h).

Furthermore, a July 1990 survey conducted by the Ministry of Labor on 6,104 firms (with 2,718 responses, or a response rate of 44.5%), sampled from among first and second section firms listed in the Tokyo, Osaka and Nagoya stock markets, as well as from companies with between 30 and 299 employees registered in cities or prefectures which had more than 50 foreigners registered as trainees, found that 10.0% of these firms were currently accepting foreign trainees (Ministry of Labor j).

Next, we will consider the question of how many workers are performing unauthorized labor using the pretext of training. To determine this it is necessary to consider the period of stay of trainees, which we found in our survey to be less than three months in 9.0% of the cases, at least three months but less than six months in 11.8%, at least six months but less than one year in 44.0%, at least one year but less than two years in 28.3%, and at least two years in 6.5% of the cases (total: 261 companies). In approximately half of the companies, the period granted was between six months and one year, and in roughly one third of cases the period was over one year.

Therefore, if we consider that roughly half of the trainees in the second and third categories above must renew their visas once a year, and the other half must renew them twice a year, we can calculate the total stock of trainees in 1991 to be approximately 26,000. Of this number, the data explained previously indicates that roughly 20,000 are in reality carrying out unauthorized labor.

Ironically, the reason why trainees face poor labor conditions despite the fact that many of them are being made to labor rather than to undergo training, is precisely due to the fact that they have been brought to Japan under the pretext that they will receive technical training.

The poverty of the working conditions that these trainees experience appears most vividly in the compensation they receive. Our own survey showed that companies paid the following total cash to trainees on a monthly basis (including allowance, and money for food and housing, but not including payment in kind) (in increments of ¥20,000): up to ¥60,000 in 17.5% of cases, between ¥60,001 and ¥80,000 in 25.2%, between ¥80,001 and ¥100,000 in 9.7%, between ¥100,001 and ¥120,000 in 11.3%, between ¥120,001 and ¥140,000 in 7.6%, between ¥140,001 and ¥160,000 in 13.9%, and over ¥160,000 in 14.8% of cases. There were some cases (3.4%) where the trainees received no compensation at all, and others (1.3%) where they received over ¥300,000 (total: 238 firms). We can see that the highest concentration was in the category between ¥60,001 and ¥80,000, which included just over one quarter of the respondents, and that there was also a sizable concentration in the category between ¥140,001 and ¥160,000.

The reason why the compensation can be this low is that it is not considered wages but rather an allowance to help the trainees meet their day-to-day expenses. In particular, the Ministry of Justice specifies that the sum of trainees' allowances must be 'within an appropriate range' (Yamagami b). What this means, essentially, is that the allowance must not exceed a certain sum. There is, however, no uniform guidance on what the appropriate range should be. Some regional immigration offices have set ¥80,000 per month as an appropriate allowance and do not permit anything over ¥100,000 (Management and Coordination Agency, p. 113).

In accordance with this situation, the Ministry of Construction once set a standard of ¥60,000 a month for trainees in the construction industry. The AOTS, which we mentioned previously, set a standard of ¥2,100 per day, adding up to a monthly allowance of slightly over ¥60,000 (Association for Overseas Technical Scholarship). Thus, for instance, the Ministry of Justice called the ¥120,000 per month allowance given to trainees at the automobile parts manufacturing plant mentioned at the beginning of this section 'evidence, to the contrary, that the trainees were being used as undocumented workers.'

This guidance that trainees' allowances should not exceed a certain sum, therefore, has the effect of giving trainees' employers a good excuse for paying low wages. In this way, the 'trainees' have become the very pictures of exploited workers.

Of course, there are also employers who, while leaving no doubt that they are using trainees for labor power, provide them with wages equivalent to those of their Japanese employees. We had the chance to speak with a Korean man named Kim Insik, a worker who entered Japan under the trainee classification.

He had come to Japan a year before the interview with three colleagues. He was a carpenter, and had been working in a construction company in his homeland along with the three other men. He had sustained his family with this job for over 20 years.

The company where Kim was accepted as a trainee had an office in Osaka with approximately 300 employees. The company's managing director said that even if the firm employed 10 workers on a daily basis, it was typical that no more than one person a month would settle into the firm. In order to secure a stable supply of labor, the firm decided to use the trainee system. In order to accept Kim and his co-workers, it set up an international division, which was given charge of all business regarding the trainees.

The application process went smoothly and took place entirely by paperwork. The company said that 'any group with know-how on the training system can receive trainees, so we would like to set up a new company to provide such know-how.'

Kim and his colleagues received their 'training' at a public works construction site in a ravine somewhere in the Kansai region. The firm had received the work as a sub-subcontractor. The person in charge of the site first tried to teach them to count in Japanese, then used them as assistants for approximately one month, and then had them work alongside the Japanese workers.

The company's assertion was that, 'In this business lectures do not help. It is only through on-the-site education that skills can be acquired.' In other words, the program was entirely conducted using on-the-job training. Kim and the other trainees worked an eight-hour day, from 8 a.m. to 5 p.m., with a one-hour lunch break. Because of occasional disruptions by the weather, they worked approximately 20 days a month.

The trainees received a daily allowance of ¥10,000, which was paid to them in a lump sum at the end of each month. In other words, their monthly allowance was a little over ¥200,000. Their salary appeared to be slightly lower than that paid to Japanese employees, but the firm justified this by saying that, 'the company paid for their air tickets from South Korea to Japan, and so it is not financially advantageous for us to use trainees.'

Just a few days before we conducted our visit, two of the trainees had returned to their country after a three-month training period. Kim and the fourth trainee, however, were planning to renew their visas and stay for an additional three-month period. The reason they had come to Japan in the first place was that it is impossible to do construction work in their homeland between December and March, as the winter cold freezes concrete. For this reason, they were planning to go home in the spring and continue their old jobs.

In addition to low wages, trainees also face the problem that labor laws and directives do not apply to them. In particular, the fact that they are not eligible for compensation under the Work Accident Insurance Act puts them into a predicament. It is possible, however, for them to use overseas traveler's accident insurance to get limited protection.

The issue of trainees being detained against their will is another large problem which lies outside of labor conditions. This problem can be subdivided into cases where trainees are inside Japan and others where they have already returned to their home countries. For the first type of case, it is important to note that most trainees sign a contract with the host company before they come to Japan. In many cases, these contracts include clauses that the trainees may not disobey the host's instructions without reason, and that they may not abandon the training before the full period is over.

These clauses give the employer an exaggerated degree of power over the trainees. For the trainees, abandoning the program means not only being deported and having to repay debts to the host company, but also carries the possibility of being sued for damages, making it for all intents and purposes impossible for them to quit. As a result, even when trainees have grave complaints they bear the training patiently, unable to do anything but to cry themselves to sleep while waiting for the period to end.

A form of bondage also sometimes takes place after the trainees' return to their home countries. Many contracts drawn up with Japanese dispatching firms stipulate that the trainees must work for the company after their training.

With regard to this, the AOTS issued a statement that, 'When trainees are compelled to work under strict contracts after returning to their home countries, there is the possibility of criticisms and complaints that this constitutes unreasonable labor conditions,' and took a policy of confronting these issues by recommending that periods of bound labor be shortened, fines for breaking contracts be abolished, and the necessity for trainees to reimburse the training fees be made clear (Association for Overseas Technical Scholarship).

As we have seen above, a significant portion of trainees seem to be working as unauthorized labor under poor working conditions. It was in order to correct this situation while simultaneously mitigating the labor shortage that the government established the Japan International Training Cooperation Organization (*Kokusai Kenshu Kyoryoku Kiko*), or JITCO.

JITCO was launched in 1991, principally by the Ministries of Justice and Labor, but with the cooperation of the Foreign Ministry and MITI, as an organization to conduct a unified supervision of trainees. It started accepting trainees in 1992, and has plans to accept 100,000 people per year in the future. Its duties include: 1) to work with public bodies in developing countries, and introduce host companies to agencies who deal with corporate trainees seeking training; 2) to give advice concerning training plans, and conduct preliminary training screenings; 3) to introduce training personnel and public facilities to firms that do not have their own capabilities; 4) to coordinate a unified insurance program for trainees; and 5) to conduct technical skill examinations on trainees who have finished their programs. As of March 1991, the JITCO had signed agreements to accept trainees from China and Indonesia (*Nikkei Shimbun*, 16 March 1992).

After finishing approximately one year of training, special trainees who pass these examinations can be given 'special activities' status stipulated under the Immigration Act and are permitted to work legally for a period of one to two years. During this period, they fall under the jurisdiction of labor insurance laws and regulations, and are covered by health and worker's compensation insurance. What this means is that public expenditures are being used to allow small- and medium-sized firms to employ trainees on a for-profit basis (*Nikkei Shimbun*, 12 December 1990, 27 June 1991).

Furthermore, as we will see in Chapter 5–1, the government, in reaction to a recommendation from the Provisional Council for the Promotion of of Administrative Reform, passed a cabinet decision in late December 1991 to establish a Technical Apprenticeship System (provisional name) which would allow trainees to work after completing their training program. In response to this, the Ministry of Labor in August 1992, in agreement with the Ministry of Justice, compiled an implementation plan for a 'Technical Intern Training Program' (*gaikokujin gino jisshu seido*) based on the following pillars: (1) that trainees would be accepted for a two-year period, and could work during the last one-year-and three-month period; (2) that 'basis levels' would be established in the technical skills examination system; and (3) that trainees would be accepted through JITCO. There are plans to accept approximately 40,000 trainees in a two-year period (*Nikkei Shimbun*, 27 August 1992). In this way, Japan has finally begun to be opened to foreign workers, albeit within limits, using the pretext of the trainee system.

In reality, however, this is not the first time that the idea of using trainees as workers has been brought up. In the period of labor shortage between the late 1960's and the early 1970's, there was also a similar misuse of the trainee category, as well as calls for using it to promote labor imports. The hiring of so-called unskilled laborers as 'trainees' was seen not only in small and medium-sized firms, but was also rampant in major companies in the shipbuilding, automobile, electrical appliances and food-stuff industries. The use of trainee nurses in hospitals around the country also became to topic of controversy. Most of these trainees were South Koreans.

This practice of hiring unskilled labor using the pretext of training was even recognized at the time by Nikkeiren (the Japan Federation of Employers' Association). In particular, a 1970 Nikkeiren report entitled *Gino Rodoryoku Busoku no Genjo to Taisaku no Hoko* (The Manual Labor Shortage: The Present Situation and Directions for Countermeasures) pointed out that an increasing number of trainees were acquiring skills or technical abilities by working together with workers at the accepting institutions, and that the difference between trainees and workers as defined by the Labor Standards Act was becoming blurred.

In the same year, the Tokyo Chamber of Commerce and Industry issued a request that foreign workers from the Asian region be introduced into Japan to alleviate the labor shortage, and called for an expansion of the trainee system (see Ochiai). This demand, however, was not powerful enough to overturn the seclusionist ideology held by the Ministry of Labor and other groups in Japan, that favored the effective use of domestic labor power, and the debate subsided with the oil shock of the early 1970's.

The layout of the present debate on opening the country to foreign labor seems to be faithfully reproducing the historical events of 20 years ago. What the two debates hold in common is that in both cases the euphemism 'training' has been used as camouflage for the introduction of foreign workers.

3 Japanese Language Schools and *Shugakusei*

The category of *shugakusei*, meaning students of language and technical schools, has become a convenient vehicle for the introduction of foreign workers. Before the revision of the Immigration Law, there were no clear rules on this category. In fact, it was a 'creation' of the Ministry of Justice (Tanaka a).

The category of *shugakusei* is given to people who come to study in a variety of schools other than the institutions of higher education specified in the School Education Law (higher than two-year junior colleges) or vocational and other special schools. Most people admitted with this status, by far, become students in Japanese language schools. There are, however, a few institutions outside of language schools that can accept them.

Some of the Japanese language schools have been set up according to the School Education Law, but there is no legal basis for their establishment, and until recently neither the Ministry of Education nor any other government agency has given them guidance or supervision. The acceptance of *shugakusei* had its origins in a 1983 speech given by then Prime Minister Yasuhiro

Nakasone, who said that 'We should accept 100,000 students by the 21st century.'

On the basis of this, the procedures for issuing these visas were simplified in 1984. In particular, it became possible for schools to go through a unified, one-time pre-screening process. These changes were immediately reflected in the number of people applying for these visas, with the number of just 4,140 in 1984 doubling to 8,942 by 1985, tripling again to 12,637 in 1986, leveling off at 13,915 in 1987, and then increasing tremendously to 35,107 in 1988 (Yamagami c).

Behind this increase has been the role of the brokers acting behind the scenes, as we saw in Section 1, as well as the recruiting slogans of Japanese language schools that 'you can get a part-time job in Japan while you study.' In particular, 795 Bangladeshis and 356 Pakistanis came to Japan as *shugakusei* in 1986 (Yamagami c), but most of them were in fact performing unauthorized labor. The Japanese language schools they were studying at were later raided by Immigration Bureau officials, and the combined total from these two countries dropped to less than 100 after 1987.

Let us now look at some typical cases of *shugakusei* carrying out unauthorized labor. In one case, a Japanese language school actually employed its own students. It kept its Filipino students in a company apartment and made them work for approximately nine hours every day at a nearby golf course. The students fled en masse because the company was only giving them ¥15,000 of their ¥120,000 monthly wage (*Sankei Shimbun*, 23 June 1988).

There have also been cases in which Korean and Taiwanese women working in the sex or entertainment trade have used *shugakusei* visas. In one case that occurred in Osaka City in April and May of 1988, the owner of an area school was arrested for having a total of 400 Taiwanese women work as hostesses in clubs while falsely registering them as 'students' in his school. In another example, a Taiwanese pub in Shinjuku's Kabuki-cho red light district was caught violating the Anti-Prostitution Act during February and March of 1988, and out of the 35 hostesses/prostitutes working there, 11 were found to have been students from a total of nine different Japanese language schools (Ministry of Justice m). There have also been cases where people in the entertainment business have set up Japanese language schools, linked with employment brokers to recruit Asian female students, and then tried to get the women to work as hostesses or dancers in their clubs (*Sankei Shimbun*, 9 May 1988).

In addition, there have been cases, which merit special attention, where companies have set up language schools specifically to secure low-wage labor. One Chinese noodle restaurant chain established a Japanese school to secure personnel, and had a large number of students work in its shops (Yamaguchi b). In another case, a food catering company enrolled Chinese-Malaysians in an affiliated Japanese language school, and had approximately one quarter of them work at its chain shops for an hourly wage of ¥600. Some worked for as many as eight and a half hours a day (Mainichi Shimbun a, Chapter 3).

Japanese language schools have mushroomed along with this influx of *shugakusei*. At the end of 1984 just 49 schools had been recognized by the Immigration Bureau as qualified to accept these students, but this number jumped to 89, 143 and 218 in the following years, and reached a level of 309 by the end of October 1988 (Yamagami c).

As we pointed out earlier, no regulation or approval was necessary before establishing a language school, and as a result a variety of ventures including real estate companies, leasing firms, travel agencies, and prep schools rushed to open language schools as profit-making ventures, sometimes going to the extreme of using an apartment or a partially remodeled store. In Tokyo this led to the so-called 'Ikebukuro War' between Japanese language schools, which then moved to become the 'Takadanobaba War,' and again the 'Otsuka War' (Azuma). It is also said that in many of these cases the schools put forward a Japanese face, but that the real owners were people of Taiwanese origin.

This is not to say that none of the schools were serious educational endeavors, but in many cases these institutions conspired, in league with brokers, to defraud the students. Schools devised a multitude of ways to take everything they could get out of the students – selling admission certificates, charging for introductions to guarantors, which are necessary for visa applications, embezzling entrance fees and tuition by accepting too many students, charging commissions for housing and part-time jobs, and charging fees to doctor attendance rates and grades to allow the students to renew their visas. Many of the schools tried to spend as little money as possible on the education itself, often using housewives as part-time teachers.

These language schools have also become a realm of activity for the brokers, who have become involved in such activities as recruiting students, creating false diplomas, making fake bank statements to show the students have the money to pay for their courses, arranging for and filling out the paperwork for false guarantors, completing applications for the language schools, and helping to find apartments and part-time jobs. These brokers received large sums of money from the students, and then went on to sell them to language schools.

Some Chinese *shugakusei* have been assisted by other Chinese, especially ex-students who settled in Japan, but mainly by other students or by agents from Hong Kong. It is said that there were at one time a dozen or so companies in Hong Kong that placed ads in Chinese newspapers recruiting such students (*Asahi Shimbun*, 18 April 1988). It is also said that Japanese brokers had difficulties working with Chinese because they could not understand the language. Some brokers also began to sell fake grade and attendance reports, which the students needed to renew their visas.

In 1988, during the first boom of Chinese *shugakusei*, we were able to speak to the management of a school in Ikebukuro, Tokyo, who said that there was no longer any need for them to run any advertisements. They said the students already enrolled in the school were encouraging their friends and relatives to come to Japan, and the school was flooded with letters from China to the effect that, 'I have already quit my job. Please hurry and accept me at your school.' The reason for this is that the Chinese government was only issuing the passports necessary for people to study abroad after the applicants had stopped working.

The JR train station at Takadanobaba in Tokyo is known as a *yoseba*, a place where day laborers gather to look for jobs. It was there that we met Lee Shiwen, a Chinese *shugakusei* who spoke Japanese quite competently. He told us that, 'I helped four people enroll in a Japanese language school. They received passports, but it has been more than a year and the visas have not yet been granted. Most people coming from Shanghai bring two or three more people over.' Naturally, the newcomers have to pay a broker's fee. In this way, many students have fallen victim to profit-seeking language schools and brokers, and have subsequently turned around to participate in the exploitation.

The influx of *shugakusei* into Japan reached a new phase in

Table 1–2 Country/place of origin of *Shugakusei* entering Japan

	1987	1988	1989	1990	1991
China	7,178	28,256	9,134	10,387	8,099
South Korea	1,470	1,733	3,858	5,346	6,487
Taiwan	1,839	1,113	1,279	1,563	1,877
Others	3,428	4,005	3,912	3,555	4,191
Total	13,915	35,107	18,183	20,851	20,654

Source: 1987–1988 (Yamagami c), 1989 (Ministry of Justice r), 1990 (Ministry of Justice u), 1991 (Ministry of Justice C).

the period following 1987. In 1988, the figure was dominated by Chinese mainlanders (hereafter the term 'Chinese' will not include Taiwanese). The reason behind this is that Chinese only gained the freedom to travel abroad in 1985, and coming to Japan with these visas became a major means of accomplishing this.

Table 1–2 shows that since 1987 Chinese *shugakusei* have continuously outnumbered the total of all other non-Chinese students. Over 28,000 Chinese, making up 80.5% of the total figure, entered the country in 1988, and this was behind the huge influx of Chinese into Japan that year. However, these visas became much more difficult to obtain after 1988, and this combined with controls imposed by the Chinese government following the Tienanmen Incident led to a sharp drop in numbers, to just one third of the previous level, in 1989. This trend continued into 1991, and the total number of incoming *shugakusei* fell to 20,654 in that year.

The number of non-Chinese *shugakusei* has risen slightly, but is still at the 10,000 level. Other countries of origin include South Korea (31.4% of the total), Taiwan (9.1%), and Hong Kong (3.4%). The growth in the numbers of Koreans merits special attention.

Incidentally, one reason that has been given for the fact that so many Taiwanese people have come into Japan with these visas is that there is no standard examination such as TOEFL, which students must undergo before being given permission to study in the United States.

We will now take a look at some interviews with people who, as we mentioned above, came from Fujian Province, many for the strict purpose of performing unauthorized labor. Zhang Liyong, a man from a farming family in Changluo, Fujian Province whom we met in Takadanobaba, seemed like a simple, good-natured man. He told us he had been in Japan for just a few months. He said he was 28 years old, but looked somewhat older. He said he had two sons, one seven and the other four years old, which seemed unusual given China's one-child-per-family policy. At the time he was living, along with his wife, in an apartment in Ikebukuro.

Before coming to Japan he had worked for an architectural firm in China. It was a profitable business, principally because the sub-contracting system that had emerged along with development. He had been living quite comfortably, and told us he had built a three-story house for his family before coming to Japan. He was able to bring ¥500,000 in living expenses which he had saved back home. In addition, he paid the school's entrance and registration fees as well as other expenses with ¥50–60,000 that he received from relatives living in the United States and in Hong Kong. When we asked him whether these were loans, he answered, 'They are close relatives, so I don't have to pay them back.'

The couple was living in a six-mat (approximately 10 square meters) apartment with a bathroom and kitchen but no bath, and the rent was ¥40,000 per month. The same friend from Fujian Province who found him his school had introduced him to the apartment. Many Japanese were living in the neighborhood, but Zhang said he had no contact with them other than greetings on the street.

He was working at a very difficult part-time job. For three or four days a week he hauled boxes for a vegetable store in Akihabara, and could only do architectural work on Sundays. He also got the job at the vegetable store through his friend. He worked a graveyard shift that went from 11 p.m. until 4 to 6 a.m. the next morning. His school hours were from 1 p.m. to 5 p.m., meaning that he only had time for a short nap between work and school. His starting wage was ¥7,000 a day, but he eventually received a raise to ¥7,500.

He told us he had found his other job, in architecture, through a Taiwanese friend. He was well-treated there because the company only hired specialists. All the other workers were Japanese. He worked from 9 a.m. to 4:30 p.m., with a one-hour lunch break, two 20-minute breaks, and received ¥9,000 per day. We were surprised to hear that he had not fallen ill even with this schedule. He was covered by his language school's health insurance program. His wife, who was attending a different language school, was also working, as a cleaning staff in a Japanese inn, and earning ¥700 per hour. She worked from 9 a.m. to 1 p.m.

They had a combined income of ¥150,000 per month, of which ¥50,000 went to their apartment and ¥60,000 to the two language schools, meaning that they had very little financial leeway. They usually shopped at a supermarket in their neighborhood, but sometimes went to Ueno. They spent a lot of time watching television.

They got their opportunity to come to Japan when they received a letter of invitation from the previously mentioned friend. That was, however, six months before they finally came. Zhang told us 'I wanted to come to Japan to learn skills from this advanced country. I am hoping to enter an architectural school within the next two years.'

His case was slightly different from most *shugakusei* in that he was able to bring his wife to Japan with him. At the time that he received the invitation it was too difficult for them to go together, so he came first and his wife followed him three months later. At first I thought that his wife had followed him over, but no, he said, they had both wanted to 'see the outside world.' They left their children with their parents, who did not oppose their plans. They promised to return after two years.

When we asked him the question, 'What is the greatest difficulty you face now?' he answered 'I worry about the children.' They called home once every two or three weeks. When we asked him what he enjoyed most, he said that, 'I like seeing the town when I ride the bus to work. I am interested in Japanese transportation. I can see the highway from my Sunday job, and it is very beautiful at night.'

In response to the problem of Japanese language schools being used as a cover by undocumented workers, in November 1988 the Ministry of Justice tightened its screening of the forms and of the contents of papers submitted by Chinese applicants for these visas. The result was the so-called 'Shanghai Incident.' A group of roughly 35,000 people who had already quit their jobs were waiting for visas in that city, and it became increasingly clear that they would not be able to go to Japan. In response, they began to hold daily demonstrations in front of the Japanese consulate.

The Ministry of Justice, partially because of this incident, passed a judgment in January 1989 against 23 Japanese language schools, ruling that they were unsuitable institutions, and revoked their ability to grant new visas as well as extensions. These restrictions were later relaxed, but at the time they caused great confusion among the people in China who had been admitted to these schools and who were waiting for their visas to be issued, as well as panic among the 5,000 students who were already living in Japan and thought that they would lose their status.

Moreover, in spite of repeated negotiations carried out by representatives of Shanghai City, as of July 1990 these schools had failed to return a total of ¥500 million, including admission and other fees, from 2,500 people, and it is believed that over ¥200 million of this sum will never be settled or repaid. There are currently moves to solicit contributions from corporations and individuals to repay this debt (*Asahi Shimbun*, 14 July, 4 September 1990).

In response to the corruption and confusion that the Shanghai Incident later cast into the spotlight, the Ministry of Justice had made an initial decision to establish an association through which it could try to control language schools. Thus, in December 1986 the Association for the Promotion of Japanese Language Education (*Gaishukyo*), with 109 member schools, was established under the sponsorship of the Immigration Bureau.

It is also likely that, in addition to control, the Immigration Bureau wanted this organization to act as its agent in dealing with the increasing number of applications and extension requests. In fact, the first two chairmen and secretary-generals were all ex-Immigration officials who 'descended from heaven' into their positions (Association for the Promotion of Japanese Language Education a). The Immigration Bureau gave special privileges to member schools, making the pre-screening process easier when their students applied for visas, and in some cases allowing them to act as agents to collectively renew the visas. For the students, this ability of the schools to handle the procedures for them, meaning that they did not need to personally go to the Immigration Bureau, was a great benefit.

However, in the end the Gaishukyo did not live up to the Immigration Bureau's expectations that it would clean up the Japanese language school industry. In theory the Association was supposed to consult the Ministry of Justice before allowing any school to become a member, but there were no set standards on what qualifications were necessary for membership. Because of this, a significant number of what were considered to be inferior businesses became members. In fact, every issue of its newsletter, *Kaiho*, seemed to include news of some school or other being expelled. One manager of a Japanese language teaching materials publications company who participated in the establishment of the Association told us that, 'there are probably 40 serious schools out of all the members.' As of August 1989, there were 223 member schools.

It has been pointed out that one major factor behind this situation is that many Immigration Bureau officials were invited to become directors of the member schools (*Asahi Shimbun*, 3 July 1988). In June 1989, the Social Democratic Party of Japan's investigation team on Japanese language schools discovered that 13 retirees from the Ministry of Justice had 'descended from heaven' into the industry. The team also found that one member school of Gaishukyo had used a current Immigration Bureau senior official to help prepare documents since its establishment. This school, in fact, had very poor attendance rates, and had problems with both facilities and in the times at which they accepted students. It could only be considered an inferior institution (*Asahi Shimbun*, 15, 22 June 1989).

In March 1987, the Ministry of Education, which seemed to be in hot pursuit of the Ministry of Justice, established the National Association of Japanese Language Institutions, Japan, with 30 language schools based on the School Education Law.

Then, in order to deal with the confusion so rampant in the administration of language schools, the 'Council for Research and Study Cooperation for the Establishment of Standard Criteria for Japanese Language Schools,' a group centered around the Ministry of Education, was founded (with Hideyasu Nakagawa, Professor of Otsuma Women's University, as chairman). In December 1988, this Council released a basic guideline for schools entitled *Criteria for Operating Japanese Language Instruction Institutions*. It included criteria for the length and beginning of the school year, number of class hours, number of students per class, number of teachers, instructor qualifications, school facilities, and building size. In fact, these standards were generally equal to or higher than those for vocational schools. They did not, however, prohibit the running of these institutions by profit-seeking corporations.

In May 1989, the Ministries of Education and Justice cooperated to establish the Association for the Promotion of Japanese Language Education (*Nikkyoshin*) (the English title is the same as for the earlier Gaishukyo, but the Japanese names are different), with the mandate of carrying out inspections and granting authorization to schools based on the *Criteria*. The Ministry of Justice, for its part, announced that it would regulate the entrance and residency of *shugakusei* based on the inspections of language school facilities carried out by Nikkyoshin (Ministry of Justice j). As of August 1992, 458 schools had been given authorization (*Asahi Shimbun*, 28 August 1992).

The real meaning of this is that the Ministry of Justice has completely abandoned its role of dealing with *shugakusei*. If we return to the analogy of the 'Whack-a-Molee' game, the Japanese language schools have become one of the holes. There are several lessons we can learn from these developments that bear on the overall issue of foreign workers.

First, we can say that because schools are involved it is only natural that the Ministry of Education should have been responsible, but because it involved immigration the Immigration Bureau took an active interest and tried to intervene in the process, and in the end it was unable to deal effectively with the situation. The direct victims of this were the 35,000 Chinese who had resigned from their jobs and who were waiting for visas. Second, not only did authorities neglect to take any action against the schools and brokers working behind the scenes who were making unreasonable profits from the system, but in fact we can say that it was the secret connections that existed between these groups and Immigration authorities that allowed the situation to develop as it did. In this case too, it was the *shugakusei* themselves and others hoping to gain this status who fell victim to this by being tricked or forced into paying large fees.

In any case, the number of *shugakusei* decreased dramatically after the introduction of controls, and Japanese language schools have fallen on hard times. Where once 60–80 percent of schools undergoing pre-screening processes were given permission to accept students, that number has now fallen to 20–35 percent, and there have been many recent examples of schools downsizing or closing down (*Nikkei Shimbun*, 9 March 1990).

Let us now consider the question of how large the stock of these students is. They are normally required to apply for alien registration cards, and as of December 1990 there were 35,595 such registrees (Ministry of Justice w). Taking the estimate, that we will mention later, that two-thirds of these students were working more than four hours per day, or 28 hours per week, there were at that time approximately 25,000 people in this category who were, in reality, workers.

The large number of *shugakusei* who entered Japan in 1988 were approaching the end of their permitted stay at the end of 1990. Partially because of the situation in China at that time, many of them did not wish to return to their homeland, and tried to extend their stay by changing their status to regular students in computer or business vocational schools, or by becoming auditors. Given this situation, some vocational schools ended up accepting up to three times more students than they could accommodate (*Asahi Shimbun*, 9 March 1990). As a result, as we will discuss in more detail later, there was a huge increase in enrollment in these schools' specialist programs. In addition, as of 1991 there were a large number, 12,678, of overstayers who had originally come on *shugakusei* visas (Ministry of Justice B). This indicates that many people who were not able to enter other schools ended up simply overstaying their visas.

As we have seen, the *shugakusei* category is one that has given rise to significant problems, and at the time of the revision of the Immigration Act the Ministry of Justice issued a ministerial directive stating that:

1) Applicants must have sufficient funds, scholarships or other sources of money, to support their daily living expenses. This support can also be given by other persons.
2) Students who wish to enroll in a vocational or specialist school program must:
    a) have spent at least six months studying Japanese at an authorized school or must have an equivalent proficiency in Japanese language;
    b) must have prospects of being employed after returning to their home country in a job that makes use of the techniques or knowledge they acquire; and
    c) the school to which they apply must have full-time

staff with the specific function of providing guidance for foreigners' lives in Japan.

3) The language schools must have received official authorization (Ministry of Justice p).

The purpose of this directive was both to forbid the reliance on part-time jobs and to weed out inferior institutions. With regard to vocational schools, it tried to ensure that students would learn skills that they could use in their home countries.

In addition, the directive changed the time limit on part-time jobs from 20 hours a week to a daily limit of four hours. It left in place the stipulation that all *shugakusei* who wanted to seek an outside job would have to receive permission from the Immigration Bureau. However, the Bureau has not been able to grasp the conditions under which students have been working, and thus has not been able to offer any guidance (Management and Coordination Agency, p. 76).

Next let us look at the situation under which *ryugakusei* (regular foreign students) work. This category includes students in Japanese universities or equivalent institutions, special courses in vocational schools, institutions aiming to prepare people who have completed 12 years of school education in other countries to enter Japanese universities, and professional colleges. Night schools and correspondence courses are not included, but *kenkyusei* (special students) and auditors are.

If we look at alien registration records, we see that in December 1991 there was a total stock of 48,715 such students. By far the greatest numbers were from China (60.3%), and South Korea (20.4%) (Ministry of Justice w). As of May 1991, 27.8% of these students were enrolled in vocational schools (or specialist courses) (*Nikkei Shimbun*, 8 February 1991). One of the reasons for the large percentage of both Chinese citizens and vocational school students is the large number of Chinese *shugakusei* who entered the country in 1988 and subsequently changed their visa status.

In order to look at how many of these students were in reality working, we can use a survey conducted in 1991 by the Tokyo Metropolitan Government. The survey took place with the cooperation of 65 universities (including two-year colleges) and 29 vocational or Japanese schools in the Tokyo metropolitan region. Responses were collected from 1,900 *ryugakusei* and 735 *shu-*

gakusei living in the city (Tokyo Metropolitan Government l). The survey found that 53.5 percent of the *ryugakusei* were working part-time, and the average working time they reported was 4.6 hours per day 3.5 days per week, meaning that they could not be classified as workers.

The ministerial directive that concerns the granting of visas to *ryugakusei* is essentially the same as that for *shugakusei*, with the exception of a minimum of 10 study hours per week that it sets for *kenkyusei* and auditors (Ministry of Justice p). Furthermore, the restrictions on these students doing part-time jobs are exactly the same as those set for *shugakusei*. An additional restriction is that no more than half of the students at any vocational school may be *ryugakusei* (*Nikkei Shimbun*, 5 July 1990).

What is the situation, then, of the *shugakusei*? According to the above-mentioned survey done by the Tokyo Metropolitan Government, the countries which sent the greatest numbers to Japan were: South Korea (41.2%), China (22.9%), Taiwan (13.5%), and Malaysia (9.3%). In a similar survey carried out by the metropolitan government in 1988, the largest group was found to be Chinese (with 49.6%), and South Koreans had only accounted for 5.5% of the total (Tokyo Metropolitan Government g).

According to the survey, men significantly outnumbered women by 56.3% to 43.7%. In terms of age, 5.7% were under 20 years old, 41.0% were at least 20 but under 25, 46.0% were at least 25 but under 30, 6.5% were at least 30 but under 35, and 0.8% were over 35, making the average age 24.8. In terms of educational background, the greatest single categories were high school graduates (45.5%), followed by university graduates (30.7%), technical college graduates (15.1%), and then by junior high school graduates (1.7%), students who had completed master courses (1.4%), with 5.6% not fitting into any of these categories. In addition, 9.4% were married.

Next we will look at the situation of *shugakusei* and part-time jobs. The survey showed that 65.4% were working part-time, meaning that approximately one third did not have a job. We must add, however, that the numbers of working hours reported by students in this survey were suspiciously short, and cannot be taken as reliable. We therefore decided to estimate the number of hours they worked by dividing the income they reported from their jobs by the typical hourly wage paid for such work. The average monthly income was ¥166,000, and the breakdown of sources for this income reported by those in the ¥150,000-¥200,000 was as follows: ¥101,000 from part-time jobs, ¥51,000 from families back home, ¥2,000 in scholarships, and ¥10,000 from other sources. This indicates that part-time jobs are an important source of income.

Since the average hourly wage received by students at the time was ¥1,090, we can infer that each student was working an average of 152.3 hours per month. Assuming that a month contains 4.3 weeks, this means that the average student was working 35.4 hours a week, or approximately six hours a day six days a week. This figure is much higher than the 4-hours-per-day or 28-hours-per-week limit imposed by the Ministry of Justice.

Nevertheless, if we look at the future hopes expressed by the students, 71.0% said they wanted to continue their studies, 20.8% said they wanted to begin working, and 8.2% said they had not thought about it yet or gave some other answer. This indicates that there is a strong thirst for education among the students. Furthermore, 84.0% of those who said they wanted to continue their education indicated that they wanted to do so in Japan. The image we get of *shugakusei*, therefore, rather than one of workers, is one of self-supporting students struggling to reach the next stage and become legitimate students in institutions of higher education.

Unmistakably, one of the real problems with *shugakusei* is that many have found themselves in a situation where they have no choice but to hold a part-time job. In the case of Chinese students, for example, governmental regulations prevent them from taking more than ¥10,000 with them when they go abroad (Group Akakabu, p. 15). What this means is that Chinese students arrive in Japan essentially penniless, and the first thing they have to do is take care of securing funds for their living expenses, especially for food and lodging, and for their tuition fees.

According to the Tokyo Metropolitan Government survey, *shugakusei*'s average monthly expenses were ¥161,000. Students who reported that their expenses were in the ¥150,000 to ¥200,000 range, the closest to the average, said this money was spent in the following areas: tuition and other school fees, ¥57,000; housing, ¥38,000; food, ¥35,000; recreation, ¥16,000;

and savings, ¥15,000. This indicates that they were leading very frugal lives.

In addition to having to pay for school and living expenses, *shugakusei* are usually burdened with loans they took out to study abroad. It is said that in 1988 Chinese students were typically paying ¥300,000 to brokers, and that in the case of Shanghai the market price for this service was between ¥500,000 and ¥600,000. This is equal to approximately 10 or 15 years' salary in China. This figure also varied from region to region and according to the student's wealth and ability to pay. The reason this system has worked, however, is that many of the people trying to gain this status believed that once they got to Japan and began working it would be easy to pay back the money. Many of these people borrowed the money to study abroad from their families and relatives (Yamaguchi a).

Up until now we have looked at the amount of labor students perform, and now we will take a look at the types of work they do. The survey conducted by the Tokyo Metropolitan Government showed that 61.2% were working as waiters, waitresses, or in other service jobs, 22.8% in manufacturing, construction or cleaning, 5.2% were doing office work, 4.5% were working as language instructors, interpreters, or translators, and 6.3 were doing other jobs that involved technical or special skills. The overwhelming majority, as this shows, were working in service industries. More than half of the students, or 56.6%, found these jobs through friends from their own countries, with the remainder (less than 10% in each category) finding them through Japanese friends, newspapers and magazines, bulletin boards and staff at their schools, and general advertisements.

The three biggest problems reported by respondents (with multiple answers allowed) of the survey were that there were few jobs which made use of their own skills and special abilities (47.0%), that wages were low (39.1%), and that the work was psychologically tiring. These problems give a good idea of the kinds of jobs that they were doing.

In closing this chapter, we would like to introduce the case of one female Chinese *shugakusei*. This example well illustrates the high levels of education, strong job experience, and desire for advancement that characterize Chinese students.

When we interviewed Yang Lienchin, she was 26 years old, and single. She had come to Japan roughly one year earlier on a *shugakusei* visa. She was attending a Japanese language school in Ikebukuro, Tokyo, and working in a coffee shop in Ochanomizu. It was the second shop she had worked for. She had found the first job through a Japanese friend (really the friend of a friend), and the present one by calling a phone number after seeing a help wanted sign outside the store.

She worked mainly as a waitress, working nine hours every day but Saturday in two shifts, the first from 8:30 a.m. to 12:00 p.m. and the second from 5:30 p.m. to 11 p.m. Her hourly wage was ¥650, which was apparently the same as that of Japanese waitresses. She thought there was another foreigner, but wasn't sure of her nationality. All the conversation was held in Japanese.

She was a university graduate, and had worked as an assistant in a computer-related college. Apparently, a friend from her university days came to study in Japan, and Yang decided she would like to try as well. She seemed to have a strong will as she told us, 'I want to enter a Japanese graduate school and study computers. I want to broaden my field of vision.'

Her father and mother were approximately 55 years old, and she had one 16-year-old sister. Both her parents were researchers in a university in the social-science field. The family lived in a 3-DK apartment where each room was approximately 12 square meters, a fairly comfortable life by Chinese standards. Her salary in China had been about ¥4,000 per month. Her family didn't oppose her coming to Japan, and in fact gave her ¥200,000. At the time we interviewed her she was not receiving any money from her family. She called them roughly once every two weeks.

In terms of living arrangements, she was sharing a home with four other friends in a city approximately one hour by train from the city center. She said she had been living in the same place ever since she came to Japan. It was a house with a bath, toilet and kitchen, and the rent was ¥130,000 per month. The house had originally been rented by the Chinese government to house publicly-funded students, so Yang was living there secretly. One of the other women was a classmate from university who was now working in a Japanese computer company, and the housemates apparently got along very well.

Yang's tuition (¥30,000) and living and transportation expenses added up to roughly ¥80,000 per month. She said she was financing all these fees with her part-time job. She usually made breakfast and lunchboxes, but often ate dinner out. Her daily schedule, of going to the coffee shop, then school, then back to the coffee shop, made this nearly inevitable. She spent her days off watching television and cooking. She also cooked and ate along with her friends.

After graduating from Japanese graduate school she said she wanted to go to the United States or to Australia. She said she didn't like Japanese men. She didn't seem to have a very positive image of Japan. She said there was no space, and the cost of living was too high. She even went so far as to say that, 'my sister wants to come study in Japan, but I won't let her come.'

2 The Situation of Workers According to Sector

1 The Sex and Entertainment Industry

In Chapter 1 we examined the question of how foreign workers enter Japan, and we will now proceed to the situation they face in different occupations. First we will consider the sex and entertainment industry. Japanese women have increasingly avoided employment in this field, but the social demand for these services remains as high as ever. Foreign women thus emerged to fill the gap. It is now quite common to find such women in amusement quarters throughout Japan.

The foreign women in this industry have become known as 'Japayuki-san' (literally 'gone to Japan'), a term derived from the similar word 'Karayuki-san' which was used in the prewar period to refer to Japanese women who had gone to other Asian countries to work in similar circumstances (Sanya). The year 1979, which witnessed the first large influx of foreign women into this trade, has become known among some commentators as 'Japayuki Year Zero.' Between that year and 1987, these women constituted the bulk of foreign workers coming into Japan. The problem of migrant workers in Japan thus in reality started with these women in the sex and entertainment trade.

It is extremely difficult to derive an estimate of how many such women exist in Japan. We can begin with the figure of 87,896 women who were said to be in Japan as overstaying as of May 1992 (Ministry of Justice C). To determine how many were working in the sex and entertainment industry, we can look at similar ratios from among apprehended undocumented workers. This is because, as we stated earlier, most of these apprehendees were overstayers who surrendered to authorities as they prepared to leave the country, and are thus believed to be fairly representative of the entire body of foreign workers.

Of all the women apprehended as undocumented workers in 1991, 54.6% were found to be working as either hostesses or prostitutes (Ministry of Justice C). If we apply this ratio to the number of overstayers above, we find that there are slightly fewer than 50,000 overstayers working in this trade.

We must add to this figure a number of Filipinas with entertainment visas who are working outside of their authorized status. In 1991, 56,851 women entered Japan under this work category. Unfortunately there is no basis upon which to estimate the number of women in this category who are in reality working in the sex industry, but some theorize that the figure may be higher than 90% (Ishihara, p. 176), and for lack of any other basis we will use this estimate. Most stay in Japan for less than six months, meaning that there are more than two 'shifts' a year, and that if we calculate by year we can surmise the existence of a total stock of a little more than 25,000 such women in the country at any given time.

In addition, there may be at least 6,000 women with *shukagusei* visas working outside of their given status (*News of the Association of International Entertainment Promoters*, 1 September 1988). A significant number of people have also used false marriages as a cover for working in Japan. We can thus theorize that more than 80,000 foreigners are working in the sex and entertainment industry. Incidentally, it appears that very few Chinese women are among them at the present time.

We will now take a closer look at the number of women apprehended while working in the industry. Of the 7,558 women caught as undocumented workers in 1991, 46.5% were working as hostesses, 14.4% in manufacturing, 8.1% as prostitutes, 7.8% as dishwashers, 4.9% as waitresses, 3.5% as domestic helpers, and 14.8% in other occupations (Ministry of Justice C). Somewhere between 50 and 60% were thus working in the sex and entertainment trade. The similar figure for 1989 was 73.9% (Ministry of Justice q), which leads us to the deduction that female employment is showing a trend toward diversification.

In many cases it is difficult to draw a line between hostesses and prostitutes. The reason for this is that, in order to avoid detection, many foreign women, with the connivance of bar owners, enter bars as if they were customers, act as hostesses, and then meet men and accompany them to hotels.

When we look at men and women together, we find that 12.5% of all apprehendees were working in this industry, a far smaller percentage than those working in manufacturing and construc-

Table 2–1 Changes in number of women apprehended as undocumented workers

	1987	1988	1989	1990	1991
Thailand	777	1,019	775	789	2,323
Philippines	5,774	3,698	2,451	2,449	1,904
South Korea	99	264	920	1,117	1,499
Chinese Mainland*	284	2	13	53	181
Others	84	402	658	1,300	1,651
Total	7,018	5,385	4,817	5,708	7,558

* The 1987 figures include Taiwan and Hong Kong.

Source: Ministry of Justice C.

tion. In 1988, however, it held the dominant position, and this downward trend is worthy of note.

The number of women caught every year as undocumented workers rose steadily up until 1987, but, as shown in Table 2–1, began to drop in the period from 1988 to 1989, though the trend reversed itself later and has begun to rise again.

Table 2–1 shows that in 1991 Thais held the lead in number of people caught, with over 2,000 apprehendees, Filipinas followed with just under 2,000, and South Koreans were next with somewhere around 1,500. The number of Thais literally exploded in the year 1991. The number of Filipinas has shown a downward trend ever since 1988. For Koreans, the decisive growth came in 1989.

Next, we will look at the number of women entering the country on entertainment visas. This category is designated for 'activities to engage in theatrical performance, musical performances, sports or any other show business . . .' It has, in actuality, been used by brokers working to bring women into the country for businesses in the sex and entertainment industry. In fact, most of the singers and dancers who enter with entertainment visas spend just a small amount of their time performing, and pass the bulk of their work hours serving drinks to and talking with their customers, or in effect working as hostesses. In the past, these visas were issued for a period of up to 60 days (starting on June 1, 1990, this changed to either three months or one year), but even people who did renew usually left Japan within six months of arrival. In addition, there was once a waiting period of six months before a person could re-enter Japan after leaving

Table 2–2 People from the Asian region entering Japan with entertainment visas

	1987	1988	1989	1990	1991
Philippines	36,039	41,357	32,636	42,738	56,851
South Korea	827	994	1,643	2,352	2,735
Taiwan	2,515	2,346	1,962	2,066	2,021
Others	1,881	3,253	2,016	2,212	2,471
Asia Total	41,262	47,950	38,257	49,368	64,078

Source: 1987–1988: Ministry of Justice a, 1989: Ministry of Justice r, 1990: Ministry of Justice u, 1991: Ministry of Justice C.

with an entertainment visa, but this provision was abolished in July 1988.

Table 2–2 shows changes from year to year in numbers of people from the Asian region entering Japan with entertainment visas. It shows that the number of entrants rose steadily until 1988, dropped suddenly in 1989, and then began growing rapidly again after 1989. It is believed that these reflect the tightening of screenings in 1988 and the announcement of new standards in 1990. In terms of nationality, the Philippines holds a commanding lead, having reached the 40,000 range in 1990 and the 50,000 range in 1991. The number of South Koreans has also increased, while those from Taiwan have been stagnant.

The numbers from South Korea grew until 1984, but decreased dramatically after 1985. The reason is that a 1983 string of suicides among Korean hostesses in Japan prompted the South Korean government to severely restrict the outflow of prostitutes using the guise of entertainment.

In July 1988, as a response to the increase in people entering Japan with entertainment visas and working in the sex and entertainment industry, the Ministry of Justice revised the application procedures for these visas. This revision sought to prevent the entry of hostesses disguised as entertainers by setting strict standards on the amount of food and drink tax paid by the employing establishment, the floor space, number of employees, and location of perfomances. It is believed that these new regulations were partly responsible for the forementioned stagnation in 1988.

At the time of the enforcement of the revised Immigration Act, the Ministry of Justice issued the following directive concerning entertainment visas:

1) The applicant must have at least two years of experience.
2) The establishment employing the applicant must satisfy the following requirements: a. It must have an owner or manager with at least three years full-time experience; b. The number of applicants must not exceed the number of full-time staff by more than ten to one; and c. It must not have performed any unlawful acts in the previous three years.
3) The place of performance must satisfy the following requirements: a. The stage must be at least 13 square meters; b. The performers must be able to use a dressing room of at least 9 square meters; c. The place of performance must have at least five full-time employees; d. Monthly sales must be at least ¥2 million; e. It must not have performed any unlawful acts in the previous three years; and f. The applicants must receive a monthly remuneration of at least ¥200,000 (Ministry of Justice p).

The intention of this ministerial directive was to eliminate the use of unauthorized labor by the 1,200 or so large and small companies in the sector as well as by individuals (Ishihara, p. 189) either acting as agencies for performers or providing places of performance. In order to do this, the directive included the strange provision that only stage performances would be allowed, thus forbidding the use of floor shows. Furthermore, in just the same way that it organized Japanese language schools into the Association for the Promotion of Japanese Language Education (*Gaishukyo*), the Justice Ministry has carried out various efforts to organize the organizations in the entertainment industry into a federation under the control of the Immigration Bureau.

Until recently there were in practice no controls on entertainers performing unauthorized labor as hostesses or prostitutes, but in July 1992 two clubs in Tokyo's Sugamo district were raided by police, and 41 Filipinas were detained for working outside of their authorized status. This incident sent shockwaves through businesses acting as agencies for foreign entertainers (*News of the Association of International Entertainment Promoters*, 1 September 1992).

In terms of the use of fake marriages, there were 237 cases of people being apprehended for violations involving marriages in the six years between 1984 and 1989. In terms of nationality, South Koreans made up almost two-thirds, with 150 cases, followed by Chinese (including an unspecified number of people from Taiwan and Hong Kong) with 67 cases, the Philippines with 13 cases, and seven from other nationalities (Ministry of Justice q).

In one classic case, the owner of a club in Fukuoka was discovered to have sent Japanese men to Korea to marry eight Korean women whom he planned to hire at his club. As compensation for 'dirtying their family registry,' he paid them ¥500,000, and in addition he was planning to have the women pay a monthly sum of ¥100,000 to their 'husbands' (*Nikkei Shimbun*, 9 May 1988).

It is important to note, after this brief examination of the overall situation of foreigners working in the sex industry, that this is a national phenomenon. In 1991, women were apprehended as undocumented workers in all 46 prefectures, with the single exception of Saga Prefecture. The major areas where these incidents occurred were Tokyo (2,224 people), Osaka (833), Chiba Prefecture (753), Kanagawa Prefecture (601), Ibaraki Prefecture (571), Saitama Prefecture (481), Aichi Prefecture (375), and Nagano Prefecture (278) (Ministry of Justice C).

Human rights violations are a greater problem among overstayers than among people in Japan on entertainment visas. Most cases reported by support groups in Japan of serious violations such as non-payment of wages, forced prostitution, and violence, involve overstayers who entered the country on short-term visas. The reason for this is that their underground status makes it very difficult for them to complain when they are victimized.

When people are using entertainment visas, by contrast, the agencies that contracted their services also fear that they may not be able to get permits from the Immigration Bureau to accept entertainers if they have troubles with the people working under their charge. There are thus many cases in this area where the wages are less than those reported to the Immigration Bureau, where the wages are paid in one lump sum at the time of departure, where time off is practically non-existent, or where unreasonable fines are levied against absences, but a certain standard of working conditions is typically maintained (*Migrant* No. 3, June 1988).

One recent case of an extremely serious abuse of human rights occurred in a Nagoya City bar called Lapin. A group of Filipina overstayers were beaten and kicked, forced into prostitution, and were confined in a jail-like room from which they could not escape. Two of them died under mysterious circumstances (ALS no Kai).

The sex industry, because of its underground nature, provides many opportunities for the machinations of brokers. There are in fact many reports and scholarly papers dealing with this issue. Among them, the following can be seen as representative works: Sanya, Ishii, Oshima and Francis, Utsumi and Matsui, Mizumachi, Tanaka and Miyoshi, Hagio, Ishiyama, Mainichi Shimbun a, Shinano Mainichi Shimbun a, and ALS no Kai.

In the following few paragraphs, we will examine the information contained in these studies while looking at the situation of people of different nationalities.

In the Philippines, an extremely well-developed supply system exists. There are agencies which work as labor recruiters, gathering women and distributing them to businesses throughout the world. Some of these agencies provide singing and dancing lessons, and it is said that more than 500 such firms exist in Manila alone.

Some of these brokers aim specifically at the Japanese market. They recruit women from agencies, karaoke bars, and from throughout the Philippines, and then pass them on to Japanese brokers. As of 1987, there were roughly 100 such Japanese brokers (*International Entertainment Association News*, 1 April 1987) who were selling these women to bars and clubs in Japan. Recently there have been many cases of businesses in Japan buying women directly from agencies and karaoke bars, meaning that the distribution route has been streamlined by eliminating the middlemen. In addition, the role of brokers, which used to be an exclusive territory for Japanese gangsters, or yakuza, has recently been taken up by amateurs.

In terms of the flow of money, the bars and clubs that are the final destinations in Japan pay the airfares and living expenses for the women, and also pay some money, either as a lump sum or a monthly commission, to the brokers. If there are several layers of brokers, the cuts become added one on top of the other. In terms of fees for the passport, visa as well as other expenses, the broker is sometimes reimbursed directly by the woman, but in most cases charges these fees to the employer in Japan through a Japanese broker. Bringing the woman to Japan is thus a significant investment for the employer, who will do everything possible, including exploitation and violations of human rights, to get the woman to work in order to recover the initial investment.

In the case of Thai women, it is said that a syndicate of Chinese Thais holds a monopoly on the supply route from Bangkok, and that they have secret links with the police. It seems, therefore, that Japanese brokers have very little room for involvement in this market. The women are typically brought into Japan by bosses who are either long-time Thai residents in Japan or by compatriots who have been to Japan several times. The women receive loans from these bosses/brokers for their passport, visa and air ticket fees, as well as the money they must show to Immigration Bureau officials to enter the country. In many cases the bosses keep their passports until they repay the initial debt.

Futhermore, there have been cases of women from these two countries marrying Japanese men and then acting as brokers either in their home countries or in Japan.

A significant number of sex industry establishments in Japan are operated by Taiwanese, and there is a network of Taiwanese residents in Japan. It is therefore common in these cases for people already working in Japan to recruit personal acquaintances and invite them to come. In particular, there is an increasing tendency for Taiwanese proprietors of membership clubs to recruit women from Taiwan to come and work as prostitutes in their clubs. Most of these women come to Japan on tourist visas, but there are cases where the club owners help them to get fake *shugakusei* or marriage visas, and brokers are often involved in these deals.

Among no group is the network as highly developed as among South Koreans. Practically all Korean women who come to work in the sex industry in Japan do so with the help of compatriots living in Japan or resident Koreans. Brokers and employers alike are mostly Koreans. It is quite common for so-called 'Korean clubs' to provide work for these women. In Tokyo's Akasaka district, the largest concentration of clubs, there are said to be 1,200 or 1,300 Korean women employed as undocumented workers in over 100 such clubs (*International Entertainment Association News*, 1 January 1988). In order to overcome the tough barriers the South Korean government has set up against foreign travel, they often use *shugakusei* visas, and occasionally, as we mentioned above, fake marriages.

We will now describe the experiences related to us during our interview of Han Heika, a 26-year-old Korean woman who was working at one of these clubs. She told us she had come to Japan one year earlier as a language school student, and had already extended her visa once. Soon she would have to renew it again. She was technically a student, but often worked until 3:00 or 4:00 in the morning, meaning that she hardly ever attended classes, which were held from noon until 3 p.m. Since she worked directly with customers, though, her Japanese was quite proficient.

There were just three people in her family: her mother (52), brother (30) and herself. At the time of the interview her brother was studying computing in Australia, and their mother was alone in Seoul, where she managed a coffee shop. Han told us she frequently spoke on the phone with her mother and brother. She said she wanted to send money home, and was thus planning to extend her stay and work in Japan. In order to renew her visa, however, she said she would have to pay the language school ¥450,000. In exchange, the school would doctor her attendance records and apply for a six-month extension.

After graduating from high school, she had spent some time studying to be a beautician, but then heard along with a friend about the possibility of coming to Japan, and had jumped at the opportunity. They heard about this chance from a talent agency with ties to a language school. They borrowed ¥2 million from the agency for air tickets and other expenses, and the company enrolled them in a language school with a resident Korean owner, and helped them to find jobs. It also helped them to pass a simple Japanese-language examination given by the Korean Immigration Bureau.

Thus, when the two women began working they were already ¥2 million in debt, and the agency kept them as virtual prisoners until they could pay back the money. During that period, they received hardly any cash for their work. They knew that as soon as they paid back the debt they would be freed and could work to earn money for themselves.

The first place they worked at was a Korean club in an amusement district. Five women lived in a sort of dormitory with two rooms and a kitchen. After approximately six months, Han gained her freedom, moved to another club, and moved out of the dormitory into an apartment. At the time of the interview she was unemployed, but apparently had a rich Japanese patron who was taking care of her. She told us that hostess jobs didn't fit her personality, and that she had left several jobs after taking a few days off and finding she had to quit. All the the employees at the Korean clubs, including a few resident Koreans from either North or South Korea, were young women like herself. The daily wages were supposed to be ¥15,000, but there were significant deductions for tardiness or absences.

At the time of the interview, she was living in an apartment with another woman, the elder sister of the friend who had come to Japan with her.

2 The Manufacturing Sector

Manufacturing industries make more widespread use of foreign labor than any other sector. The bulk of the workers are Latin American Nikkeijin, but there are also overstayers as well as *shugakusei* and trainees who are in reality working outside of their authorized status.

The greatest souce so far of information on Nikkeijin is the survey of workers conducted by the Overseas Nikkeijin Association, which we looked at in the Introduction.

According to their survey, 79.7% of these workers were employed in factories, 0.9% in retail stores, 7.0% in offices, 5.3% at construction sites, and 7.0% in other places. The division by industry was as follows: 33.5% in automobile or auto parts, 19.9% in electrical appliances or assembling, 10.6% in metals and metal processing, 14.2% in other manufacturing industries, 6.1% in construction, 6.8% in office work, and 8.9% in sales and services. It is clear that most of the workers were concentrated in the automobile and electrical appliances industries (JICA, p. 113).

We can make use of data compiled by the Ministry of Foreign Affairs' Consular and Emigration Affairs to get a picture of their countries or places of origin. According to this data, there were 148,700 Nikkeijin working in Japan as of June 1991, and according to the survey on Nikkeijin, 80.7% came from Brazil, 12.1% from Peru, 5.7% from Argentina, 1.0% from Bolivia, and 0.5% from Paraguay (JICA, p. 69). Of the people from Brazil, 79.3% were citizens of that country, 11.9% were Japanese citizens, and 8.9% held dual citizenship. For Peru, the equivalent figures were 78.0%, 11.0%, and 11.0%. This means that nearly 20% of these people held Japanese citizenships.

The survey gives the following statistics for Nikkeijin: 67.8% were males, and 32.2% females, meaning that there were twice as many men as women; by age, 4.9% were in their teens, 47.9% in their twenties, 23.8% in their thirties, 11.2% in their forties, 5.8% in their fifties, and 0.8% in their sixties, meaning that there was an overwhelming preponderance of the 20s group. Furthermore, 88.3% were of fully Japanese parentage, and 11.7 of mixed blood, with the level of mixture highest among the Peruvians.

Of the people of fully Japanese parentage, 6.7% were first generation (meaning that they had migrated from Japan themselves), 62.1% were second or second-and-a-half generation (this half would mean, for instance, that their father was first but their mother second generation), 30.9% were third or third-and-a-half generation, and 0.2% were fourth or fourth-and-a-half generation, showing that second-generation Nikkeijin were dominant (JICA, pp. 72–).

Because Nikkeijin can work legally, even prestigious manufacturers have been among their employers. The largest concentrations of registered Nikkeijin are in Aichi, Shizuoka and Kanagawa Prefectures. It is believed that many of them are working in companies affiliated with Toyota (in Aichi), Suzuki, Yamaha and Honda (in Shizuoka), and Nissan (in Kanagawa). There is also a large concentration in the Tomo region of Gunma Prefecture, which is a base for Fuji Heavy Industries and Sanyo Electrics Co.

Next we will look at overstayers. As we did earlier for the sex and entertainment trade, we can base an estimate on the numbers of people apprehended. In 1991, 9,596 people (1,087 of them women) were caught while working as employees in manufacturing, making up 29.2% of the total number of apprehendees (a smaller figure than the 36.6% for the construction industry). If we apply this ratio to the total number of 278,892 overstayers believed to be working as of May 1992, we can guess that slightly more than 80,000 overstayers are working in manufacturing.

If we turn to people performing unauthorized labor, we first encounter the 25,000 people registered as *shugakusei* but who are in reality performing labor. According to the survey conducted by the Tokyo Metropolitan Institute for Labor (Shutoken survey) which we looked at in the Introduction, 20.7% of these people were working in manufacturing, indicating a total population of slightly more than 5,000. In regards to trainees, our own survey which we presented in Chapter 1–2 showed that 83.3% of these people were working in manufacturing, implying that a little over 15,000 of the slightly more than 20,000 people performing unauthorized labor were doing so in manufacturing. Hence, there are probably more than 260,000 foreigners working in this sector who are either Nikkeijin, overstayers, or people performing unauthorized labor.

We will now look at the situation of Bangladeshi workers, quoting from our conversations with Babu, Masoom and Farooq whom we introduced in Chapter 1–1.

Q: Where, and what kind of work are you doing?

A: We are producing lip cream cases at a factory in Yokohama. We work together with Japanese, but we are given work such as carrying heavy boxes and performing dirty jobs. We just do what the Japanese tell us to do. For the hard work we receive just ¥580 per hour, but the Japanese get ¥800 per hour for the light work they do.

Babu was working from 2 p.m. to 2 a.m., Farooq from 2 a.m. to 2 p.m., and Masoom from 8 a.m. to 8 p.m. They each worked 12 hours straight with no breaks at all. The Japanese workers, naturally, were given breaks. Furthermore, when we asked the three where in Yokohama the factory was located, they were extremely reluctant to provide an answer. They were afraid we would report them to the Immigration Bureau.

Farooq and Masoom were in Japan on tourist visas, but Babu had *shugakusei* status. He had received it at the time he had gone to renew his visa, thanks to the president of his Japanese language school, who was an ex-Immigration Bureau official with 15 years' experience. At the time of the interview, Farooq and Masoom had registered for classes at the same school.

Q: With your busy schedules, can you really find time to go to the school in Ikebukuro?

A: Of course we can. But it means that we have practically no time to ourselves.

For instance, Babu's days passed roughly as follows. At 7 a.m. he woke up and left for the school in Ikebukuro. He attended class from 8 a.m. to noon. In order to have his visa renewed, he had to have an attendance rate of at least 90%, so he could rarely afford to skip classes. After class, he went back to Yokohama (about one hour by train) and started work. Then, 12 hours later, he stopped work, and walked all the way to his apartment, a roughly 40 minute walk. He then slept for a mere four hours, and the cycle began again. This routine was so tiring, he told us, that on Sunday, his day off, he typically slept from morning to evening.

Q: Aren't there any better jobs available?

A: Not really. One of my friends works in a family restaurant, and he works from 8 p.m. to 8 a.m. On top of that, the salary is low.

We asked several other questions about their working conditions. They received some food during their 12 hour shifts, but if they spent in excess of ¥500 it was taken out of their salaries. They made sure not to overspend that amount.

Furthermore, the company deducted ¥15,000 from their salaries every month for 'taxes.' There was no insurance at all. When they caught colds they had no choice but to buy the medicine themselves. Their living costs included rent and food (¥60,000), school tuition (¥36,000), train fares (¥35,000), for a total of ¥130,000 per month. They transferred the rest by postal order to Bangladesh.

They added that 'The boss doesn't care about our visa status, but we don't have any document such as a labor contract to guarantee our status.' They meant to tell us that their employment situation was very uncertain, that they could be laid off at anytime.

Q: Why did you come to Japan?

The natural response was 'for money,' and 'for my family.' It seemed to be common knowledge that Japan was a place where one could make money. They said that if they had the chance to bring family members they would choose their male siblings and have them work with them.

Babu, however, graduated from university in Bangladesh with a degree in natural science, and told us his dream was to study in a Japanese university, in whatever field, and then find a job in Japan. He said that he was attracted to this country because of its advanced position in many academic fields. He said he planned to work in Japan for five or six years, and that once he returned to Bangladesh he could work in a Japanese factory and receive a high salary.

Q: Did you work in Bangladesh?

Babu was the only one with any working experience prior to coming to Japan. 'I worked as a waiter for just one or two months,' he said. 'But I didn't have a father then, and it was a difficult time.'

We asked them about their impressions of Japanese people, and Babu began speaking in Japanese, repeating, 'Strange!' over and over. The company owner made them work too hard, and made them do all the hard work. This is why he said, 'strange.' The only thing they ever spoke about with their Japanese co-workers was work.

The three men were all Muslims. Believers of Islam must pray five times every day, but Babu, Masoom and Farooq had neither the time nor the space to fulfill their duties. Masoom once complained to the boss, saying 'There is no space at work to pray,' but the boss answered back curtly, 'I'm the God in this place.'

As we can see by this example, the advance of foreign workers into small- and medium-sized manufacturing companies was brought about by the acute labor shortage with which these firms have been confronted.

In order to understand this situation, we can make use of the 'Survey on Technical Improvements and Environment Changes in Industry in the Capital Region' conducted between February and April 1989 on small- and medium-sized manufacturers in the Tokyo metropolitan area (Shutoken Survey) (Iyotani and Naito).

This survey was conducted without sampling by mail on 2,923 small- and medium-sized firms in Tokyo's 23 wards and in the adjacent cities of Kawasaki and Kawaguchi. The survey was limited to companies in the following eight fields: casting, metal processing, welding, gilding, ironworking, machine industry, electrical appliances, and bookbinding. Responses were received from 266 companies, a response rate of 9.1%, and the average number of employees in the respondant firms was 20.3, a figure considerably higher than the average for manufacturers in the Tokyo metropolitan area (11.6 persons per factory in 1986).

Of these companies, 58.3% said that 'It's impossible to find employees even when we place help wanted ads,' implying that the labor shortage is very serious for small- and medium-sized firms. A great number of respondants (59.4%) complained of a 'labor shortage of young men.' The next largest number (20.0%) complained of a 'shortage of skilled workers.' Furthermore, 13.2% said that 'Young workers will not stay long with our firm.' Also, the average age of employees among these companies was 40.4 years old, a very high figure.

Because of the labor shortage, the average age of employees in the Kansai area has also risen dramatically. According to a company survey conducted in 1986 on 208 small- and medium-sized firms in Higashi-Osaka City, the average age of employees in these companies reached a figure of 44.3 years. Incidentally, if we look at business fields as reported in company statistics, this aging of employees is particularly advanced in companies which said they were in the following lines of business: 'wire-netting, machine tools, casting, and forging,' 'steel and non-steel wire-making,' and 'machines and tools,' in that order. The fields where the most aging has taken place in the past five years are 'plating and painting' (Onishi).

The reason behind the labor shortage in small- and medium-sized manufacturing firms is that the labor conditions are much worse than in other places, and the origin of these poor conditions can be found in the sub-contracting structure of the Japanese economy. This structure refers to the pattern that arises as firms decide that it is cheaper to contract out parts or processes to other companies than to carry out these processes in-house. In the manufacturing sector, there is even a distinction between the first line of subcontractors and the second and lower ranks of sub-contractors below them.

Most of these subcontractors are small- and medium-sized firms, and in fact make up roughly two-thirds of all smaller manufacturers. One of the characteristics of this structure is that the contractors tend to be continuously linked to one single parent company. This means, essentially, that the parent companies hold a great deal of power over the subcontractors under their umbrella. These contractors can be roughly divided into three categories: parts suppliers, piecework contractors, and in-house contractors. The piecework pattern is typical in the textiles industry, and in-house contracting is common in ship-building.

In recent years, the control exerted over subcontractors by parent firms has become ever stronger, as manifested by caps on order prices, shortened delivery times, orders for smaller lots, and demands for higher part quality, and this coupled with increasing numbers of entrants from other industries, has resulted in an increasingly severe process of stratification among the subcontractors. Because of this, an increasing number of piecework subcontractors have begun to change their lines of business, and in-house subcontractors have closed down in rising numbers (above data from the Small and Medium Enterprise Agency, Chapter 2).

In this way, labor conditions, including wages, working hours, and working environment in subcontracting firms have by necessity become worse than ever. Because of this, as we mentioned earlier, younger workers have become almost non-existent, and the aging of the workforce has brought about an acute labor shortage.

Smaller firms have thus been forced, however reluctantly, to rely on foreign labor. In the Introduction, we used data from two surveys focusing on smaller companies, the first conducted by KSD (*Chusho Kigyo Keieisha Saigai Hosho Jigyodan*), and the second by the Tokyo Metropolitan Institute for Labor, or Toroken. In the first survey, 37.6% of all respondents in the manufacturing or assembly sectors (31.3% in all sectors) said they hoped to employ foreign workers (KSD). In the second, 35.0% of all manufacturing firms which were not employing foreigners at the time said they wished to do so, the highest percentage for any sector (the figure was 25.2% for all firms) (Tokyo Metropolitan Government k).

A much higher percentage of smaller manufacturers than is commonly believed have used foreign workers. According to the KSD survey, 17.8% of firms in the manufacturing and assembly sector said they were employing foreigners. The equivalent figure in the Toroken survey was 12.4%. According to the previously mentioned survey conducted on technical improvements and environment changes in capital region industry (Shutoken survey), 12.8% of respondents said they were currently employing foreign workers, 11.3% said they had in the past, adding up to a total of 24.1%, or nearly one-quarter of the total.

What needs to be emphasized is that the question of whether or not a firm hires foreign workers bears a strong connection to its number of employees. In the forementioned Shutoken survey, 8.0% of firms with under four employees, 23.0% of those with between 5 and 9 employees, and 36.6%, or over a third, of those with at least 10 employees, had hired foreign workers.

In reference to these results, Iyotani and Naito concluded that, 'Among smaller firms, it is generally those with more than 10 employees that are most enthusiastic about technical innovations, and who, because they feel the labor shortage so acutely, feel most strongly the necessity of hiring foreign workers . . . It has often been said that the introduction of migrant workers slows the rate of technical innovation, but it is important to note that it is precisely those firms that are enthusiastically working to upgrade their technology that most strongly feel the necessity of hiring foreign labor.'

In regard to the question of mechanization, however, Inagami, in the People's Finance Corporation (*Kokumin Kinyu Koko*) survey which we described in the Introduction, interviewed managers from small- and medium-sized corporations and found that there were two contrasting patterns: one involving reliance on both technical innovation and foreign labor, and the other involving dependency on technical innovation with a constrained hiring of foreign labor. He described other patterns as well: 'no use of foreign labor,' 'maintenance of the status quo/ad hoc,' 'training foreign employees,' and 'internal transfers within transnational corporations' (Inakami, Kuwabara et al., pp. 134–).

Next, we will look at the industries in which foreign workers have found employment. According to the Shutoken survey, 26.8% of companies in the five metal-related industries had some experience with foreign workers, as did 20.7% in the bookbinding, and 15.8% of firms in machinery and electrics. We can see from these results that foreign labor has become particularly common in metals industries.

If we look at the 9,596 undocumented production workers apprehended in 1991, we find that 37.7% were working in metal processing-related jobs, 14.1% in the processing of rubber or plastic, 7.5% in metal parts manufacturing, 7.5% in food processing, 7.4% in appliance assembly, and 4.6% in fields relating to printing or book-making (Ministry of Justice C).

Ministry of Labor documents also show that foreign workers are concentrated in metals-related occupational categories. In March 1988, the Ministry sent personnel, including staff from local Labor Standards Inspection Offices, to question owners of construction and manufacturing firms in large cities, where foreign workers tend to work in large numbers. A total of 43 firms admitted using undocumented workers, and 29 of these appeared to be in the manufacturing sector.

In terms of the occupational categories in which the foreigners were employed, ten were in metal product manufacturing, four in food manufacturing, four in automobile repair, three in electrical appliance parts manufacturing, two in bookbinding, one each in paper processing, general machinery manufacturing and ceramics, stone and clay manufacturing, and three in other manufacturing industries, meaning that metals constituted by far the largest single category (Ministry of Labor a).

Some insights into the use of foreign workers in small- and medium-sized manufacturing firms can also be gleamed from the results of a series of on-site inspections carried out by the Tokyo Regional Immigration Bureau against 19 parts subcontractors in Tokyo's Keihin industrial district in November 1987. A large number of undocumented foreigners, mostly Bangladeshis and Pakistanis, were apprehended during the raids. Most were working in plating, auto parts manufacturing, electrical appliance parts manufacturing, and can-making, and the average number of employees per firm was 40.

A common feature of these firms was that they confronted chronic labor shortages. They faced a lack of Japanese applicants, and even those who came to work did not tend to settle into the job. Two reasons cited for this lack of interest were the inconvenient locations of the factories and the fact that they were mostly considered high-pollution industries. The firms had thus been driven to a point where they had no choice but to hire foreigners. The workers had spent between 11 days and one year and ten months on the job, worked for an average of nine hours a day, and received hourly wages of between ¥700 and ¥900.

The owners listed the following merits of hiring foreigners: 1) they worked hard even at unskilled and dirty tasks which Japanese disliked; 2) they did not usually miss work, making it easy to complete work on schedule; 3) there was no need for the troublesome paperwork necessary when hiring Japanese workers; 4) there was no need to worry about social insurance; 5) foreign workers tended to introduce replacements when leaving the job; and 6) they tended to accept jobs even at relatively low wages.

The companies listed as demerits, however, that because foreigners often could not understand Japanese it took extra time to teach them how to perform jobs (Ministry of Justice d).

In the following section, we will examine the situation of foreign workers involved in small- and medium-sized sub-contractors in representative occupations in the manufacturing sector. In terms of metals, we will introduce examples from the plating and casting industries.

In May 1990, the Institute for Social Affairs in Asia (*Asia Shakai Mondai Kenkyujo*) carried out hearings on some 30 plating companies in the Tokyo metropolitan region, and heard from 109 workers. The respondents included 33 Chinese, 20 Pakistanis, 18 Bangladeshis, 15 Indonesians, 9 Ghanians, 6 Nigerians, 4 Sri Lankans, and one person each from Egypt, South Korea, the U.K., and the Philippines. The largest number, 49, had tourist visas, followed by *shugakusei* (26), trainees (15), and *ryugakusei* (10) (Institute for Social Affairs in Asia).

We ourselves conducted some interviews in a plating factory in Tokyo's Katsushika Ward. Even though plating has been heavily mechanized, much of the work relies on the intuition of the operators, and it is said that it takes ten years to master the necessary technical skills. Moreover, the work involves dangerous chemical agents, and the labor conditions can therefore not be said to be good. As a result, young people tend to steer away from it, and the factory we researched was experiencing labor shortages for both unskilled and skilled labor.

In response to this, the firm had come to rely on foreign labor. It was currently employing 8 Bangladeshis and 2 Pakistanis. Its experience with foreign labor had begun several years earlier when the management hired one Bangladeshi with the help of a job broker, but nobody remembered who the broker was. They had never used a broker again, since after that new workers learned about job openings by word of mouth.

All of the foreigners were *shugakusei* studying at Japanese language schools. The schools were in relatively faraway places such as Kita and Toshima Wards, so the employees attended classes in the mornings. They began work at 2:00 or 3:00 p.m., and worked for roughly 6 hours, finishing their day at 8:00 or 9:00. They also worked all day on Saturdays, meaning they had a working week of over 40 hours.

The foreigners were working at polishing the completed pieces, which came out blackened. It was a job which could not be mechanized, but which Japanese disliked because of its unskilled nature. Some of the foreigners received ¥200,000 per month, roughly on par with their Japanese counterparts, but the employer did not have to worry about bonuses or welfare expenses, making it economically advantageous.

The foreigners worked very diligently, and seemed to be sparing of every moment of the day. There were apparently occasional troubles between them and the Japanese, but the employer did not take sides as both sides were usually at fault. The foreigners were polite, and had a very good reputation in the factory.

Next we will look at casting. There is a major industry in Kawaguchi City, Saitama Prefecture, which is sometimes called the representative area of this business, but it is currently in decline, and the downfall has been accelerated by a severe labor shortage. We interviewed one manager of a very small casting business, who told us that 'All of my business is subcontracting, and the contractors are very severe in the prices they demand. I've tried to rationalize as much as I could, but it doesn't solve the problem. I have no alternative but to cut personnel costs.' The industry sends a caravan through the Tohoku District every year to recruit workers, but does not seem to have much success. The director of the Kawaguchi City Employment Security Office said that, 'Even when the industry places advertizements calling for 100 workers, they are lucky if they receive applications from ten old men' (*Asahi Shimbun*, 2 April 1988).

One major factory in the old section of the town has hired some 10 Ghanians and Nigerians. The president of the company said that, 'They are all on tourist visas, you know, illegal workers. We cannot find workers, so there's no other way' (Mainichi Shimbun a, Chapter 3). Furthermore, in 1990 a group of roughly 20 industry-related companies from the same city set up a Nikkei Human Resources Center in San Paolo, Brazil (Yamashita, p. 62).

Many foreign workers have been employed in the automobile industry as well. Gonoi's reportage on a small auto parts subcontractor gives a vivid description of conditions in the industry. The company was in the outskirts of Isezaki City, Gunma Prefecture, and the owner, an older man, worked alongside the 12 employees. Eight of the employees were undocumented Filipinos, and all the Japanese workers were already in their late 40s. The Filipinos did none of the skilled work, but simply picked up the finished pieces and packed them into boxes.

'Hiring the Filipinos was a move of desperation,' the owner said. 'For a small sub-contractor like this, cutting labor costs is the only way to survive.' He said of the Filipinos that 'They work hard. To be quite frank, the Japanese ought to learn from them.' On the question of hiring undocumented labor, he stressed that, 'There's absolutely nothing I can do if somebody informs on me and we are raided by the police or the Immigration Bureau. I don't have any means to defend myself. And the factory? It's stupid to even ask that question. Of course it would have to close down' (Gonoi, Chapter 1).

Many of the Nikkeijin work in auto parts factories. Most of them are employed by in-house sub-subcontractors that assemble pieces to be used on the assembly lines of the subcontractors who serve the major manufacturers. These firms receive guidance and orders directly from the companies above them, and are normally paid on a formula of price-per-item times volume of production. The workers are managed by other Brazilians who are able to speak Japanese.

Adult men normally receive a daily wage of between ¥8,000 and ¥10,000, to which is added an allowance for the two or four hours of overtime they typically perform. Many take advances from the companies to get the money for their airfares, and in most cases repay the sum with deductions from their monthly paychecks. Single workers are typically housed in groups of four or five in single-room apartments rented by their employers, who share the cost of the rents with the workers. Some of the workers have Japanese citizenship, and so must return to their home countries every two years to avoid losing their permanent residencies there. For this reason, many work for less than two years (Ministry of Justice o).

We would now like to present the results of a survey we conducted by interview on Nikkeijin working in the manufacturing sector. We interviewed Tomoo Oshiro, a 31-year-old, single second-generation Japanese Brazilian. Before coming to Japan he graduated from university in a field involving electrics, and had worked as an engineer. He had moved to Brazil when he was six years old. His parents were currently living 300 kilometers from Sao Paolo, but he had been living independently in Sao Paolo.

Oshiro was working at a factory in the automobile industry on a one-year contract. The company was employing Nikkei Brazilians as short-term workers, and had a representative in Sao Paolo who did recruiting. Approximately 130 Brazilians were living in the company dormitory. Their basic daily wage was ¥10,000, but they typically earned over ¥300,000 a month because of overtime, late-night, and holiday work benefits, and rewards for perfect attendance. In addition, workers who finished their contracts successfully and who had perfect attendance records received a bonus and subsidies for their travel back to Brazil. The conditions were generally the same as for Japanese temporary staff, and were better than those at many other factories which employed Nikkeijin.

Oshiro was working assembling rear axles. There were two eight-hour shifts, one in the daytime and one at night, with a break in each. He usually worked one hour overtime.

He learned about the job from a friend who saw an advertizement in a Japanese-language newspaper. He came to work in Japan partly because of the money but partly because he wanted to learn about Japan. He had come on a tourist visa three months earlier, but had then changed his status to a three-year permanent residence.

Because he had just arrived, he was not yet sending money back to Brazil, but said he had plans to do so. The money was to be spent on payments for an apartment he and his brother had recently bought. He did not yet have any Japanese friends. His relationship with other Brazilians was basically confined to some colleagues in the company. He never called his family, but wrote a letter once every week.

He said he did not plan to return to Brazil until he had made all the payments on his apartment, and added that this would probably take four years. Once he returned to Brazil, he was planning to open a restaurant or other such business.

In the next section, we will look at the situation in the printing and bookbinding industry. The *Asahi Shimbun* carried a story on a printing factory in the southern part of Saitama prefecture which did work as a subcontractor for a major company from Tokyo. The factory also contained, however, a small sub-subcontractor doing in-house bookbinding using leased binding machines. A total of 12 workers were employed in this small firm, most of them foreigners from Bangladesh, Pakistan, and the Philippines. The owner, whom they all called 'shacho' (president), said that 'Our parent company told us not to hire foreign workers, but no matter how much we advertize we just can't find Japanese applicants. We are in a predicament. We wish they'd amend the law, but . . . Anyway, we are always prepared for a police raid' (*Asahi Shimbun*, 31 March 1988).

In this way, companies have been driven into a corner by the labor shortage. There have even been instances of managers being apprehended for hiring undocumented workers again and again; and yet they simply cannot afford to give up the practice. In June 1989 the Tokyo Regional Immigration Bureau raided a spring manufacturing factory in Kawaguchi City, and caught a total of 14 foreigners, including eight Pakistanis, five Bangladeshis, and one Filipino. The company had been raided three times before, and had already had a total of 60 workers apprehended. It was trying to enlarge a new business division, and was simply hiring new undocumented workers to replace those who had been caught. When the company suspected that a raid was imminent, the managers hid most of the foreign workers inside the factory; some Japanese workers hid the foreigners in their work stations (Ministry of Justice 1).

We will now introduce the experience of a Filipino whom we were able to interview. Ernie, who is 31 years old, came from the island of Cebu. He left a wife and two children behind. He came to Japan with the help of a cousin whose father was Japanese. He had studied management in university, and after graduating worked in stocks and later as a salesman. At the time we met him he was living in a small, less than 3-tatami mat (approximately 4.5 square meters) apartment in Kotobukicho, a day laborers' town in the city of Yokohama.

His job involved packaging machinery, and consisted of putting machines in plastic bags and then placing them in cardboard boxes. He found the job through the introduction of a fellow Filipino who lived in the same row of dormitory houses. It was a mere 10-minute walk from his room to his job.

One other Filipino was working in the same factory. Ernie got on quite well with him, because they both came from Cebu, and got along with the boss as well, who he said was a nice man. His daily wage was between ¥12,000 and ¥14,000 (including overtime). He was paid ¥1,000 for each hour of overtime. This means he typically worked two hours extra every day.

In the past he had worked both as a construction worker and had engaged in frame dismantling work. He had also worked removing rust from the inside of ships using sandpaper, but said it was almost impossible to breathe even with a dust mask.

He told us his dream was to work for a while in Japan, just to make money, then go to America, buy a machine for gold placer mining, and go home. He called his family about twice every month. The cost was ¥3,000 for roughly five minutes, so each telephone card evaporated quickly. He sent money back to his family on an irregular basis, but sent approximately ¥300,000 every three months.

He had a cold during the interview. He said his joints ached and that his body felt listless. In spite of this he wasn't taking time off from work. When we asked him why he quickly pointed to the watch on his left wrist, and answered:

'I got this watch as a souvenir from my brother who went to work in Saudi Arabia. When I go back to the Philippines, I want to do the same and give presents to my family. Then they'll talk about me as a success.'

In the Kansai region (to the west of Tokyo), small- and medium-sized manufacturing companies have tended to employ large numbers of Korean workers, and we will look in some detail at this situation.

The dramatic increase in Korean workers started in 1988, and has been particularly remarkable in Osaka, Kyoto, and in Shiga Prefecture, all in the Kinki region, as well as in Gifu Prefecture. According to the Immigration Bureau, this is because 'Many resident Koreans of Japan live in these same areas, and they have often been the ones to bring the workers to Japan or hire them here' (Ministry of Justice n). Moreover, 36% of all Koreans apprehended in the first half of 1988 were in Osaka, and the next largest region was Gifu (Ministry of Justice m).

In 1987, the Osaka Regional Immigration Bureau apprehended a total of 215 undocumented South Korean workers from six prefectures in the Kinki region including Wakayama Prefecture. The largest number, or 54.0% of these workers were employed in manufacturing factories, followed by hostesses (14.0%) and construction workers (13.5%). South Koreans made up 63.4% of all factory worker apprehendees, a figure that demonstrates that

Koreans make up the bulk of foreign workers in the Kansai manufacturing sector. There were 62 men and 54 women, meaning that women were close to men in numbers. Incidentally, 54.0% of the apprehendees were over 40 years old, showing that there has been significant aging even among these migrant workers (Ministry of Justice c).

The basis for these large numbers can be found in the communities of Korean residents of Japan (known as *Zainichi*), from both North and South Korea, who have a long history in the Kansai region. For Koreans, having connections with these resident Korean communities has decisive meaning in terms of finding jobs and accommodation. Ties range from some people who have relatives or friends in the resident communities, to others who have simply heard the name of a company owner from somebody else on their way back to Korea. In any case, the workers come to rely on these networks when they arrive in Japan. The next part of the puzzle is that many of the resident Koreans run manufacturing companies.

Many of Osaka city's small- and medium-sized factories are located in Ikuno Ward. It is within the Ikaino section that one finds the greatest concentration of resident Koreans in Japan, and hence the factories they run. Most commonly they are engaged in fields such as metal, plastics, rubber, and vinyl processing, as well as sandal manufacturing. In the following section we will give an overview of the small businesses in this area, based on our own visits.

The factories in this area face an extremely difficult environment, because of stringent cost-cutting demands from the prime contractors as well as due to falling domestic demand for such items as sandals. They had once relied on Japanese and resident Korean workers, but in recent times low wages and hard work have combined to keep these people away. As a result, the owners have come to rely on Korean migrant workers.

At the time of our visit most of the foreign workers were employed in the industries outlined above, but some of the women were working as tailors or seamstresses. In most cases they stayed for a period of less than six months, because they came as tourists, telling immigration authorities that they were 'visiting immediate relatives.' This status gives a maximum stay of 90 days, and can usually be renewed just once. In addition, in many cases the wife would come as soon as her husband returned, meaning that there was a constant stream of visits.

At the time of our study, the market rate for labor was ¥500-¥600 hourly. Working hours were often 12 hours per day, since the factories tended to run two shifts in order to keep the machinery in operation 24 hours a day. Even in cases which did not fit into this pattern, the workers typically wanted to perform as much labor in a short period of time, so they tended to work long hours. Many of them were bearing all their living expenses from their overtime wages, and were sending all of the rest back to their home country. Moreover, quite a few were living with relatives in order to bring expenses down to an absolute minimum.

As we saw earlier, the poor working conditions in Japanese small- and medium-sized manufacturing plants lead inevitably to high rates of workplace accidents. However, as we mentioned in the Introduction, applications for worker's accident compensation insurance are very rare, since the foreign workers fear deportation and the employers fear being caught for hiring undocumented workers.

Between April 1987 and March 1990, there were only 200 cases in which Labor Standards Inspection Offices received insurance applications and paid compensation in which they believed the applications came from undocumented workers (89 of the cases were in FY1989). In 1991 this number increased to 221, eclipsing the total of the previous three years, and the number of countries from which these claimants came increased by six to 24. However, this must be seen in the light of similar figures for Japanese workers. Approximately 2% of all Japanese workers become insurance recipients every year. The total for foreigners is still an order of degree lower.

In the four years leading up to 1990, there were 345 cases in which the workers' fields of employment were clear. The breakdown was: 286 in manufacturing, 52 in construction, and seven in other fields. Most accidents, by far, took place in manufacturing industries. Within this sector, the largest numbers were in metal parts manufacturing or metal processing (138), transportation machines and equipment manufacturing (29), general machinery and equipment manufacturing (19), and chemicals (13). It is thus in the metals parts and metal product manufacturing field that accidents have been most prevalent (Japan Occupational Safety and Health Resource Center b). A total of 55 of the foreigners were injured while using machinery (presses, planes, or circular saws), 17 suffered burns from hot water or other materials, and five were involved in falls (Ministry of Labor g).

Starting in 1990, one non-governmental organization (NGO) has published an annual *White Paper on Labor Accidents among Foreign Workers* based on its consultations with workers. In 1991 it registered a total of 129 consultations, up three times from the previous year. Of these cases, 67 were accepted for workmen's accident compensation insurance, but in a mere 15 of these cases were the cases filed prior to the intervention of the NGO. Most of these cases (64) were in manufacturing, including 24 involving workers operating presses, and 39 were in construction. Moreover, of the 66 cases in which it was known how long the worker had been employed, 39 took place within three months of initial hiring, and 5 occurred on the first day of work (Japan Occupational Safety and Health Resource Center b).

We will now introduce a number of labor accident cases. First, we will examine a small number of instances in which the worker successfully received worker's compensation.

Case 1: A Bangladeshi man (21 years old) entered Japan on a tourist visa, and was working in a metal processing plant in Chiba Prefecture with four or five employees. His right hand was caught in a drill one day while he was working. His thumb was severed and he suffered a fracture in the hand. He initially returned to Bangladesh, but then came back to Japan just before the expiration date of his visa, applied by himself for worker's accident compensation insurance, and received a payment of ¥2,740,000.

Case 2: A Bangladeshi man (24) entered Japan on a tourist visa. He had just started working in a press processing factory in Chiba Prefecture (with roughly 20 employees) when his right thumb was severed in an accident. He applied for compensation, received a payment of ¥1,320,000, and was then deported (both cases 1 and 2 from *Asahi Shimbun*, 19 June 1988).

Case 3: A Pakistani man (28) was working as an undocumented worker in a press factory in Saitama Prefecture. During his second day on the job, he inadvertantly stepped on the machine's pedal while his arms were in the press. His right hand was severed from the wrist, and he lost his left arm up to his elbow. At the time the data was published he was undergoing therapy in a national rehabilitation center. His application for worker's accident compensation insurance was granted, and he received ¥3,200,000 for medical treatments, and a monthly unemployment payment of ¥84,000. In addition, he will probably get yearly disability payments of roughly ¥1,000,000 (Mainichi Shimbun a, pp. 264–265).

Next, we will look at cases where the victims did not apply for compensation.

Case 4: A 22-year-old Pakistani man was working at the above-mentioned printing factory (with 12 employees) in Saitama Prefecture. The glove he was wearing on his right hand got stuck in the roller of a bookbinding machine, and his index finger was crushed. He underwent an operation, and the finger had to be removed at the second joint. Because he was an undocumented worker, however, no claim was filed for worker's compensation. The man's boss stated that he would pay the hospital bills as well as 60% of wages during the time the man could not work (*Asahi Shimbun*, 26, 31 March 1988).

Next, we will present the example of a South Korean woman who was employed in a Korean-run small plastics factory (with four workers) in the Ikaino District. She was still in the hospital as of March 1989 due to injuries she suffered on the job. We were unable to interview her, however, because of the strong wishes of the factory's owner, and we heard her story through the words of the boss and from an officer at the Labor Standards Inspection Office.

She was 53 years old, and came from Cheju Island, where she had worked as a farmer. She was married, and had one son and four daughters. She came to Japan on a one-month visa which permitted her to visit relatives.

She found her job through the mother of the owner of the company where she was working. She had been living in the house of the mother-in-law of a resident Korean woman who was friends with the owner's mother, and relied on the relatives and other connections she had in Japan to seek employment. The factory, for its part, was facing a dilemma since the new year's holiday had just ended and one worker had not yet come back to work. The factory's owner decided to hire her.

She was hired to do such jobs as removing plastic pieces from their molds, for which she was paid ¥570 per hour, a wage equivalent to what the other employees were receiving. She worked 12 hours a day, but this factory did not, unlike many others, have two shifts in order to run the plant 24-hours-a-day, and so she did not have to work at night.

She could hardly speak any Japanese at all, but she could communicate with the owner in Korean, and so this was not particularly disadvantageous. She ate her meals at her relatives' house. The factory fed its workers with noodles (udon) in the late afternoon, but she didn't seem to like it, and usually brought her own soup. She didn't seem to have many acquaintances among either Japanese or the resident Korean community, but she occasionally visited the woman who introduced her to the owner's mother.

Her factory job ended and she ended up in the hospital after just three days on the job, when her hand got stuck in a machine. The accident seems to have happened in the following way: the most dangerous part of a plastic molding machine is the place where the mold is housed, and because of this there are administrative rules requiring machine manufacturers to install door lock-type safety devices. Apparently the woman somehow put her hand through the space above the door which serves as a safety device.

Soon after the accident the Labor Standards Inspection Office conducted an investigation, and the woman was able to claim worker's compensation insurance. They said that when she went back to her home country she would be able to receive the same payments and conditions that she could get in Japan. At the same time, however, it became clear to the authorities that she was an undocumented worker. The owner was called in for questioning by the Immigration Bureau authorities, and he was also given a variety of warnings. They threatened him that, 'If this happens again, it could have an effect on your own residency status.'

At the time of the interview, the woman's one-month visa had expired, but she was applying for extensions while she was in the hospital. She could not do the paperwork herself, so her husband's sister, who was married to a Japanese man, was doing the work for her. She still did not have free use of her hand, and the doctor could not estimate when she would be able to leave the hospital and go home.

3 The Construction Industry

The construction industry is another major user of foreign labor. In the same way as we did for other sectors, we can estimate the number of undocumented workers employed by extrapolating from the number of apprehendees. Of the 32,908 people who were caught in 1991 as undocumented workers, 12,057 were listed as 'construction workers.' This means that this category accounted for 36.6% of all apprehendees, a figure higher than those for either factory workers or people involved in the sex and entertainment industry.

We can estimate that a little more than 100,000 of the estimated 278,892 overstayers in Japan as of May 1992 were working in the construction industry. In addition, the survey conducted by the Tokyo Metropolitan Labor Institute found that 3.4% of all the *shugakusei* in Japan who were in reality working were doing so as construction workers, adding up to fewer than 1,000 people. Furthermore, our own survey found that 5.5% of all trainees were working in this sector, adding slightly over 1,000 people. In terms of Nikkeijin workers, the study by the Overseas Japanese Association found that 6.1% of Nikkeijin working in Japan were doing so in construction, and we can infer from the total of 147,800 Nikkeijin working in Japan as of June 1991 that slightly less than 10,000 were involved in construction work. If we take the total of all the above groups, we find that more than 110,000 foreigners were working in this field.

There are three general reasons for the prominence of foreigners in the construction industry. The first is that the relatively light weight given to the character and background of workers makes it easy for them to find employment. The second, as we mentioned above, is the complex structure of labor management in the industry, which makes it easy for foreign workers to penetrate it. The third, which is much more important, is the particularly severe labor shortage which has hit the industry in recent years.

Beginning in the latter half of 1986, Japan's growing domestic demand added fuel to construction industry activities, and the sector emerged from the doldrums and into a boom. The industry lacked, however, a sufficient stock of workers to cope with the situation. As a result, there was a rash of bid failures on public construction projects, meaning that the bid prices were too low and the contractors found themselves unable to fulfill the contracts. The largest reason behind these failures was rising wages brought about by the labor shortage in the industry.

The labor shortage was above all one of skilled workers, but applied to workers willing to carry out unskilled labor as well. Many of the people who entered the industry during the boom period at the time of the Tokyo Olympics (1964) were forced out when it later went into recession. In addition to this, very few young people were seeking employment in the field. As a result, there was a nearly unbelievable aging of the industry's workforce.

For instance, in 1989 outdoor workers employed by private construction companies with more than five regular employees fell into the following age categories: 2.0% were in their teens, 11.8% in their twenties, 19.9% in their thirties, 24.5% in their forties, 29.4% in their fifties, and 12.4% in their sixties. Incredibly the largest category consists of people in their fifties (Ministry of Labor i, p. 21).

What were the causes of this shortage? The first thing that must be pointed to is Japan's decreasing labor supply. Traditionally, people going into the construction industry have been unemployed people rather than recent graduates. What this implies is that workers in industries in the midst of structural recession were absorbed into construction. This supply has now, for all practical purposes, dried up.

Secondly, we can point to the falling number of migrant workers from agricultural villages. Public works projects have tended to be concentrated in two specific periods of the year – between August and October, and between February and March – as a result of governmental budgetary policies which encourage agencies to spend all their allocated funds in a given fiscal year. Migrant workers from the countryside once played an important role in filling this cyclical demand. The supply of workers has grown smaller, though, and is currently practically non-existent. The reasons for this can be found in the increasing depopulation of rural communities and the flow of younger people into the cities.

A more important reason for the labor shortage, however, is the fact that labor conditions in construction are terrible in comparison to other industries. Much of the work is done outdoors and at elevated heights, which increases the risk of accidents. Moreover, traffic regulations in major cities have increasingly made construction work a nocturnal task, and weather conditions make it impossible to predict numbers of non-working days. At the same time, construction schedules sometimes make rush work necessary.

In spite of these factors, wages in the construction industry are extremely low, and the employment is unstable. The basis for this is the industry's peculiar 'structure of stratified contractors,' a hierarchy of exploitation. Under this structure, purchasers give contracts to the general contractors, who then place orders with a first tier of subcontractors, who then place orders with a second tier . . . on and on downward. As a result, the number of firms in the industry has proliferated, and there are said to be over 500,000 at present.

Under this system, labor is typically supplied as squads of five to ten men working under an 'oyakata,' or foreman. These squads can be generally divided into those who are tied directly to one contractor, and those who work temporarily on contract. When companies face a labor shortage, they usually react by either going out or sending out a foreman from one of their squads to hire day laborers, or hiring a temporary squad.

Under this structure of stratified subcontracting, pressures from seasonal and economic adjustments or falling prices caused by competitive pressure can filter down through the successive ranks of subcontractors. The top contractors at the apex of the pyramid, who gain large profits from the system, are huge corporations known as 'general contractors.' The consequence, however, of this system, has been an overall worsening of labor conditions and a drop in wages for employees in the industry, and this in turn has led to many people leaving the business and to stagnation in the number of young people entering it.

It is generally said that there are 5.5 million people involved in the construction industry, out of which three-fourths, or 4.1 million, are outdoor workers. In the following section we will examine the kinds of jobs that are being performed by the 110,000 foreign workers among them.

The tasks on construction sites are usually organized around skilled laborers, and are divided into the following occupational categories: earthworkers, who dig out foundations and lay concrete; scaffold workers, who build frames; form assemblers, who build molds into which concrete is poured; concrete block builders, who install reinforcing rods in the concrete blocks; chippers, who dismantle the molds and chip away the unnecessary parts, and plasterers. In addition, there are a variety of unskilled workers who perform such labor-intensive tasks as cleaning the construction site, digging the foundations, tearing up roads, and carrying materials. As of 1989, the percentage of workers doing the different tasks were as follows: earthworkers: 29.1%, form assemblers: 3.7%, scaffold workers: 2.6%, concrete block builders: 1.8%, chippers: 0.5%, and handymen: 11.9% (Ministry of Labor i, p. 19).

Most foreign workers are employed as assistants to concrete block builders or chippers, or as handymen doing light work. It is said that some parts of the concrete block and chipping work can be learned in two or three days, but that Japanese people do not want to perform these dirty tasks. Producing the reinforcing rods requires cutting and bending, and many foreigners are working in the shops which process these parts. It is said that half of all chipping work is done by foreign workers (National Federation of Construction Workers' Unions, Kanto Region Committee, p. 76).

In the following section, we will report on the experiences of a form maker's assistant whom we were able to interview.

We met Luis, a 36-year-old Filipino, in a flophouse quarter of Kotobukicho in Yokohama. He told us he had come to Japan on a *shugakusei* visa, and enrolled in a photography school in Kawaguchi City. He did not use the services of a broker, and so had very few expenses other than his air ticket. He was introduced to his job by another Filipino he met at a party at a Filipino pub.

His workplace was in Hachioji, and he had to commute from Yokohama every day. He said he felt himself lucky to have found a job which gave him daily work for such a long period of time. He did not have any particular problems with his employment. His one holiday was on Sunday, and he used it to go to church with other Filipinos.

Luis' initial aim in coming to Japan had been to go to photography school. He had been working as a police officer in the Philippines, but had also been active in photojournalism and had managed a photography shop. He was married, and his wife had come to Japan twice to visit him. He told us he called home every Sunday.

Next, we will look at the case of a group of foreign workers employed in a reinforcing rod-processing shop.

Four Pakistanis and one Taiwanese between the ages of 21 and 33 were working cutting rods for apartment buildings in the materials depot of a construction company in southern Saitama Prefecture. The five foreigners were housed together in a small one-room prehab building in a corner of the company compound. At first they had received a daily wage of ¥6,000, but the sum had risen as they acquired technical skills, and at the time of the interview they were getting between ¥8,000 and ¥9,000 per day, with additional payments for overtime, adding up to a monthly salary of approximately ¥200,000 (Mainichi Shimbun a, pp. 170–171).

During the industry's recession, handymen were in little demand because skilled workers were forced to do the auxillary and unskilled tasks themselves. When the shortage of skilled labor emerged, however, it became necessary for the specialists to rely on others to carry out these tasks, and the industry began to take on foreign workers. This trend was further spurred as the supply of workers from industries with structural unemployment and of migrant workers from the countryside began to decrease.

We will now introduce the situation of two Filipino workers we met in a construction camp. They were working carrying materials, digging wells, and clearing away extra soil at a sewage works site in Tokyo.

The first, Ben, was 33 years old, and had three children, the eldest a 14-year-old daughter. The second, Romy, was 22, the second of three sons, and he was living with his parents. Ben had come to Japan roughly one year earlier on a tourist visa, and had wandered from work camp to work camp. Romy had come to Japan three months earlier on a *shugakusei* visa, and this was his second work camp. They told us they had met at a '*yoseba*' (a place where day laborers gather to look for work) and had worked together since.

They were receiving a daily wage of ¥7,000 (the Japanese workers were given ¥8,000). Their view of this differential was that 'Wages are pretty good here, and the working conditions are not so bad. We're happy, and would like to continue working and making money here. If you (the interviewers) make a big deal out of it we won't be able to work here any more, so please don't say anything. We think it's fine here.' When we insisted, they reluctantly told us that the boss of the last camp had mocked them, saying, 'Filipino, Filipino,' and that he had refused to pay them any more than ¥4,000 per day. Because of this, it seemed that the wage discrimination in the present site did not bother them much, that they were simply happy to have found a place with reasonable conditions.

They told us they had heard about this job from another Filipino. This is a common practice, in which Filipinos exchange information from compatriots in the hope of finding jobs with even marginally better conditions. Most of the information they exchanged concerned wages, but the discussion sometimes focused on the personalities of bosses and even the food served at different camps. They told us they looked for jobs on the basis of such information.

Ben told us that there were often gaps betwen what he was told by labor recruiters and the real conditions at construction camps. The stated and real wages were sometimes different, at other times there were no breaks, and at still other sites he received no overtime pay despite the fact that he worked late into the night. The worst thing he had ever experienced was being sent from one construction camp with ties to the yakuza to another, but he had finally managed to escape. We asked him why he continued working when it meant having such terrible memories, and he answered, 'When I get back to the Philippines I want to open a store, and get a house where I can live with my whole family.'

One month after the interview we saw them again, and asked if they had received their proper wages. They answered simply, 'Never mind.' No matter how many times we asked they refused to say any more. When we finally asked about their future plans, they said, 'What do you think? We will go back to the *yoseba* and look for other work.'

In spite of the fact, as we have just seen, that many foreign workers are currently employed in the construction industry, the Ministry of Construction is dead set against the practice. A Ministry circular issued in November 1988 laid out its position, that 'Not only may the increase of illegally employed foreign workers in construction cause a drop in the public's trust and appraisal of the industry, but it may also obstruct efforts to hire young people who will sustain the future industry as its basic workers, and may hence impede efforts to restructure the business' (Ministry of Construction).

In spite of the Ministry's attitude, most of the public entities which issue contract orders have not enforced penalties against businesses using undocumented workers, and have basically taken the position that this practice may exist, but that it is an effect of the subcontracting system. There is, however, one exception to this general attitude. The Ministry of Construction's Kanto Regional Construction Bureau, which issues orders for up to 1,000 projects a year, instructs firms found to be using undocumented workers to fire them immediately, and has also made it known that firms carrying out such practices might be penalized with a possible demerit on their 'works evaluation score,' which might lead to a decrease in the number of works for which they would be given authorization to issue bids (*The Daily Engineering and Construction Industry News*, 8 March, 1988).

One major issue stemming from the use of undocumented workers is workplace accidents. Responsibility in construction work is placed upon the master contractor, and the original bidder in any project must file the compensation claims. If an accident involves an undocumented worker, the master contractor must file a claim which reveals the fact that the worker was undocumented. This can lead to great damage to the firm, and can hurt the corporate image. According to a Ministry circular, in more than 60% of cases the reason that industry companies cover up accidents is either to protect a perfect 'no accidents' track record, or in consideration for the reputations of the master contractors (Japan Occupational Safety and Health Center c).

We will now look at one case involving a workplace accident. A 45-year-old undocumented Filipino worker employed in an apartment building construction site in Tokyo was severely injured when a more-than–100 kg panel was caught by a sudden wind and landed on top of him. His spinal cord was damaged and he received multiple fractures in his right leg. A support group for foreign workers gave him assistance, and as a result the master contractor was forced to take responsibility for the accident. As a result, he was able to receive compensation insurance, and a precedent was set as he was guaranteed that the payments would continue even after his return to the Philippines (Kalabaw no Kai b, Chapter 2).

The president of one construction company that was using

foreign workers told us that, 'When I think about the possibility of workplace accidents, I'd really much rather use Japanese. This may sound strange to say, but I feel much more comfortable dealing with injuries to the Japanese workers, and I'd rather see them get hurt.' One worker told us, 'I'm in Japan on a tourist visa, so I can't get health insurance. . . . When I think about the possibility of injury, I hesitate before taking on any dangerous work.' These two opinions bluntly demonstrate the problems concerning foreign workers and accidents.

In the Kanto region, thus, there are very few foreigners working at big project sites being run by the general contractors or on large-scale work on official government buildings. In the outlying regions such as Chiba, Saitama, and Kanagawa, however, it is reportely quite common to see foreigners working on ten-or-so-story building projects (*The Daily Engineering and Construction Industry News*, 5 April 1988).

In terms of the quality of the work done by foreigners, one boss we interviewed gave solid approval, saying that, 'They're much more serious about their work than Japanese kids today. They can learn how to do the work, if you take a little time.' Another gave a different opinion, however, saying that, 'We put a lot of money into them, and if we could get Japanese to work for the same wages there's no question we would. Foreigners don't understand Japanese, so they're inefficient. The Chinese, they make fun of bosses who can only speak Japanese, and they don't work. Filipinos are better. They're serious, and work harder than Japanese.'

Next, we will look at how major corporations conduct checks to find whether undocumented workers are being employed in their own construction sites. We will use the information gained by the Kanto Regional Council of the National Federation of Construction Workers' Unions (Zenken Soren) during its contract negotiations with the 53 general contractors which form the bulk of master contractors' as well as 16 housing construction firms (compiled from data collected by the National Federation of Construction Workers' Unions, Kanto Region Council).

Checks for the presence of foreign workers seemed to be much more rigidly enforced by the general contractors than they were by the housing firms. Of the 53 general contractors, only 12 said that they had not carried out such inspections. For the housing firms, the figure was much higher, reaching 9 out of the 16 companies. It is believed that this reflects the fact that public works make up a large part of the contracts for general contractors, whereas most contracts fulfilled by the housing firms come from the private sector.

The process by which general contractors conducted checks to discover whether foreign workers were being used or not could be divided into the following six steps in accordance with the severity of the check: 1) warnings to subcontractors or foremen to cease the practice; 2) semanding lists of workers employed; 3) Patrolling sites; 4) conducting inspections as workers entered the sites or during morning assemblies; 5) conducting checks during the training of new employees; and 6) addressing workers or asking them to write in Japanese language. Generally speaking, checks of a given severity included elements of a less severe step. In other words, general contractors that collected worker lists had usually already given warnings to the foremen, and in most cases where language checks were given the firms had already gone through the five earlier steps.

The 41 general contractors who had conducted such checks reported the following breakdown of actions: six had issued warning, six demanded lists, five conducted patrols, ten given inspections at site entrances or during morning assemblies, four given checks during training, and ten given language inspections. It is not generally believed that the first two steps are in reality effective. The third and fourth checks are not particularly effective against foreign workers who look Japanese. Therefore it is only the last two steps that can in reality have some effect, but only 14 of the 53 firms had taken such measures.

Similarly, just three of the seven housing firms which conducted checks had asked the local builder's office to provide them with lists of workers, three had asked site foremen conduct checks, and just one had carried out both measures. In other words, no checks for foreign workers were conducted at sites belonging to more than half of these companies, and even in places where they were it was merely a formality.

The labor shortage in the construction industry has led to a rapidly increasing chorus of people calling for the legal introduction of foreign labor. The Associated General Contractors of Japan, Inc. (*Zenkoku Kensetugyo Kyokai*), which represents the business, has lined up with the positions of the Ministry, but there have been strong calls for legalization from its regional branches. The first such call came from the Associated General Contractors of Kanagawa Prefecture (*Kanagawa-ken Kensetsugyo Kyokai*), which called for the development of a system to employ foreign workers, but one with braking mechanisms, as well as legal studies on a system to fit the Japanese cultural background (*The Daily Engineering and Industry Construction News*, 25, 29 March, 1988).

In addition to this, one industry magazine emphasized that in the 21st century one-third of all workers in the business would have to be migrant workers, including foreigners, in order to respond to the waves inherent in construction projects (*Gekkan Kensetsu*, May 1989, p. 16). The reinforcement rod sector also adopted a stance strongly promoting the acceptance of foreign laborers.

Moreover, the Japan Federation of Contractors, Inc. (*Nihon Kensetsugyo Dantai Rengokai*), a group made up of the 52 largest firms, created a public corporation which has begun discussions on the possibility of asking the government to accept foreign workers provided that the numbers and periods of stay are controlled (*Nikkei Shimbun*, 20 October 1989).

Furthermore, the National Federation of Construction Worker's Unions (*Zenken Soren*), a group made up of carpenters, plasterers, and small builders, had long held a strong position that, 'Illegal foreign workers should be prevented from working at sites, and unscrupulous businesses that carry out such acts should be expelled from the industry,' but in February 1989 this was toned down to the much softer position that, 'We are opposed to the acceptance of foreign workers until there is agreement in the industry on how to stop confusion from arising in the labor market.' It is believed that the opinion issued from the union's members, who are also bosses, was influential. The Japan Federation of Construction Workers' Unions (*Kensetsu Domei*), which is made up principally of the labor unions of listed corporations, also issued a statement that, 'At the present we do not accept the presence of foreign workers, but in the future it may well become inevitable' (*Asahi Shimbun*, 1 August 1988). In this way, the labor shortage has prompted the construction industry to increasingly come out publicly in favor of a national open door policy.

Foreign workers are generally hired into the construction industry through the following routes: 1) They are directly hired by subcontractors or labor bosses; 2) they are introduced by brokers; or 3) they are hired through the day laborer market. Workers are typically lured into the industry through networks of compatriots where they exchange information on jobs, wages, and bosses. Some also come as trainees. In the following section, we will examine the ways foreigners enter the industry, and their working situations.

The following case involves two foreigners who were hired directly (route 1) into a job building concrete blocks.

Case 1: In February 1988, two Filipino brothers, one 28 and the other 34, were working at a housing construction site in the Tama section of Tokyo. Their boss, who was 43, introduced them as his 'Filipino carpenters.' One of the brothers, who was a college graduate, had worked for a company, and the other had been a sailor. They had come to Japan four years earlier on tourist visas, found carpenter apprenticeships in Kanagawa Prefecture with the help of a friend, and then began working for the present boss two years later. The boss praised them, saying that, 'It takes six years to make a full carpenter. They're about eight tenths of the way there, so I can entrust them with simple jobs.' The brothers, who spoke Japanese with almost no difficulty, said that, 'We are Japanese carpenters. It's hard for anybody to tell the difference.'

They were living in an apartment near the boss's house, and were sending approximately half of the ¥200,000 or so they made every month back to their family in the Philippines. The one who had once been a sailor said he had already bought one fishing boat, and that he planned to work for at least five more years, then go back to his country and manage a fishing company (Mainichi Shimbun a, p. 169).

The second case, which involves a group of Thai workers who found work through a broker (route 2), is slightly dated, but is a well-known example.

Case 2: In November 1984, a construction company in Toyohashi City hired 13 Thai men who had come to Japan on tourist visas and had them work not only in the Chubu region, but sent them from Kanto, the nation's center, out to Kyushu and Chugoku in the south to work assembling vinyl houses on farms. The men were paid ¥9,000 for each nine-hour day, receiving a monthly salary of ¥150,000, but there were monthly deductions of ¥10,000 for housing and ¥30,000 for food, meaning that they were left with approximately ¥80,000-¥100,000 to repay their travel expenses and send back to their families.

Their presence was discovered in September 1986, when there was a traffic accident involving a group returning from a worksite in Mie Prefecture to their lodgings in the company's office in Yokkaichi. Four of the workers were killed, and one was seriously injured. They were farmers from northern Thailand, and had received passports and air tickets to Japan after paying a fee of ¥450,000 to a Thai-Chinese broker in Chiengmai. The fees, however, were in the form of high-interest loans. The workers were met at Narita Airport by employees of the company (*Chubu Yomiuri Shimbun*, 28 September 1986, *Chunichi Shimbun*, 10 October 1986).

As we can see from this example, in most cases where the foreign workers find their job directly or through brokers, they are housed in company housing or apartments, and are transported to their work sites.

It is important to take a careful look at route 3, the day labor markets, since many of the foreign workers engaged in unskilled work as assistants or handymen use this route. The approximately 600,000 temporary or day laborers working in construction make up roughly 15% of the total industry workforce. This percentage is the largest among all industries, and shows the importance of day labor for the business.

A large number of the day laborers look for and choose their workplaces in the early mornings at places known as *yoseba*, directly selling their labor power. The workers hired in these markets are generally believed to be of the worst possible quality. They can be characterized as follows: most are single, anonymous, and possess a high degree of mobility in many different ways. The *yoseba* are thus convenient places for foreign workers who are both undocumented and who do not possess special skills.

Japan's four largest *yoseba* are Sanya in Tokyo, Kotobukicho in Yokohama, Sasajima in Nagoya, and Kamagasaki in Osaka. All four of these areas include special housing areas called '*doya-gai*' (flophouse quarters) in Japanese. In Osaka, almost all day labor hiring is concentrated in Kamagasaki, but in Tokyo and Yokohama there are several smaller marketplaces in addition to the main areas. Tokyo's Ikebukuro and Takadanobaba are particularly well known smaller markets.

Workers at *yoseba* are generally hired in the three following ways: 1) through public employment security offices; 2) directly, in a quasi-contractual way, often when the company knows the worker; and 3) through labor sharks. The second route is most common for workers with some stability in their employment; whereas route 3 is most common for those with little stability. The labor sharks, who recruit workers and then receive a commission in exchange for sending them to work for workplace foremen or companies, are said to control 90% of the *yoseba* labor market. It is also said that many of these people are criminal gang members or have links to such gangs, and that in the Kansai area there are quite a few resident Koreans.

There are very few foreign workers living in the flophouse quarters with the exception of Kotobukicho in Yokohama. This is partly because these areas are easy targets for Immigration Bureau surveillance, partly because many of the lodging managers will not allow foreigners to stay in their buildings, but also because building improvements conducted recently in Sanya and Kamagasaki have pushed up lodging prices.

In contrast to this, Kotobukicho has a population, in addition to Japanese workers, of resident Koreans as well as a large number of Filipinos, South Koreans, and other foreign workers. One of the reasons for this is that building renovations have proceeded only slowly, meaning that lodging is still inexpensive, but it has also been said that about 90% of the lodging owners are resident Koreans who feel sympathy not only toward others in the own community and to South Koreans, but toward other foreign workers as well.

It is impossible to determine the exact number of Filipinos living in the Kotobukicho neighborhood, but roughly 250 show up on Sundays at a local Catholic church (*Asahi Shimbun*, 15 April 1988). The number of Koreans began to increase around 1988, and it appears now that there are several hundred people.

With the exception of Kotobukicho, most foreigners found in *yoseba* commute there from apartments in other residential areas.

Even in *yoseba* one finds that foreign workers are ranked below their Japanese counterparts. It usually takes them longer to find jobs. One foreman told us that, 'You can't teach these kinds of jobs with just gestures. It doesn't help that foreign workers are cheap, because you can't use them.' It is important to remember, though, that at least 10% of all workers dispatched by labor sharks are foreigners. It seems, therefore, that companies looking for high-quality laborers have no choice but to go to the *yoseba* themselves.

In this way, 'well-meaning' labor sharks, because of the belief that foreign workers do not perform well, have begun to avoid hiring them. There are, however, some who deal exclusively with foreigners. They typically provide labor to sites who need to hire a certain number of laborers, and for whom foreign workers can be a cheap source. It is said that in many cases these labor sharks have some connection, through marriage for instance, to the workers' source countries.

In addition to dormitories, apartments and flophouses, foreign workers are housed and fed in construction camps, or '*hanba*,' which are prehab or other buildings set up near construction sites, usually when the work will continue for several weeks or months. They are often used in cases where commuting is difficult or excessively expensive, as in for sites located in mountainous areas. Labor camps, because they are very inaccessible to Immigration Bureau checks, are at the opposite end of the spectrum from the flophouses quarters.

Next we will look at how foreign workers are regarded at their worksites. In many cases, as exemplified by Case 1, bosses treat foreigners identically to their Japanese counterparts. It is also said that at present Japanese workers generally are indifferent to the foreigners. They typically have complaints, such as 'Our wages will fall,' or, 'We can't communicate, so if we work with them our squad will not be able to work as fast as other groups,' but these complaints are rarely voiced and so do not translate into troubles.

There have been, however, increasing instances of insulting behavior against foreign workers, and in particular against Filipinos.

Case 3: A Filipino who was working at a construction company in Yokohama was spoken to derogatorily and even forced to serve meals. At the worksite he was unable to understand the Japanese orders, and was often shouted at rudely. He was later transferred to another worksite, and when on one occasion he became faint from exhaustion after working long hours the foreman threw a large rock at him, which struck him in the thigh; he collapsed. His recollection was that, 'At that time, I thought that that job would end up destroying my body. I couldn't stand the humiliation of being treated like a menial servant' (*Asahi Shimbun*, 3 July 1987).

In the Kansai region, the labor shortage became pronounced when the construction industry went into its boom. The situation is bound to become even more serious when projects such as the Kansai International Airport, the Bay Area Development Project, the plan for a new city center, and new office buildings, go into full-scale construction. In response to this situation, the Kansai industry has begun in earnest to hire South Koreans, who have had fewer work opportunities since the end of the construction boom in their country at the time of the 1988 Seoul Summer Olympics.

Construction firms under the ownership of resident Koreans are more likely than those under Japanese ownership to hire South Korean workers. One reason is that newly arrived workers tend to find jobs through information passed by word-of-mouth from others who are already employed. Another is that many of the people who run construction camps are resident Koreans, and they are naturally receptive to Koreans. There are already some camps where everybody, from the owner to the cook all the way down to the workers, are either Koreans or resident Koreans, and where one cannot find a single Japanese.

In addition, some Korean workers can be found in the Kamagasaki *yoseba*, seeking employment in either construction or longshoreman jobs (*Asahi Shimbun*, 14 October 1988).

In the following section, we will look at the example of a South Korean whom we interviewed at a mountain workcamp in Nara Prefecture.

Case 4: Chong Mu (50), a native of Kyongju, worked in his home country in a variety of jobs, including as a steelworker, machine repairman and construction worker. He had lived with his mother, wife, his son (29) who was a restaurant cook, and his high school-age daughter (17). He had an aunt who was a resident Korean living in Osaka. At the time of the interview he was in Japan under the pretext of visiting this aunt, but was in reality working at a construction site.

This was Chong's second stay in Japan. On the first occasion he had only been carrying ¥100,000 in 'show money,' and as a result had been granted a mere 15-day visa. He told us that his calculations showed that he needed to work in Japan for at least two months in order to break even. To prevent a second failure, he had enlisted the help of a friend who had experience working in Japan; the friend helped him to fill out immigration forms and find work in Japan. Chong told us his friend had not charged him any fees for these services.

At the time of the interview, Chong had resigned from his first job and was working for a construction firm with about 80 employees to which he had been introduced by an acquaintance. Most of the work involved carrying materials in order to improve the efficiency of the Japanese workers. He could not speak Japanese, but could understand enough to follow simple orders. He said there were other Koreans working for the same company, but that there was a very high turnover rate. At some times there were none at all, but at other times two or three came together. There were also some Filipino and Taiwanese workers.

He was receiving ¥12,000 a day for his work, but there were deductions for meals (¥2,000), lodging (¥2,000), as well as a total of approximately ¥2,000 for taxes and as cuts for the team leader and the broker. He was usually left with roughly ¥7,000. He said that the Filipinos, by contrast, received a net wage of just ¥3,000. When Japanese students worked for the firm, they typically received between ¥9,000 and ¥10,000.

Chong was living with one other South Korean in a room arranged by the company, but there were also Japanese workers living in the camp. The company prepared three meals a day for him. He told us he had not really cared for Japanese food at the beginning, but had grown used to it after a month.

On Sundays he usually went shopping at department stores and called his family back in Korea. He said that he had spent approximately ¥100,000 so far on such items as a camera, watch, a rice cooker, and some tools he planned to use back home. He called home roughly twice a week, and wrote a letter once a month. He complained about using up his money on Sundays, but in spite of the shopping he managed to save about ¥120,000 out of his monthly wage of ¥150,000. He said he would not send the money in regular intervals, but would keep it with him and carry it all back to Korea. He did not have to use the money for food or lodging, and had very few living expenses.

Chong told us that beginning with his first trip to Japan and the curtailed stay granted to him he had come to fear the Immigration Bureau, and he was careful about doing anything that might seem suspicious to the police. He did say, though, that he planned to come back to Japan after some time, and he also told us that, though it seemed impossible under present law, he hoped to become a long-term resident some day. If it were possible, he remarked, he would like to bring his whole family to Japan.

Next, we will introduce several examples involving Korean construction workers who were apprehended while in Japan.

Case 5: A construction company headquartered in Kyoto hired a group of 12 South Korean workers who had come to Japan on tourist visas, lodged them in a company dormitory in Ashiya city, and had them work in apartment building construction sites in the cities of Kobe, Osaka, and Nara. The workers were paid ¥3,000 per day plus meals (*Yomiuri Shimbun*, 12 May 1988). In addition, the same company individually hired a total of 40 Koreans and 3 Malaysians who had entered Japan on tourist visas, lodged them in a dormitory, and used a microbus to transport them to road construction and archeological excavation worksites in Kyoto (*Mainichi Shimbun*, 16 June 1988).

Case 6: A resident Korean-owned construction company in Amagasaki city lodged a group of 15 South Koreans who had come to Japan on tourist visas in a company dormitory, and had them work at building sites it had received contracts for in Kobe and Takarazuka cities. The workers were paid between ¥2,200 and ¥5,000 per day (*Mainichi Shimbun*, 15 March 1988). Such examples of mass hirings of South Korean workers have also taken place outside of the Kansai region.

Case 7: The resident Korean owner of a construction materials company based in Sunto-Gun, Shizuoka Prefecture, hired 39 Korean men and one woman (a cook) to come to Japan under the pretext of visiting relatives. They were lodged in the company dormitory, and received ¥5,000–7,000 a day for working at civil engineering work sites (Ministry of Justice f).

Let us next look at the question of how much foreign workers receive in wages compared to their Japanese counterparts. In the past, there were many cases in which it was impossible for them to receive anything other than low wages. For Filipinos, in particular, there is much information suggesting that the wages they received were very low. In fact, in some sections of the construction industry it is said that Filipino workers have been called 'Manila.' Their wages were set according to what was called the 'Manila market,' and were significantly lower than those for Japanese workers (Utsumi and Matsui, pp. 186–187). In Chiba

Prefecture, for example, the going rate in the 'Manila market' was ¥4,000 per day (Kalabaw no Kai a).

As we have seen in previous examples, however, foreign workers are increasingly being given the same wages as Japanese in response to their increased skills. The background for this situation is the exchange networks, which foreign workers have used to avoid poorly-paying jobs.

In addition to the three routes which we listed at the beginning of this section, there is another way in which foreign workers are employed: the legal, and poorly paying trainee system. It has been used aggressively in the construction industry.

Case 8: At a general meeting of the Japan Reinforcement Contractors' Association, the president of one company which was using foreign trainees stated that at the time his company had 20 trainees in the concrete form assemblers, and 20 making reinforcing rods, all from China. The Japanese firm had accepted them through an architectural public corporation in China. The trainees had received six-month visas, and had already renewed them once, but they did not think they would be able to renew a second time. The company had been very careful, and had hired one interpreter and one cook from China, as well as a Japanese language instructor and lecturers to give workshops on technical matters. It had not found many worksites which would accept the trainees, however, and had concluded that this kind of training would be difficult to do in the future.

The Chinese workers looked the same as their Japanese counterparts, making it difficult to distinguish the two, but when they were addressed by officials of the contractors all they could do was to smile back. They were caught one time, and the official suddenly shouted, 'They' re a group of monkeys, aren't they?' and this created a major scene. The young workers, however, had been selected from within a large group, and so they were not low-quality people. Moreover, many of them already had experience in their occupations, and they worked diligently and were of great benefit to the Japanese firms (*Gekkan Kensetsu*, June 1989).

According to the report from the National Federation of Construction Workers' Unions which we introduced earlier, five out of the 53 general contractors were using trainees. In addition, one firm said it had declined to accept trainees since they were unskilled. Among the 16 housing firms, two reported having accepted Chinese trainees (data gathered by the National Federation of Construction Workers' Unions, Kanto Region Council).

The experience of Hiroshima City can be instructive in terms of the large-scale hiring of foreign workers in major private sector projects. In 1980 an organization was launched around a local medium-sized corporation, with the participation of some experts. As of 1988 a total of 218 foreigners had come to receive training in form assembling or reinforcement rod building, and had already finished their training and gone back to their home countries. The three major countries of origin of the trainees were the Philippines, Thailand and China (*The Daily Engineering and Construction Industry News*, 20 April 1988).

There are, however, many problems with the trainee system in the construction industry. According to the Ministry of Justice document we introduced in Chapter 1–2 (Ministry of Justice k), three out of the 40 companies with 547 trainees which were suspected of being problematic were in the 'architecture/construction field,' and 12 were in the 'steel reinforcing rod processing field,' meaning that the construction industry accounted for a total of 37.5% of the problematic firms.

Moreoever, 11 of the problematic steel reinforcing rod assembly plants were in the jurisdiction of the Nagoya Regional Immigration Bureau, and all of them were using Chinese trainees. The reason for this is that the businesses in this region worked together to sign an agreement with China in February 1988 under which they would accept trainees from that country. Incidentally, the trainees in this project were receiving an extremely low daily renumeration of just ¥2,000 (*The Daily Engineering and Construction Industry News*, 7 April 1988).

4 The Service Sector

By 'service sector' we refer to a wide range of manual labor-intensive businesses such as restaurants, distribution, and building maintenance. In this sense our definition differs slightly from that used in Japanese industry classification standards.

As is well known, the concept of the 'service sector' under standard Japanese industry classifications is an extremely diverse category. To give an idea of the its breadth, we can enumerate some businesses that fall within its purview: product leasing, lodging, housework services, laundromats, barber shops, bath houses, personal services, movie theaters, entertainment, parking lots, automobile repairs, other repair services, industrial services, industrial waste disposal, broadcasting and information services, organizations in the medical, religious, and educational fields, and other specialized services. In this section we will omit such businesses as medical organizations, but will include the following major classifications: wholesalers and retailers, and certain portions of the restaurant, transportation, and communications industries. We will not consider, however, the sex and entertainment industry, since we have examined it previously.

We can make use of the Ministry of Justice data we used previously in this chapter to estimate the number of foreign workers involved in this sector (Ministry of Justice C).

In 1991, 4,321 people working in this category were apprehended as undocumented workers, including people working as cleaners, dishwashers, waiters and waitresses, cooks, transportation workers, and domestic helpers. They made up 13.1% of all apprehendees, lower than other categories such as construction (36.6%), and manufacturing (29.2%), but higher than the sex industry (12.5%). Only 8.1% of all apprehendees did not fit into any of these four large groupings – agriculture, for instance, accounted for just 0.4%. If we apply this percentage to the total number of overstayers as of May 1992, we find that there were slightly over 35,000 overstayers who fit into the service sector as we define it.

In addition to undocumented workers, there are many *shugakusei* doing part-time work in this sector. As we saw in Chapter 1–3, there are roughly 25,000 such students who are, in reality, performing labor, with approximately 50%, or a little over 10,000, working in the service sector. Our own survey showed that only 8.8% of all trainees were working in services if we discount information processing and services, meaning that no more than 2,000 people are working outside of their given status in this area. In terms of Nikkeijin, the previously quoted survey found that some 8.8%, or somewhat more than 10,000 people, were working in the retail and service industries.

If we add up the following figures, we find that more than 50,000 foreign workers are employed in this sector.

We will begin our examination of the situation of foreign workers in this sector by looking at the KSD survey which appeared in the Introduction on firms in the capital region. It found that 28.7% of companies in the restaurant, 13.9% in the service, 6.9% in the retailing and wholesaling, and 4.8% in the transportation industry had employed foreign workers. It thus appears that an incredible 30% of the metropolitan area's restaurants are employing foreigners.

The Toroken survey which appeared in the same section found that the following percentages of small firms in different industries had hired foreign workers: wholesalers/retailers: 5.9%; restaurants: 40.5%; transportation/communication: 2.7%; services: 12.9%, showing that more than 40% of restaurants in the region had such experiences. These two surveys also pointed to the fact that the employment of foreigners has not reached significantly into the transportation, communication, and wholesale/retail sectors.

In addition, the survey conducted by the Shinagawa Ward Labor Administration Office in Tokyo which we introduced in Chapter 1–2 found that 33.6% of firms in the service sector were currently employing foreign workers, and that 10.5% had done so in the past. Similar figures for retailers/wholesalers were 33.2% and 8.3%, and for transportation and communications 14.1% and 7.1%. The figure rose when larger companies were included because of their ability to hire legal workers with working visas.

In the following section, we will proceed to the question of gender, nationality and the types of specific occupations in which these workers are employed.

Ministry of Justice data shows the presence of 1,243 men, compared to just 717 women, working as undocumented workers in this sector. Incidentally, the only occupation for which women were predominant was that of 'domestic helpers.' The ratio of men to women among *shugakusei* was also roughly 3:2, meaning that in the service sector as a whole it can be surmised that there is a preponderance of men.

In terms of nationality, the largest group of apprehendees in 1989 who were working in the service sector came from South Korea, with 26.5% of the total, followed by the Philippines, with 19.1%, Taiwan with 12.8%, Bangladesh with 9.7%, Pakistan with 9.6%, Malaysia with 8.9%, Thailand with 7.3%, with other countries accounting for 6.0% (Ministry of Justice q). If we apply these ratios to the total of slightly more than 10,000 people surmised earlier, we find the following numbers: 2,000–3,000 South Koreans, a little over 2,000 Filipinos, and approximately 1,000 each from Taiwan, Bangladesh, Pakistan, and from other countries.

To these figures we can add the following numbers of *shugakusei*: 4,000–5,000 Chinese, 3,000–4,000 South Koreans, and 1,000 Taiwanese, with 2,000–3,000 of other nationalities. We can therefore estimate that Koreans hold the top spot with 5,000–7,000 people, followed by approximately 4,000–5,000 Chinese, 2,000 Taiwanese, and 2,000 Filipinos. In this way, Koreans and Chinese hold a salient position in the service sector, and most of the remaining workers are also from Asian countries.

Incidentally, Korean women and Filipinas make up an extremely large share of domestic helpers, whereas most cooks are Taiwanese men. In the next section, we will examine the situation of He Yaoji, a cook in a Taiwanese restaurant.

At the time of our interview, he was 38 years old, and had come to Japan from the suburbs of Tainan. He was living in Japan with his wife, but she had returned temporarily to their home country to give birth to a child. He had first come to Japan in 1986 on a *shugakusei* visa, and was currently working as a live-in cook in a restaurant in Ibaraki Prefecture. He was the third of six children (two girls and four boys). His family operated a tiny factory, where they worked alongside a handful of employees, producing room ornaments for export. He came to Japan to escape family disputes and marriage pressures.

When he had arrived in Japan three years earlier, the Japanese language schools were still in a completely unregulated state. He just received the visa, and became an overstayer when it expired. At the time we interviewed him he was not attending school at all. Japan was no more than a refuge for him. It seemed that he had had no other reason for coming to Japan other than the fact that it was nearby and that he could get a visa.

He had not come to Japan specifically to work, but had not come for study either. He had living expenses to worry about, however, and found that he had to work to sustain himself. He lingered in the Tokyo area for about one year, making a living through an assortment of jobs, including one, which he remembered vividly, selling goods on the street in Shinjuku. He moved from the uncertainty of Tokyo to Ibaraki Prefecture in the summer of 1987, after a Taiwanese acquaintance introduced him to the job he still held at the time of the interview one-and-a-half years later.

The restaurant owner was aware that he was an overstayer. He had never been a cook in his home country, and learned all the necessary skills while working at the restaurant, so that now he was doing all the cooking himself. His working hours started at 5:30 p.m. and ended at 4:00 the next morning, but in reality he had to do preparations and clean up after work, so he ended up working about one extra hour every day. He received ¥200,000 per month. The small restaurant was run by just three people: He Yaoji, and two Taiwanese women: the owner and her helper. The three got along quite well. The store was also an apartment, and the three lived together there along with the owner's son, all Taiwanese. He said he was satisfied there.

He had married another Taiwanese woman who often came to the restaurant, but they had not yet registered their wedding. She had gone back to her parents' home to give birth to a child, but was planning to leave it with them and come back to Japan. His life was extremely monotonous. He had no holidays, and even during his off hours only slept or watched television. He could not speak any Japanese, with the exception of the few words that were necessary for his work. He hardly ever ventured outside of the restaurant, so did not know anybody in the neighborhood. His three compatriots made up his whole world.

Because he lived and worked in the same place, there were relatively few concerns in his daily life. It could neither be called difficult nor could it be called enjoyable. The reason he rarely ventured outside did not seem to be because he was scared of the police or immigration officials, but simply because that was his personality or his mood. Most of the restaurant's patrons were Japanese, but it seemed natural for them that the cook of a Taiwanese restaurant should be Taiwanese; most of them called him 'chief,' and treated him no differently from other Japanese.

His family often told him that they wanted him to come home. His passport was set to expire, and his status as an undocumented resident prevented him from properly marrying his common-law wife. Now that he had a child, he was finding it increasingly useless to be living in Japan. He was planning to return home within six months or a year. He planned to manage the family factory that had been entrusted to his relatives, since it required little capital.

Next, we will take a look at the sorts of occupations being performed by foreign workers in the service sector. According to Ministry of Justice data, of the 4,321 apprehendees in 1991, 1,551 were manual laborers, most involved in cleaning, 1,103 were dishwashers, 764 were waiters and waitresses, 337 were cooks, 302 were transportation workers, and 264 were domestic helpers. According to this data, cleaning workers and dishwashers made up a large part of the total (Ministry of Justice C).

The Toroken survey, which considered the question from the viewpoint of companies, found that among 204 small- or medium-sized firms which responded, the following numbers were employing foreigners in service-sector occupations (with multiple responses possible): 42 had waiters, waitresses, or dishwashers; 16 had cooks; 14 had shop clerks; 13 had salespeople; 11 had cleaning staff; and 10 had other handymen. It is clear from this data that restaurants are the major users of foreign service workers in the Tokyo region (Tokyo Metropolitan Government h, Chart 1–12).

Actually, the situation we have examined up to now may not reflect the expectations that corporations have of foreign workers. According to the survey we just quoted from, the five largest service sector work categories in which companies wanted to employ foreigners were (with multiple responses): delivery, warehousing: 26; cargo handling, warehousing: 20; assisting in cooking, washing: 11; cleaning: 11; sales clerks: 8; sales: 7; and drivers: 7. Jobs such as delivery, warehousing, and cargo handling were the highest, eclipsing jobs relating to the restaurant industry (Tokyo Metropolitan Government j, p. 41).

Furthermore, a manager from a job information magazine whom we interviewed confirmed that most help-wanted ads aimed at foreigners were for jobs with poor working conditions which faced labor shortages: for instance, newspaper delivery, guards, building maintenance, drivers, delivery workers, restaurants, and jobs measuring traffic volume. Foreign workers are also employed in *pachinko* (a type of Japanese slot machine which resembles pinball) parlors and convenience stores.

Let us next look at how foreign workers find employment in the service sector. The previously mentioned survey gives an idea of how 223 firms hired workers in a variety of fields (with multiple answers permitted). Of the 47 restaurants, 42.6% said they had done so 'through the introduction of other foreign employees,' 31.9% that 'the workers personally came to seek employment,' and an identical 31.9% that they had found them 'through newspaper help wanted ads or employment magazines.' Within companies which described themselves in 'service industries' (57 firms), the response, 'through newspaper help wanted ads or employment magazines' was most popular, with a 45.6% share. In restaurants it is most common for new workers to enter through the introduction of friends and by direct contact (Tokyo Metropolitan Government k, p. 17).

In the following section, we will look at the example of two Filipinos employed disposing used oil, a job which falls under the category of waste disposal within the service sector.

Andy's (33) job involved disposing used oil from excavating equipment. He woke up every morning at 5:00 a.m., ate some rice which he received from the Philippines, and at 7:00 jumped into his employer's minivan and travelled from his flophouse in Yokohama to Funabashi, Chiba Prefecture. He received ¥10,000 per day, the same as that given to his Japanese counterparts. He worked from 8:00 a.m. to 4:00 p.m., with a one-hour lunch break and a fifteen-minute break at 3:00. He hardly ever worked overtime, and usually arrived back in Yokohama at about 6:00.

The job left him sweaty and smelly, so he always took a shower as soon as he returned home. He usually worked 15–20 days a month, but had been working on Sundays since he was planning to return to the Philippines soon and wanted to save as much money as possible. He ate dinner after taking his shower, but was usually tired from working and just went to a local lunch box shop to buy some white rice and one side dish.

After dinner two or three Filipinos who lived in the same neighborhood usually came to his small room. They talked about their hometowns and consulted each other on problems. They also exchange bits of information such as, 'Such-and-such job site is very sunny,' or 'I wouldn't get work from such-and-such labor shark if I were you.' They also worked to protect their rights using the *Asian Worker's Handbook* (Forum on Asian Migrant Workers a).

On Sundays, Andy went to services at a nearly church. After church he returned to his room and listened to music or took a nap. His days off seemed devoted to rest. He said he was afraid of Immigration Bureau officials, and hardly ever ventured outside.

While we were talking the company boss came into his room and said, 'I want you to work tomorrow. I'll pick you up in the morning.' Andy said he would go. The boss spoke to us a little, and said that 'I wouldn't be able to do business if it weren't for Filipinos. We'd go bankrupt.'

Andy also told us that in addition to supporting himself he managed to send ¥100,000 back to his family every month. He communicated with them by letter or telephone. He had a home in Manila, and before coming to Japan had lived there with his wife, son and two daughters. In the Philippines he had worked as a painter, but had found it difficult to find jobs. He had come to Japan in order to pay for his children's secondary education. He had come on a tourist visa, but had never bothered to try to renew it, and had simply stayed on for over two years. His two eldest children were both high school students, and he repeated several times that, 'I need money to send them to school.'

Andy was actually living with another Filipino named Rick, who was 32 years old. Rick was the third son in a family of six children, and was single, though he had a girlfriend in Manila. He had been living in an apartment in Kita-Senju with several other Filipinos, but had found the rent prohibitive and, with the introduction of a friend, had come to live with Andy. The rental fee for the small flophouse room was just ¥1,100 a night, but the two men were sharing it, so it was ¥550 each, a much lower fee than what Rick had been paying at the apartment.

At the time of the interview, he was working, like Andy, in a job that left him covered with oil. In fact, he had been introduced to his job by Andy. It was his second trip to Japan. The first time he had come as a dancer on an entertainment visa, but had been forced to shell out ¥220,000 to an agent. He had borrowed the sum from his family and from relatives. This time he refused to go through an agent, and had simply bought a plane ticket (¥40,000 one way).

During his first trip he had worked for roughly one year in the frame dismantling business, but had found the job to be very difficult. He had gone back with many bad memories, including being called 'stupid' and being addressed with racial slurs. But he really liked his current job, since the boss was a nice man, and he said he wanted to continue working there if possible.

Unlike Andy, Rick could speak almost no Japanese. The only words he knew were simple greetings and terms connected with his work. He grumbled several times that, 'I can't speak Japanese, so I can't find a Japanese girlfriend.'

Next, we will take a short look at the situation of trainees in the service sector. The previously mentioned Toroken survey looked at companies in the Tokyo region which had accepted trainees, and found that, among 220 firms in the service sector, 16.4% currently had trainees, and 13.2% had accepted trainees in the past. Among wholesalers/retailers and restaurants (217 firms), similar figures were 12.9% and 10.1%, and among 85 firms in the transportation and communications field, the figures were 4.7% and 3.5%. There was thus a considerable number of trainees in this area.

The largest occupational category (with multiple responses) was sales, which led the pack with 14 instances, followed by cooks with five instances, assistant cooks/washers and clerks, with four each, cargo work, warehousing, delivery/warehousing, drivers, and waiters/waitresses/receptionists with two each, and cleaners and guards, with one each (Tokyo Metropolitan Government h, pp. 31–32). In other words, in the service sector like other areas the use of foreign workers under the pretext of training is becoming increasingly common.

In the following section, we will look at the situation in restaurants and building maintenance, two representative fields of the service sector. In recent times, growing numbers of restaurants have begun hiring foreign applicants on the spot without asking any questions. This is because they fear that questions on reasons for coming to Japan, family status, and future plans may drive the applicant away (*Nikkei Shimbun*, 20 September 1989).

One newspaper article showed that a large chain of family restaurants had approximately 80 foreigners working in its stores. All were from Asian countries, and most were Chinese *shugakusei*. They were mainly employed as dishwashers or assistant cooks, but those who could speak even a small amount of Japanese were assigned as waiters and waitresses. They received the same wages as their Japanese counterparts, and worked a strictly observed 20 hours per week. The company's president justified the situation by saying that, 'It's extremely difficult to find part-time workers, especially for our stores in the central areas of Tokyo. In order to keep up the quality of our service, we need to hire people' (*Asahi Shimbun*, 4 January 1989).

There have also been cases of companies in the restaurant industry trying to use training programs as a cover for employing foreign workers. One restaurant chain has been trying to get Filipino trainees since the spring of 1990. Its plan is to hire them at chain stores in the Philippines, bring them to Japan for a six-month training program, and then send them back to work in the Philippines after the end of the program (*Nikkei Shimbun*, 20 September 1989).

From September to October 1989 the Ministry of Agriculture, Fisheries, and Forestry conducted a survey on 25 firms selected from among major food industry companies with over 200 employees. It found that 20 of the firms were employing foreign workers, and that half of the workers were Chinese (Ministry of Agriculture, Fisheries, and Forestry).

We can get additional insights from a survey conducted by the Japan Food Service Association (*Nihon Food Service Kyokai*), an industry group made up of Japanese taverns (*izakaya*), and fast food and family restaurants. In September 1988 it conducted a mail survey of its 324 members, and received 182 responses (a response rate of 56.2%).

A total of 61.5% of respondents said they were currently employing foreigners, 9.3% said they had once done so, but were not at the present time, 13.7% said they had never done so, but hoped to in the future, and 15.4% said they had never done so, and did not have any future plans, showing that many firms hoped to hire foreigners. A great majority, or 45.0% said that the reason behind these plans was the 'shortage of Japanese workers.'

In May 1990, on the basis of this survey as well as research and debate, the association issued its 'Proposal from the Restaurant Industry on the Employment of Foreigners,' which contained plans for the use of migrant workers under the control of an organization to regulate this employment (Japan Food Service Association).

Next we will look at the building maintenance industry, a city-based service sector category which includes cleaning, air conditioning, and the management of energy supply equipment for buildings. The use of foreign labor in this business, reportedly mostly Chinese *shugakusei*, increased dramatically starting sometime near the spring of 1988. In order to cope with this increase, in the spring of 1989 the Japan Building Maintenance Association distributed a 'Manual of Procedures and Applications for Employing Foreign Students' to its 2,550 member companies (*Asahi Shimbun*, 10 April 1989, Japan Building Maintenance Association).

It seems that over 100 companies in this business are using foreign workers, and that many of them are experimenting by hiring just two or three foreigners. There have been reports that one single major company, however, was using approximately 80 foreigners. Almost all were Chinese *shugakusei*, and in fact 20 were working as janitors in the metropolitan government hall. Not only did the company have interpreters, but had even published a picture book called *The Work of Building Maintenance* and a Chinese glossary of 'Terms Used in Simple Building Cleaning Tasks.' It has an internal study group on 'problems of hiring foreign workers,' and was holding Chinese language classes twice every month (*Nihon Biru Shimbun*, 7 November 1988).

In addition, one building management and cleaning company in the Unazuki hot spring area in Toyama Prefecture overcame the shortage of handymen in the area by hiring 13 Bangladeshi overstayers for ¥600 per hour and sending them to work cleaning and changing *futons* (Japanese bedding) in customers' rooms (Ministry of Justice 1).

There have also been some moves in the hotel and inn (*ryokan*) industry to hire Nikkei Brazilians. The Hokkaido Ryokan Association introduced a plan to hire foreign workers, beginning in 1991 with an initial target of 200 people, to work centrally in occupational categories such as cleaning and maintenance inspection (*Nikkei Shimbun*, 9 August 1990). The Toyama Hotel and Inn Environmental Sanitation Trade Association conducted introductory meetings in Sao Paolo, Brazil, with the idea of hiring 150 people to work cleaning hotel rooms and working at reception desks (*Asahi Shimbun*, 31 August 1990).

We will now briefly introduce two other service sector occupational categories. The first, Tokyo's Tsukiji Central Wholesale Market, has experienced a severe shortage of young workers because the early work hours and the smell of the fish, especially during the summer, make it a '3D' job. A survey conducted by Tosha, a guild of purchasing brokers, found that roughly 230 foreign workers were being employed in fish brokers' shops in the market. However, if companies working outside of the market were included, it is believed the number would have reached 500 or even 1,000. Most of the workers were Chinese college students or *shugakusei*. They did not work long hours, but still received ¥7,000–¥8,000 per day (Aoyama).

Next, we will look at the situation of four Chinese *shugakusei* who were employed washing taxis late at night in an LPG (liquefied petroleum gas) stand in Tokyo's Shitamachi area. They received roughly ¥170,000 per month for working eight hours in a graveyard shift. 'It's a simple tedious job. Japanese young people just can't do it,' said the foreman (Mainichi Shimbun a, pp. 163–164).

In closing this section, we will introduce one case of a labor accident which occurred in paper recycling, which like oil disposal is included in the waste disposal industry. In December 1990, a 12-year old Iranian boy was pulled into rollers and killed while removing foreign objects from piles of old newspapers. His father had come to work in Japan, and the boy had followed along with his mother and a younger brother. He had lied about his age to begin working, saying he was 18, and had worked alongside adults, receiving ¥650 per hour (*Asahi Shimbun*, 16, 21 December, 1990).

5 Other Industries

Foreign workers are increasingly moving into many industries other than the sex and entertainment, manufacturing, construction, and service sectors that we have discussed earlier. These industries include agriculture, fishing, forestry, sea transportation, and computer software. In the following section we will look at the advances they have made into these fields, and will then proceed to a summary and analysis of the results of this chapter.

If we look at agriculture, we find that 134 people, or just 0.4% of those apprehended as undocumented workers in 1991, were working in this area (Ministry of Justice C).

How do foreign workers become employed in agriculture? The information on this question comes mainly from Ibaraki Prefecture. Many young men, mostly Filipinos, are working in farming areas in the southeast and western parts of the prefecture, either living with farming families or traveling from one farm to the next, carrying out unskilled tasks such as planting and harvesting vegetables, and breeding pigs and chickens. It is said that more than 500 Filipinos are working in the vegetable-growing areas in the western part of the prefecture.

One farm owner said that, 'Up until about two years ago very few farms had ever hired foreign workers. The ones that did were mainly places that knew job brokers with connections in the Philippines. The number increased dramatically in the past year, however, and so has the number of foreigners. Filipinos work briskly, and have a good reputation.' There were certain limitations, however, in that the farmers could not let the foreigners work in conspicuous places for fear of being caught, and the undocumented workers could not drive vehicles since they could not obtain driver's licenses.

One large-scale farm in the region, with over 100 hectares planted with burdock and Chinese cabbage, hired 14 Filipinos in Japan with tourist visas to perform harvesting and packaging tasks. The practice had begun three years earlier with three Filipinos recruited from a nearby lumber factory.

These workers received approximately ¥80,000 per month, or ¥3,000 per day, a very low wage, lower than the ¥5,000 given to part-time housewives. The foreigners were given, in addition, a daily ¥500 food allowance and free rice and vegetables. The farm's owner said that, 'At the beginning, there was resistance to the idea of hiring foreign workers. It was difficult to get housewives to work during the planting and harvesting seasons, however, and there were all these people in the nearby factory. Without the Filipinos we wouldn't have been able to manage.'

Another farm in the same region, which was raising approximately 80,000 chickens, was employing four Filipinos to perform such tasks as collecting eggs, feeding the birds, and cleaning. They were paid roughly ¥100,000 a month plus housing and food, or about ¥50,000 less than their Japanese counterparts (*Mainichi Shimbun*, 19 March 1989).

Next we will look at the routes through which these workers found their employment. One *Asahi Shimbun* article featured a farm in the western part of the prefecture that was employing three Filipino overstayers. The practice had begun three or four years earlier when the farm hired 16 foreigners including Filipinos, Sri Lankans, and Ghanians. The first group was introduced to them by a company in the scrap business, and later they used brokers to find workers from construction and real estate companies in Tokyo and in nearby Saitama Prefecture. The farm paid an introduction fee of ¥200,000 for each worker, but found that workers often left after working just one or two months of a three-year contract, so they changed their policy and began paying the brokers a fee of ¥500 per day per worker. At the time of the article, they had begun to find workers by word of mouth, and had even gone to the Philippines to recruit (*Asahi Shimbun*, 4 August 1989).

To understand the situation of trainees working in the agicultural sector, we can make use of data obtained by a Ministry of Agriculture, Forestry and Fisheries survey conducted in 1988 on 16 public corporations. The survey found that these corporations were using a total of 1,150 trainees. Of this total, 110 were living on farms doing agricultural work, and were involved in training programs that lasted between seven months and one year (Ministry of Agriculture, Forestry, and Fisheries).

Next we will examine the situation in the forestry industry. One resident Korean-run company in Gifu City was found to be employing 82 South Koreans who had entered the country on tourist visas in tasks such as logging and golf course construction. The company was paying very low wages, ¥7,000 per day for men and ¥4,000 for women, in contrast to the market rate of ¥12,000-¥13,000 for Japanese workers. The work hours began at 6 a.m. and ended at 5 p.m., meaning an 11-hour workday. This was one of the largest cases yet of a single company hiring Koreans on such a large scale (*Yomiuri Shimbun*, 21 April 1988, Ministry of Justice n).

In terms of fisheries, the case of *ama* (women who go diving for shellfish with primitive diving equipment) is well known. The number of women working at this job has decreased, and the age of the divers has also risen. In order to fill this gap, *ama* have been brought from Cheju Island in South Korea.

In the midwestern part of Kumanonada, a fishermen's association rents turban shell and abalone fishing grounds to businesses introduced by its members, and the companies employ highly-skilled Cheju Island women who they hire at low wages. In May 1988, 16 Korean *ama* were apprehended in Mie Prefecture, and they stated that their wages 'are less than half of what Japanese receive, since we only get ¥200 or less, for instance, for a kilo of turban shells.' They had rented a house to live in, and were cooking their own meals (Kataoka).

Most of these women had come to Japan on visas allowing them to visit relatives, and found work for traders owned by resident Koreans. Their wages range between ¥100,000 and ¥400,000 per month, most of which they send home to Korea. They return home when their visas expire, and are replaced by others, meaning that there are several women employed at any given time (*Asahi Shimbun*, 13 May 1988).

The deep sea fishing industry has also shown a tendency toward introducing foreign labor. Because of severe labor conditions, there has been a pronounced aging of the workforce in this occupation, accompanied by a dearth of young workers. A September 1988 report released by the Fishing Industry Problems Study Group (*Gyogyo Mondai Kenkyukai*), an advisory panel to the director of the Fisheries Agency, took a positive position on the question of hiring foreign sailors, making statements for instance that 'sailors' lives are typically based in their home countries, and there are many cases in which countries ask our companies to hire their own nationals when the ships are fishing within their 200-mile exclusive economic zones (EEZs) (Fishing Industry Problems Study Group, pp. 44–45).

In practical terms, the recommendation made by the report is that Japanese ships based in foreign ports hire sailors from that foreign country. What this indicates is a relaxation of the Fisheries Agency's traditional stance of forbidding the hiring of foreign crews. The Overseas Fisheries Labor-Management Council (*Kaigai Gyogyo Sen'in Roshi Kyogikai*), a group made up of both labor unions and companies in the industry, has reported a rapid increase in the hiring of foreigners in the industry, and that as of March 1992 there were at least 2,100 foreign workers, making up roughly 10% of the workforce. Approximately 60% of these sailors were Indonesian, 20% were Filipinos, and 10% were Peruvians (*Asahi Shimbun*, 24 April 1992).

The hiring of foreign crews has been particularly strong in the ocean transport industry. There is in fact a cabinet stipulation requiring that Japanese-flag ships in the industry employ only Japanese nationals. Because of the relatively high wages demanded by Japanese, however, a variety of methods have been used to get around this and employ foreigners.

The first method traditionally used has been to give the ship, in name at least, a foreign registry, an arrangement known as flag-of-convenience, allowing it to freely hire foreign workers. The second, called '*maru* ship' in Japanese (*maru* is the prefix added to the names of ships in Japan), has been to temporarily lend the ship to a foreign firm, hire foreign crew members, and then have it returned to the Japanese firm. This second form has mainly been used on coastal vessels, where the Law for Ships' Officers sets a requirement of at least 9 Japanese crewmembers. For this reason, foreigners have usually been hired as part of crews of mixed nationalities.

The International Mariners Management Association of Japan (*Kokusai Sen'in Kyokai*), which is made up of Japan's 32 largest shipping companies, has reported that as of October 1991 its members were employing 9,028 foreigners on either flag-of-convenience or '*maru* ships,' with these crewmembers coming from the following countries: 6,847 from the Philippines, 2,059 from South Korea, 41 from Myanmar, 29 from Indonesia, 18 from Sri Lanka, and 34 from European countries. Filipinos are far ahead of the rest of the pack. Moreover, there were just 2,455 Japanese nationals employed on these and on Japanese-flag ships.

Because the Japan Seamen's Union (*Zen Nihon Kaiin Kumiai*) has claimed that the use of mixed crew in so-called '*maru* ship' arrangements leads to unemployment among Japanese sailors, in the past there were no foreign crew on these ships. As a result, however, 70% of Japan's roughly 1,900 merchant ships became flag-of-convenience ships, and the number of Japanese crew fell drastically. In October 1989 the union accepted the '*maru* ship' system for newly built ships, with the condition that each ship have at least 9 Japanese crewmembers on board (*Asahi Shimbun*, 26 October 1989).

Next we will examine a few examples of '*maru* ships.' One 53,500-ton bulk carrier was lent to a paper company in Panama. Up until the time of this transaction in the summer of 1986, the entire crew was Japanese. At the time of the report, however, there were nine licensed Japanese crewmembers, including the captain and the first mate, and the remaining 12 sailors, including the cook and the deckhands, were Filipinos.

The hiring of the Filipinos was done through Japanese manning agents who specialize in ship crews and by recruiters in the Philippines. The sailors were hired under one-year contracts, with the strict condition that they would be immediately taken off the ship if they disobeyed any order given by the captain (Mainichi Shimbun a, pp. 174–).

Another industry with a significant labor shortage, the computer software business, is slightly different in that it does not involve unskilled labor. Because of this, there has been a large increase of foreign workers entering under the pretext of training. The Ministry of International Trade and Industry (MITI) has suggested that 'It seems there are several thousand people involved in this' (*Asahi Shimbun*, 24 August 1989). Incidentally, there have been many complaints among trainees that, 'we have been treated simply as cheap labor, and have not been taught the things we wanted to learn.' Some consider there is a possibility that the system is being used to use trainees as low-pay workers in software factories (Shimoda).

In order to deal with this situation, in which private companies have not been consistent in their introduction of software technology to trainees, MITI worked out a plan for FY1990 in which it would unify the system for accepting and supervising trainees under a new single office, and would make ODA (official development assistance) available for such programs. The Ministry has stated that it hoped to make the software industry a model for using foreign trainees as a vehicle for promoting technology transfer (*Asahi Shimbun*, 24 August 1989).

One of the outstanding characteristics of the employment of foreign workers that we have examined in this chapter is that they have been firmly incorporated into the lower strata of Japan's industrial structure. It is also true, however, as we saw earlier, that the labor shortage which has continued until recently has affected even major companies' operations, leading to the appearance of foreigners, especially in the auto parts and electrical appliance industries.

The great majority of the workers in the manufacturing sector, however, are not employed by major corporations, but rather by the medium- and small-sized subcontractors that make up the lowest echelon of the contracting structure. In the construction industry in particular they have found themselves employed by the labor sharks who occupy the lowest rank in its special hierarchical structure.

In addition, we cannot ignore the fact that the workers in these two sectors have increasingly been concentrated into specific occupational categories. In the case of manufacturing, the concentration is in metal-working, auto parts manufacturing, printing, and book binding, and in construction they are working in concrete form assembly, frame dismantling, and as handymen, all jobs that require relatively little skill. The common characteristic of these categories is that they are all among the '3D' jobs that Japanese workers tend to avoid.

Much of the service sector is also composed of small and unstable businesses, meaning that they generally fit into the lower strata of the Japanese industrial structure. The foreigners in the sector are mainly concentrated in jobs such as those in the restaurant business, '3D' jobs which also involve late working hours. The sex and entertainment industry, which on the one hand fulfills a function which Japanese society cannot do without, at the same time is excluded from the mainstream industrial structure.

Individual foreign workers may enter and leave from their jobs in these different industries and occupations, but an increasing number are now ever-present in these areas. What this means, essentially, is that these workers have already been incorporated into the industrial structure. In Japan, however, a special labor market for foreign workers does not yet exist. The dual labor structure which exists in Euro-American countries has not yet emerged here.

What we must emphasize is that the entrepreneurs who employ foreign workers tend to be those who occupy the lower ranks of Japan's industrial structure. The subcontractors at the bottom ends of the hierarchy of the contracting chain which exists in the manufacturing and construction sectors are in a position where they simply cannot hire Japanese workers, and they are under constant pressure, in good times, to produce at lower prices, and in bad times to deal with shrinking contracts. The managers in the service and sex industries also find themselves in situations that are far from stable. For these people, using foreign workers as a control valve is only natural.

It has become normal today to treat these overstayers and out-of-status workers in the same way as part-time housewives and students and as employees in small-sized businesses. It may appear at first glance that we are proposing that there is no gap between foreign workers and Japanese, but the Japanese workers whom they compare to are those in the lowest ranks of the labor market, meaning that foreign workers have not been able to attain a rank higher than that of their Japanese counterparts in the lowest echelons of Japanese society.

In conclusion, we can make the judgement that the influx of foreign workers has acted as a sort of patch to cover up contradictions in the Japanese industrial structure. These contradictions have caused the emergence of a double control mechanism to regulate economic cycles. The first regulator is the small-sized firms, and the second is the foreign workers employed in these companies. Mass hirings during booms and mass firings during recessions is the natural result of this structure. Once these workers enter Japan, however, they have shown little tendency to later return to their home countries.

3 Foreign Workers' Housing and Living Situation

1 Housing

In the previous chapter we touched upon the issue of housing patterns among foreign workers, and will now look at this question in greater detail. Many companies in the manufacturing and construction sectors offer accommodations to their workers, and in these cases the living quarters are often adjacent to the work sites. Many *shugakusei* are also housed in dormitories owned by their language schools. Workers without access to such housing must seek out their own living arrangements, and they tend to find themselves extremely limited in their choices, as they must find places which are both low-cost and which will accept them. The search for housing often poses a greater challenge than looking for a job.

As we mentioned in Chapter 2–3, it is very rare nowadays to find foreigners living in '*doya*' or flophouses outside of the Kotobukicho section of Yokohama. There are instances of foreign workers living in one-room concrete apartments, but it is much more common to find them in cheap and easy-to-enter wooden apartments. Some women in the sex industry, however, receive fairly high wages and live in the more expensive concrete buildings.

In addition, there exists a growing category of cheap housing known as '*gaijin* houses' ('*gaijin*' is the Japanese word for 'foreigner'). They typically consist of a single floor of an apartment complex or building that has been divided into small rooms and equipped with bunk beds. They are typically equipped with shared kitchens and pay washing machines. In addition, they play a role as a place for exchanging information. There are at least a dozen such places in Tokyo, in areas such as Itabashi, Ikebukuro, Okubo and Nippori, with some of them accommodating up to 200 people (Hinako b, p. 33).

In the following section, we will take a look at the housing and living situation of Ernie, the Filipino we mentioned in Chapter 2–2 who was living in a flophouse in Yokohama's Kotobukicho.

His quarters consisted of a single room of about 5 square meters, but it was at the corner of the building and a steel rod jutted out from the wall, reinforcing the idea of how small the room really was. In addition to his work clothes and futon, the room contained a television set and a shelf that he had received from Filipino friends. In the corner was a pile of things he was planning to send back to his family. For his daughter there was a big stuffed rabbit, for his son a radio control car, in addition to some chocolate bars which his children relished. He was waiting for a friend to bring over a videotape player the following day, and was going to pack it and send all the things together. The previous month he had bought a television set in Akihabara and had it sent to the Philippines. He told us it had cost him a total of ¥200,000, including freight charges and taxes.

Every day, after coming home from work, he took a shower and ate dinner at 8:00. He often cooked his own meals. After dinner he spent time with Filipino friends passing around the English-language newspapers, and went to sleep at around 10:00. The television was usually on, but he did not understand Japanese and so had no clear idea of what was being shown. He said that if he had more money he would buy a television set which could receive bilingual programs.

Incidentally, most of the cheap wooden apartment buildings still on the rental market today were built around 1965 (very few have been built since then), meaning that the last ones are now approaching the end of their 30-odd-year useful lifetimes. In recent years, increasing numbers of these apartment buildings have been destroyed because of soaring land prices or to make way for city development projects, and there has been a dramatic decrease in their number. As a result, these buildings exist only in limited areas, and foreign workers have found themselves forced to live in these same places.

In Tokyo, we can use the distribution of registered foreigners to gain an idea of where foreign workers are living. The great numbers of overstayers are naturally not registered, however, and this places significant limits on the use that can be made of this data. College and *shukakusei* students as well as trainees are, however, normally registered.

The nationalities of these registered foreigners can be classified into the following categories: South and North Koreans/Chinese (including Taiwanese), Philippines/Thailand/Malaysia, and others. The first group, who made up 22.6% of the entire population of Tokyo, constituted at least 25.0% in the following wards: Toshima, Chuo, Nakano, Shinjuku, Suginami, Itabashi, Kita, and Bunkyo. The second group, which makes up 5.7% of the total, held over 6.2% in Sumida, Taito, Koto, Bunkyo, Kita, Meguro, Minato, Shinagawa, and Edogawa wards, in that order (Watado).

In other words, with the exception of Chuo Ward, the Chinese group is concentrated in the two major amusement quarters of Ikebukuro and Shinjuku and their surrounding wards. This leads to the interesting observation that this group is conspicuously absent from Tokyo's third such quarter, Shibuya. The second group, by contrast, is concentrated, with the exception of Bunkyo and Kita wards, in the riverfront areas traditionally known as Joto (east of the castle) and Jonan (south of the castle).

There are concentrations of foreign workers in some specific areas, but in general they are scattered throughout the capital region. The reason for this is that the low-rent wood housing that they tend to live in is spread in a low-density pattern throughout the city. They are most commonly found along the railway lines, and have spread out to the limits of commutable distances.

Many foreign workers find their accommodations through real estate agents. When *shugakusei* were asked in a survey who had introduced them to or helped them to find housing, 35.8% responded 'a real estate agent,' 26.3% 'a Japanese friend,' 21.0% 'a compatriot,' and 16.9% 'other' (Tokyo Metropolitan Government g, p. 46).

In recent years, there has also been a proliferation of troubles involving foreign workers' living arrangements. Most of this information is held by real estate agents, and the most common complaint is the practice of subletting, where the person who signed the initial contracts disappears and a completely unknown person is found to be occupying the apartment.

One apartment rental agency near the west exit of Ikebukuro Station told the *Asahi Journal* that, 'The biggest complaint we receive concerns many people living in the same room. Then there is the problem of putting out garbage. Chinese tend to use a lot of oil in their cooking, and it is smelly. They stay up late at night conversing loudly, and for Japanese people the fact that they are speaking in a foreign language makes it even more disconcerting. The kinds of cheap apartments the foreign workers seek have all had this sort of experience' (*Asahi Journal*, 20 October 1989).

One real estate agent whom we interviewed in Oji, Kita Ward, told us that, 'Recently, we had an incident where a South Korean rented an apartment, invited his friends to share the place, and would not pay rent. Neighbors complained about people gathering in his apartment. As a last resort, we took him to court, and finally got an eviction order. When we went into the room, it was an incredible mess. The landlord lost something like a million yen on that one person. We will never let a foreigner live there again.'

Another real estate agent said that, 'Foreigners collect all sorts of trash – televisions, stoves – and leave them in the halls outside their rooms. It causes trouble to the other residents. They leave packaging from instant foods scattered in their rooms, and the air gets stale' (*Asahi Shimbun*, 25 September 1988). As these kinds of trouble have become common, landlords and real estate agents have begun to think twice before allowing foreigners to rent rooms. The rental agent from Ikebukuro whom we mentioned above was quoted as saying that, 'Three years ago, it was easy to find landlords who would happily rent rooms to foreigners. Now it has become extremely difficult. Landlords who have just one bad experience change their minds right away. It is particularly difficult in the Ikebukuro area' (*Asahi Journal*, 20 October 1989). In addition, a group of landlords along Okubo Dori street in Shinjuku Ward gathered in the spring of 1989, making a decision to 'not lend rooms to foreigners under any circumstances,' and notifying real estate agents of this decision (Hatada).

In this way, it has become extremely hard for foreign workers to find rooms. It is said that many real estate agencies have a policy of not dealing with Asian foreigners. In FY1989, the Center for Domestic and Foreign Students (*Naigai Gakusei Center*) found that only 14% (450 cases) of all student housing locations in the metropolitan region said they would accept foreign college students, and that of the students that the Center introduced to these places, only 16% (78 people) were actually able to move in (Shinano Mainichi Shimbun b, p. 197). Moreover, 69% of foreign college students said they had been refused a contract at least once because they were foreigners (Watado, p. 56). On top of this, the situation is more difficult in cases where the landlord asks for proof of the student's status and for a guarantor.

There are also some who profiteer from the misfortunes of these foreign workers. One broker took out an advertizement in a newspaper aimed at Chinese college students, and offered to rent space in a small 2DK apartment he owned for ¥2,500 per night. He had dozens of people stay in the small place (*Asahi Shimbun*, 9 September 1989).

This situation, of sharing a small space with several other people, is a usual state of affairs for foreign workers. This is naturally partly a result of high rents, but it is also due to housing discrimination which makes for an extremely limited supply of apartments. The close networks that have proliferated among these workers have also spurred this tendency. Newcomers stay with friends or relatives who are already settled in and stay until they, too, gain a footing.

We will now examine the living arrangement of the three Bangladeshis – Babu, Masoom, and Farooq – whose case we looked at in Chapter 1–1.

Q: Tell us about your accommodations in Japan.

A: Five of us live in a five-mat (six square meter) room. Normally we have different working hours so it's not that bad, but on Sundays all five of us are at home. The rent used to be ¥50,000 a month, but the landlord found out there were five of us and raised the rent to ¥54,000. Our boss acts as our guarantor, but we're the ones who pay the rent. In addition, we have to pay an extra ¥200,000 charge every year as "key money." '

At first we thought that this 'key money' referred to the deposit and initial fee normally paid when renting an apartment in Japan, but they emphasized that they had to pay '¥200,000 every year.' We had no way of knowing who was receiving this money. They also said that, 'Our room does not have a bath, so we either go to the public bath or use the shower at work once or twice a week. For meals, we buy spices in Ikebukuro and cook our own food. We can't understand Japanese very well, so our only communication with our neighbors (Japanese, Koreans, and Chinese) is basic greetings.'

The problem of insufficient equipment is another problem, besides overcrowding, that should not be overlooked. In one survey, *shugakusei* were asked about the facilities in their rooms, and 70.4% said they had their own kitchens. The results for toilets were nearly split, with 49.4% saying they had their own and 49.1%, saying they were sharing. For baths, more than half, or 45.4%, said they did not have one, compared to 37.8% who said they had their own (Tokyo Metropolitan Government g, p. 45).

2 The Formation of Zones of Concentrated Housing

As foreign workers have settled in Japan, they have begun to concentrate in certain zones. In the following section, we will look at areas representative of this trend.

Many Asian foreigners have moved into the large slice of land running from Kabukicho in Shinjuku through Okubo and ending in Ikebukuro. It is essentially a pleasure quarters, and is a relatively good place for finding jobs. In Kabukicho, for example, half of all workers appear to be foreigners. In addition, there are many language schools in Ikebukuro, making the area convenient for *shugakusei*. The zone is also characterized by a horseshoe-shaped ring of low-rent wooden apartments and other housing facilities surrounding a bustling center. The area has thus become a concentration of Asian workers.

One real estate agent in Okubo who we interviewed told us that, 'a long time ago, about 60%–70% of the people who visited our office were Japanese hostesses, 25% or 35% were businessmen or students, and the remaining 5% or so were "people from third-rate countries". But now nine out of ten people are from the "third-rate countries." ' The expression *daisankoku-jin*, of 'people from third-rate countries,' was a common derogatory term referring to people from China, South Korea, and Taiwan, and this illustrates clearly the mentality of the agent.

In Ikebukuro, the enormous increase in the number of Asian foreigners has prompted local residents to sometimes refer to their area self-deprecatingly as 'Little Hong Kong' or 'Chinatown' (*Asahi Journal*, 20 October 1989). In addition, inns have recently appeared geared specifically at long-time foreign residents (Watado, p. 52).

Okuda et al. conducted a very interesting survey in the Shinjuku and Ikebukuro areas, and we will introduce their results here. They held interviews in Ikebukuro between 1989 and 1990, and in Shinjuku in 1991, and received 156 and 158 responses respectively. In Ikebukuro, by far the largest group of people (84) were from China, followed by Taiwan (27), then in smaller numbers from South Korea (15), Hong Kong (6), Malaysia (6), Bangladesh (5), Thailand (3), and others (10). In Shinjuku, South Koreans were the largest group, with 57, followed by Taiwanese (46), Chinese (40), Thais (5), and others (10), showing a slight difference from Ikebukuro since Koreans and Taiwanese held the top slots.

In terms of profession, the respondents from Ikebukuro were mainly *shugakusei* (110), followed by college, graduate, and specialty school students (25), full-time workers (9), with 12 responding 'other' or not answering. In Shinjuku, by contrast, 63 were *shugakusei*, 47 college students, 16 full-time workers, 13 unemployed, and 19 responded either 'other' or did not give a response.

In terms of housing situation, most of the respondents from Ikebukuro were living in wooden apartments. In two-thirds of all cases the rooms were under six tatami mats (seven square meters) in size, and 49 of the respondents said they were sharing these rooms with at least two other people. In contrast, 88 of the Shinjuku respondents were living in wooden apartments, 65 in concrete buildings, with half of these people in smaller than six mat rooms, and with 37 sharing their rooms with at least two other people. The situation was clearly better in Shinjuku than in Ikebukuro (Okuda and Tajima a, pp. 40-; Okuda and Tajima b). In addition, the market value for rental fees to foreigners in Shinjuku Ward was said to be 10% higher than that for Japanese (Okuda and Tajima b, p. 138).

Some of the peculiar features of this data are the complete absence of Nikkeijin, who make up a large percentage of foreign workers, the relatively small presence of Southeast Asians, as well as the preponderance of college students and *shugakusei*. This seems to indicate that the area is becoming a center for students, and, as we already pointed out, it is believed that the reason for this is the combination of relatively low rents, the presence of Japanese language schools, and the existence of service sector jobs in the vicinity.

Furthermore, as of July 1990, there were roughly 8,000 Chinese legally registered in Toshima Ward, which includes Ikebukuro. There were 52,364 Chinese students registered in Japan as of the end of 1989 (Ministry of Justice s), indicating that one in seven of them were living in this single area.

As foreign workers flow into Japan in an inevitable stream, how will their living situations change? The number of cheap wooden apartments, which make up the bulk of low-cost housing, is clearly decreasing in Tokyo, and housing discrimination is on the increase. What this means is that the supply of housing available to foreign workers is decreasing, and that their housing situation is worsening.

There is, however, a compensating trend. Because the numbers of foreigners are too large to ignore, they have, in particular in the Okubo area, become valuable customers for real estate agencies. Some agencies have even begun to build housing especially aimed at foreigners.

As we saw in Chapter 2–2, Nikkeijin workers have tended to concentrate and settle in local cities and near areas where automobile manufacturers are located. We will now examine a few representative cases of this phenomenon. First we will look at two municipalities in Gunma Prefecture's Tomo region, Oizumi-machi (pop. 40,000), the site of Fuji Heavy Industries and Sanyo Electric Company factories, and neighboring Ota City (pop. 140,000), where there is a population of Nikkeijin and other foreign residents.

As of the end of 1991, 1,382 of Oizumi-machi's more than 2,000 registered foreign residents were Nikkei Brazilians, and in Ota City they made up 1,359 of the city's 2,200 registrees. There is, in addition, a considerable number of undocumented workers. Small- and medium-sized businesses in Oizumi-machi organized the Tomo District Employment Promotion Council in order to hire Nikkei Brazilians, and as of 1992 its 72 member companies were employing a total of 683 Brazilians (Iida).

In a November 1990 survey carried out by Kitagawa on 182 Nikkeijin in Oizumi-machi, 20.0% of respondents said they were living in company dormitories or apartments, 57.1% said they were living in apartments rented by their companies, 11.9% said they were renting an apartment themselves but received some financial aid from their employer, 7.9% were paying all the rent themselves, and 1.1% responded 'other.' This demonstrates that they were relying overwhelmingly on their employers (Yamashita, p. 122). The single largest housing pattern was for a company or employment agency to either own or rent an apartment complex and to make into an exclusively Nikkeijin residence. In an effort to minimize problems with the outside, there have been cases of companies housing their workers within the factory grounds. This shows that purely Nikkei communities have begun to form.

In Toyota City, the headquarters of Toyota Motor, there were as of October 1991 a total of 2,730 registered Nikkei Brazilians. Their places of residence were concentrated around Toyota's main office, the company's sub contractors, as well as prefectural and housing corporation residences contained in one major housing complex. It is said that at the time there were 700 or 800 Brazilians in the complex, which had a total population of roughly 10,000. Their companies or employment agencies acted as guarantors for the rooms with rented furniture and appliances which they stayed in, but the workers themselves were responsible for paying the rent, deposit, and key money. Their rooms were not necessarily in the same tower or same floor, but in spite of this they had very little contact with neighbors. The reason for this is that the employment agencies effectively erected a fence around them, using company buses to transport them not only to work, but to nurseries, schools, and hospitals.

Hamamatsu City in Shizuoka Prefecture is the site of such auto makers as Honda, Yamaha, and Suzuki, and many of these firms' sub contractors are concentrated in the nearby cities of Toyohashi and Kosai. As of February 1991, there were 3,880 registered Brazilians in Hamamatsu, 2,047 in Toyohashi, and 728 in Kosai. Moreover, it seems that a significant number were commuting to Kosai from one of the other two cities.

Another concentration of Nikkeijin workers can be found in Kanagawa Prefecture's Ayase City (pop. 78,000) and Aikawa-machi (pop. 40,000), the sites of many of Nissan Motor's sub contractors as well as a relatively new factory complex.

3 The Increasing Role of Local Governments

The settling of foreign workers has been accompanied by an increasing role for local governments in their lifestyles and work. Under the Local Government Law, these bodies are required to operate public organizations to look after the safety, health, and welfare of those, including foreigners, who live in the cities, towns, and villages which make up their areas of jurisdiction. These administrations must protect people as workers, of course, but also as residents. They must offer information and consultation, as well as measures for social security, education, family protection, housing, and cultural exchanges. It is impossible for them to provide these services to foreigners, however, if they are not able to deal with people who cannot understand Japanese.

Many local bodies are still not up to par in providing services to foreigners. The amount of money spent by all local governments on foreigners in 1991, if calculated at the same per capita basis as the top four groups, should have reached ¥28.3 billion, but in reality only came to ¥5.4 billion (Ministry of Labor n).

In order to understand the situation, we should begin with the question of how much Japanese language foreign workers can understand and speak. In terms of Nikkeijin, we will make use of the results of the previously mentioned survey conducted by the Overseas Japanese Association, since there were questions on hearing, speaking, reading, and writing Japanese. The number of people with relatively high ability in each of the four areas was 43.5%, 27.9%, 14.0%, and 11.2%, respectively, whereas the number of people with no ability at all in the same categories was 14.1%, 12.3%, 29.1%, and 24.6%. This shows that many could understand, but that reading and writing were quite difficult for them (JICA, p. 102).

In terms of Iranians, we can use the survey mentioned in the Introduction of 17 people which was conducted by Kitagawa et al. in Ota City, Gunma Prefecture. Seven of the respondents said they could speak 'a little' Japanese, six said 'none,' five said they could speak at least 'some' English, and eleven said they could speak 'a little.' It thus appears that most have some command of broken Japanese (Yamashita, p. 234).

Statistics for other groups of foreigners, with some variation, are basically similar to these figures. This leads us to conclude that local governments will not be able to deal effectively with foreigners unless they are able to use foreign languages.

In 1991 the Ministry of Labor conducted a survey on 290 municipalities with at least 1,000 foreign residents in 15 prefectures or metropolises primarily in the Kanto, Chubu, and Kinki regions. Of these local bodies, 29.3% were providing information or consultation in foreign languages, 28.0% had handbooks for living published in foreign languages, and 7.3% had interpreters (Ministry of Labor n).

The town of Oizumi-machi, which we mentioned in the previous section, hired two second-generation Nikkeijin on a part-time basis to provide interpretation and counselling (Watanabe and Mitsuyama). In Matsumoto City, Nagano Prefecture, the city government worked with the local medical association to produce a guidebook for emergencies in ten languages. Ayase City in Kanagawa Prefecture produced a form for medical emergencies in 15 languages (*Ashita*, June 1992, p. 29).

The need for classes to teach foreigners Japanese language is also pressing. In Tokyo, the following local governments have such classes: the wards of Minato, Meguro, and Katsushika (aimed at returnees from China), and the cities of Musashino and Kunitachi (Tokyo Metropolitan Government e, f). In Kawasaki City, where there are many resident Koreans, a social center was set up, with the aim of teaching basic Japanese mainly to first generation Korean women in Japan, but many foreign workers have also made use of its services (All Japan Prefectural and Municipal Workers' Union, p. 67).

In terms of consultation services for foreign workers, the forerunner was a service set up in 1988 in Tokyo's Toshima Ward. One of its five regular staff members could speak English, and another Chinese. In terms of content, 19.0% of cases involved 'living,' which included questions on facilities and where to go for certain problems, 14,7% involved 'immigration and residence status,' 13.4% 'education and leisure,' 12.6% 'administration,' including public relations brochures and taxes, 11.7% 'family problems' such as marriage and childbirth, and 11.2% 'welfare,' including questions on nurseries and compensation for medical treatment. It thus seems that most counselling involved the problems that accompany long-term residence (*Ashita*, June 1992, pp. 24–25).

Medical services, which fall under the responsibility of local governments for social security, have become a major problem.

Foreign workers, as could be expected from the hardship of their daily lives, tend to experience a multitude of medical problems, but one illness, tuberculosis, stands out. In 1988, the Tokyo Metropolitan Government's Bureau of Public Health, at the request of 92 Tokyo-based Japanese-language schools from among the 116 that belonged to the Association for the Promotion of Japanese Language Education (*Gaishukyo*), conducted a screening for T.B. on a group of 13,117 students. They discovered 57 people who were in need of treatment, which indicates an infection rate of 0.43%. The same rate in 1987 for pupils in Japanese schools was only 0.01%, meaning that foreign workers were 43 times more likely to be infected with T.B. than were Japanese children (Tokyo Metropolitan Government d).

Furthermore, Inamura et al. conducted a survey on 84 *shugakusei* and other foreigners working in small- and medium-sized companies in the Kanto region, and found that 74.4% registered above average on the GHQ score which measures mental stability (normally, only 50% should be above average). This indicates a high rate of nervous disorders. It was also reported that many of the workers said they had increased their intake of cigarettes and alcohol, and that many experienced feelings of isolation (*Nikkei Shimbun*, 29 May 1992).

We should also add that one of the results of overcrowded housing has been a prevalence of skin disease (National Institute for Research Advancement, p. 122). This situation is related to the overall lack of shower and bath facilities. One well-known example of the problems they face is that Pakistanis are not accustomed to undressing in front of other people, and when they do not have their own showers have no choice but to go to public baths, although they enter the baths still wearing their underclothes (which is considered inproper in Japanese custom). This had earned them the nickname of 'underwear men.' They do not go into the bath itself, but use the showers, and change their clothes carefully with a towel wrapped around their waist (*Asahi Shimbun*, 6 April 1988). It would seem obvious that people in this sort of situation would avoid going to the bathhouse whenever possible.

Many foreign workers are not covered by medical insurance,

which imposes an extremely heavy financial burden on them when they become sick or are injured. Under present law, legal foreign workers employed in businesses are covered under medical insurance and fraternal insurance systems, and others can be covered under the National Health Insurance system. The benefits of the national system, however, are limited to registered foreigners who have a residence status of at least one year or who are planning to stay for at least one year.

Undocumented workers are not covered under any of the medical insurance systems, and there are also a considerable number of foreigners who could be covered but who do not enter the programs because of the high costs. The survey of local governments by the Ministry of Labor which we introduced earlier, for example, showed that even among legal Nikkeijin only 23.4% were enrolled in a medical insurance program, and that only 19.6% of those whose residency period was under one year were registered on the National Health Insurance list, despite the fact that the costs for these short-term stayers were quite low (Ministry of Labor n). The Management and Coordination Agency, in a survey of the 56 medical institutions working under it, found that of 1,396 foreigners who had come to see doctors at these institutions, only 53.3% were enrolled in a public medical insurance program, and that 2.4% had failed to pay their medical bills (Management and Coordination Agency, p. 176).

Another survey conducted by the AMDA International Medical Information Center, a private medical assistance organization, found that 57.3% of the 5,198 foreigners who had visited 64 hospitals and medical clinics mainly in the Tokyo metropolitan region were not members of health insurance plans (*Asahi Shimbun*, 1 June 1992). The Japanese Red Cross Society also reported that in 1991 there were 108 cases among its 92 hospitals nationwide of foreigners not paying their medical bills, with the total amounting to 80% of the total costs of ¥37 million for foreigners. The national office reported that, 'There seems to be a mistaken belief spreading by word of mouth that there is no need to pay bills to the Japanese Red Cross' (*Asahi Shimbun*, 10 July 1992).

In the past, these unpaid medical bills have been covered by public assistance, and in fact, medical expenses have made up a large portion of this aid. In the summer of 1990, however, the Ministry of Health and Welfare indicated to the Tokyo Metropolitan Government that providing public assistance to short-term stayers or illegal foreign workers was a breach of the 1954 directive from the director of the Social Welfare Bureau. This directive forbade the application of public assistance any foreigner who could not produce an alien registration card unless the person was truly in financial distress (*Asahi Shimbun*, 5 December 1990). Furthermore, in October of the same year, the Ministry of Health and Welfare gave oral instructions to the same effect to all local governments throughout the country (the contents of this order are contained in Forum on Asian Migrant Workers b, p. 416).

This notification led to an increasing number of cases in which medical institutions were forced to bear the costs of emergency treatment they had provided to undocumented workers. This may have led, moreover, to the widely-reported cases of patients being transferred from hospital to hospital or being refused treatment. According to the above-mentioned survey by the AMDA International Medical Information Center, 13 of the 54 institutions said they would not accept patients without medical insurance.

In order to relieve the burden on medical institutions caused by foreign workers not paying bills and by the national government's refusal to apply public assistance to these cases, some local governments including the Tokyo metropolitan government and Ibaraki Prefecture revived the 'Law on the Treatment of Sick and Dead Travellers' which was enacted during the Meiji Period. This is a vivid example of where local governments, in the face of a national policy that does not even recognize the right to life, have tried to protect the foreign workers who are, after all, residents of their jurisdictions.

In terms of educational establishments, which fall under the responsibility of local governments, the increasing settling-in of foreign workers has brought with it the urgent necessity of establishing systems for their childrens' education. One particularly pressing problem is the increasing number of children who cannot understand Japanese.

According to a survey by the Ministry of Education, there were as of September 1991, 5,463 foreign children who could not understand Japanese language attending a total of 1,923 public elementary or junior high schools. The most prevalent of these children's 43 mother tongues was Portuguese, with 35.4% of the total, followed by Chinese with 29.7%, Spanish with 10.9%, and Korean, Vietnamese, English, and Tagalog (Filipino). The schools did not have either sufficient staff or teaching materials to deal with these children (Ministry of Education b).

In the areas with significant concentrations of foreign workers that we looked at earlier, the local governments have made various attempts at providing education to the children of these workers. In Oizumi-machi, for instance, there were at the time of Watanabe's survey 23 Brazilian Nikkei children enrolled in municipal nursery schools, and 80 such pupils in the town's elementary and junior high schools. In order to deal with this, the town had set up Japanese language classes in all four elementary schools as well as in one of the town's junior high schools which had a high percentage of Nikkei pupils. The town had also hired three Portuguese speakers to assist with Japanese language instruction as well as special part-time teachers (Watanabe).

In Hamamatsu City, there are now more than 200 Brazilian Nikkei school-age children, most of them in elementary schools. In order to deal with this situation, the city set up a special 'Language Classroom' both to teach them Japanese and to help them with Portuguese to prepare them for returning to life in Brazil. The children were given transportation to and from the classroom by the employment agency, the Japanese was taught by city employees, and the Portuguese by staff of the employment agency (Watanabe and Mitsuyama). In Toyota City, one public nursery school located near the housing complex with a concentration of Nikkeijin had 23 Nikkei Brazilian children, and the nearby elementary school had between 20 and 30 of these children. A special Japanese language class staffed by volunteers was being held twice a week (Tsuzuki). In Aikawa-machi, Kanagawa Prefecture, which has also seen a great increase in foreign workers, Spanish- and Portuguese-speaking children are enrolled in local schools, and the town has set up special classes for these children as well as classes aimed at teaching Japanese to adults (Tezuka, Miyajima et al., p. 171, p. 226).

In contrast to these examples, however, the town of Zentsuji-machi in Kagawa Prefecture refused for nine months to admit a Brazilian Nikkei student under the pretext that the student could not understand Japanese (*Asahi Shimbun*, 3 August 1992).

The responsibility of local governments to set up facilities for cultural exchange has been another area where foreigners have made strong requests to these bodies. In 1988, Tokyo's Toshima Ward conducted a survey of 600 foreign residents asking their demands toward local government administration. A total of 60.7% of the respondents complained of having no exchanges with others in their neighborhoods, and 75.4% expressed a desire for such exchanges. The largest category of requests to the Ward government was that it provide them with opportunities for cultural exchanges and for participation in social groups (Tokyo Metropolitan Government c). In addition, the Ward government added three foreigners to its group of 'ward administration monitors,' (Shinano Mainichi Shimbun b, p. 261), thus attempting to involve foreigners in the local administration.

Oizumi-machi had a group of mostly young Brazilian Nikkeijin participate in the town's summer festival as a samba team, and the group was warmly applauded by the townspeople. In addition, a Brazilian photo exhibit and cultural exchange party were added to the town's culture day events (*Ashita*, June 1992, p. 27).

We should add, also, that the use of telephones to call home is one of the major comforts in the lives of foreign workers. At present, however, few public phone booths allow international phone calls, and these booths are usually found near or in the large stations. In many areas with large populations of foreign workers, it is common to see the workers gathering around these telephones to call their families back home late on Saturday nights, after their work week has ended and after 11 p.m., when the rates go down. The foreigners gathered in these places often take advantage of the opportunity and either chat with their friends or exchange information on work (*Asahi Shimbun*, 22 April 1988).

4 Foreigners and Crime

In the last section of this chapter, we will look at the problem of crimes committed by foreign workers. In the *1990 White Paper on Police*, which focused on 'police responses to an increasing population of foreign workers,' the issue of crimes committed by foreign workers was dealt with as an omen of a threat to public security. The following year's white paper followed this trend, with its special issue, 'Changes in Crime in a Borderless Age,' and focused on changing crime patterns among foreigners. It reported that in 1991 there were 6,990 cases involving 4,813 people, of foreigners being arrested on criminal charges. The number of cases was 1.72 times higher, and the number of people 1.62 times higher than 1990, which was itself a record-setting year.

In terms of the nature of the crimes, 64.5% involved theft. In the past violent crimes tended to involve disputes between foreigners working as brokers, and Japanese nationals were not usually targets, but in recent years these disputes have been accompanied by a rising number of murders, armed robberies, and rapes directed at Japanese. In 1991, there were 126 foreigners arrested in Japan for heinous crimes, and in 37, or half of the 69 cases of arrests for armed robbery, the victims were Japanese.

If we look at criminal offenses by nationality, we see that the largest number, 83.4%, were committed by people from the Asian region. Of the crime from this region, 37.8% was committed by Chinese nationals, followed by North and South Koreans, with 31.0%, and Iranians with 10.1%. What stands out concerning the Iranian crime is that it jumped 4.9 times compared to one year earlier (National Policy Agency d, pp. 42–43, e, p. 16).

It must be stressed however, that most foreign workers come to Japan to earn money, and they tend to stay well away from crime since arrest would almost certainly lead to deportation.

For Pakistanis, there is a high incidence of fraternal crime. In March 1988, in an apartment in Kawaguchi City, Saitama Prefecture, a fight between Pakistanis broke out into a major brawl. Then, in March 1989 in Tokyo's Itabashi Ward there was a fatal stabbing incident also involving Pakistanis, caused, like the incident in Kawaguchi City, by disputes between rival groups. Since 1988 there have been seven such incidents in the Tokyo metropolitan region, and the National Police Agency has estimated that there are seven or eight rival groups in the capital region (*Asahi Shimbun*, 4 April 1989).

The judge who presided over the trial in the Tokyo District Court for these incidents pointed out that, 'The victims in these incidents could not report anything to the police because of the fear of deportation, and so had no other choice but to rely on the strength of their group' (*Nikkei Shimbun*, 8 November 1989). In other words, the status of foreign workers as overstayers puts them into a situation where they become outlaws, and this seems to lead them, when confronted with problems involving other groups of the same nationality, to take their defense into their own hands.

In another incident, a group of *shugakusei* from Fujian Province in China formed a group to carry out armed robberies, and began a series of attacks against Shanghai students living in Saitama and Kanagawa Prefectures. The students were having difficulty repaying the debts they had accumulated to come to Japan, and so turned on a group of compatriots from a relatively affluent region. One said the choice was made because, 'They were also Chinese, so we didn't think we'd get caught' (*Asahi Shimbun*, 6 October 1989). A similar incident of internecine violence between Chinese during a theft occurred in September 1989 in Tokyo's Akishima City (*Asahi Shimbun*, 14 September 1989).

There have been other incidents as well, not limited to Chinese or Pakistanis, involving injuries caused by fights between co-workers of the same nationality.

Another series of incidents has involved the manufacture and use of counterfeit telephone cards (prepaid cards) by foreign workers. By the end of March 1992, roughly 20 people had been arrested for this crime, and 90% were Iranians (*Asahi Shimbun*, 26 March 1992).

Meanwhile, some very interesting points emerged from the survey conducted by Yoshihiko Yamazaki et al., which we looked at in Section 4 of the Introduction. We will quote here some comments made by a 23-year-old Iranian man:

'Iranians are not dangerous people. If you accepted more of us into the country, you would see that we are really wonderful people . . . Before the Revolution, there were Iranians all over the world and many foreigners working in our country. The situation has changed, now, the economic situation has deteriorated, and Iran is no longer popular among foreigners.

'The reason so many Iranians have come to work in Japan is because its economic and social status has fallen. The Iran-Iraq War contributed to this. But what I really want to say is this: even if some people have caused problems, it doesn't mean that all Iranians are bad people. Please get the Japanese government to understand that' (Yamazaki, Wakabayashi et al., p. 21).

Incidentally, we need to take note of a recent increase in indictments levied against Asian foreigners for minor offenses. It is believed that the reasons for this are not to be found in an increasing crime rate, but rather in the fact that prosecutors have become stricter and are now issuing indictments for crimes that they once overlooked. There have also been reports of extremely tough investigations in cases involving Asian foreigners. One Bangladeshi, who was arrested on suspicion of murdering a compatriot, complained that he experienced torture, including a beating with a wooden stick, while being interrogated in the Shinagawa Police Station in Tokyo. The Tokyo District Court ordered the police station to release the transcript of the interrogation, but the police refused. The suspect's lawyers claimed that this formed the basis for speculation that the torture did occur (*Asahi Shimbun*, 8 July 1989).

A significant number of human rights violations against foreign defendants occurs because of language problems, both during the periods in which they are suspects and during trials. This may be caused by a lack of interpreters, by interpreters with below-par ability, or because of prejudice on the part of interpreters (Ebashi, p. 126). Another problem is that state-appointed lawyers have been reluctant to represent foreigners, and even when they have accepted have tended to neglect the cases, leading to convictions even on minor charges (Takahashi, p. 37).

On top of this, it has been pointed out that foreigners have often been given unreasonably heavy sentences. Between April 1985 and March 1988, for instance, 88.1% of Japanese defendants convicted of pickpocketing and 100% of those convicted of shoplifting in Tokyo District Courts and summary courts were given suspended sentences. Similar figures for foreign defendants were 14.0% and 21.4%, respectively (Onuki, p. 62).

In one incident, a Thai woman who severely injured a Filipina in a hostess club in Nagoya was given a three-year prison sentence for attempted murder. The reason for this heavy sentence was, according to the judges, that 'We must consider that she was in Japan illegally at the time of the crime, and her punishment should therefore be heavy.' It is quite clear from this sentence that the punishment was unreasonably heavy, and that it was meant to be an example to other foreign workers in Japan. For this reason, it attracted much concern from support groups (*Migrant*, 20 October 1989).

Examples like this suggest that there are cases in which the Japanese police and judicial administration aim to punish foreign workers and then subsequently deport them. Using the Immigration Act to deport foreigners or refuse them visa extensions has served to make criminal trials meaningless, since the suspects are deported and subsequently denied the opportunity to defend themselves (Ebashi, p. 123).

4 The Third World's Structuralized Labor Exports

1 The Stages of Asia's Labor Exports

In this chapter, we will look at the conditions in exporting countries which drive workers to go abroad. Some of the factors usually mentioned are the great gap in income between Japan and these countries, the population explosion, and the problem of unemployment. It hardly needs to be pointed out again here, but in 1988 Japan's per capita GNP was 5.8 times that of South Korea, 10.8 times larger than Malaysia's, 9.7 times larger than Brazil's, 21.0 times that of Thailand, 33.4 larger than the Philippines', 47.8 times larger than Indonesia's, 60.1 times that of Pakistan, 63.7 times greater than China's, and an incredible 123.6 times that of Bangladesh (World Bank, Table 1).

Basically, it is undoubtable that this situation is a factor in the migration of labor to Japan. More fundamentally, however, the emergence of migrant labor on a large scale happened in a specific historical context, and the conditions mentioned above are basically symptoms of this underlying structure.

If we restrict our analysis to the post-World War II period, we can roughly divide the structure of labor flow from Asian countries into three stages. The first involved movements from the ex-colonies to the centers of the former empires, and included, for instance, the migration from India to England or from the Philippines to the United States.

The second stage was brought about by the money accumulated in the Middle East after the first oil shock, and involved as its main feature the migration of labor to that region, mainly in pursuit of the construction boom that was occurring at the time. At the time, the construction industry in those countries constituted 60% of total labor demand. It is fair to say that it was during this period that labor export was instituted as national policy in Asian countries, who found that the remittances from these overseas workers could help to mitigate pressure from actual and latent unemployment and population growth, as well as to improve their balances of international payments.

The third stage began when the Middle East started to lose its significance as a place to find work. In the latter half of the 1980's, the oil-producing countries of the region suddenly set policies aimed at nationalizing their labor forces. This happened concurrently with the end of the oil boom and the virtual death of the construction demand that had accompanied the boom. The demand for labor in the construction sector fell by more than half, and there was an increase in jobs involving maintenance, services, and house work. Despite this fall in exports to the Middle East, however, Asian countries continued to export labor on a large scale, though on a smaller scale than during the peak years. In other words, the Asian countries began desperately to seek new destinations for migrant workers. The fact that Japan became a major target of attention is only natural.

We will leave our examination of the first stage to the later section on countries of origin, and will now look at the situation of workers in the Middle East during the second phase. We will base our observations on the excellent survey conducted by Ogawa (Ogawa) in this regard.

Table 4–1 shows the number of migrant workers leaving selected countries to work abroad, including of course the Middle East. It shows that the real wave of migrant workers from Asia began in the late 1970's, and that their numbers continued to increase until the early 1980's.

In 1983, the peak year for migration to the Middle East, the Philippines occupied the first spot with 380,000 people, followed by South Korea with 162,000, Pakistan and Indonesia with 128,000 each, with smaller numbers coming from Thailand, Bangladesh, and China. It is not clear how many Sri Lankans left their country that year, though there was a considerable number the previous year. Ogawa has estimated that in the middle of the 1980's an annual total of 1,200,000 Asians went to work abroad, including 500,000 from South Asia and 700,000 from Southeast Asia.

Most of these workers were headed for the Gulf region. In 1983, for instance, it was the destination of 85.1% of all the Filipino migrant workers. For Koreans the figure was 92.6%, for Pakistanis 95.5% (in 1978), for Thais 94.8%, and for Bangladeshis 98.2%. In 1983, there were 3,156,000 Asian workers in the

Table 4–1 Numbers of migrant workers originating in Asian countries (1,000 people)

	1976	1977	1978	1979	1980
(South Asia)					
Pakistan	41.7	140.5	130.5	125.5	129.8
Bangladesh	1.0	15.7	22.8	24.5	30.6
Sri Lanka	5.6	8.1	9.4	25.8	28.6
India	4.2	22.9	69.0	171.8	236.2
(Southeast Asia)					
Philippines	19.2	36.7	61.0	92.6	157.4
Thailand	1.3	3.9	14.5	9.1	20.9
South Korea	37.9	69.6	85.0	105.7	131.1
Indonesia[2]	n.a.	n.a.	n.a.	n.a.	145.9
China	n.a.	n.a.	n.a.	n.a.	n.a.

	1981	1982	1983	1984
(South Asia)				
Pakistan	168.4	143.0	128.2	n.a.
Bangladesh	55.8	62.8	59.2	n.a.
Sri Lanka	57.3	48.0	n.a.	n.a.
India	272.0	239.5	119.0[1]	n.a.
(Southeast Asia)				
Philippines	210.9	250.1	380.3	371.1
Thailand	24.7	108.1	67.0	75.0
South Korea	163.1	171.2	162.0	152.7
Indonesia[2]	159.4	180.7	128.1	69.2
China	17.0	31.0	30.0	47.0

Notes:
[1] January-June.
[2] Numbers of people abroad at the end of each year.

Source: Ogawa, p. 296.

Middle East, 2,310,000 from South Asia and 846,000 from other Asian countries.

The largest country of origin for these workers was Pakistan, with 1,200,000, followed by India with 900,000, the Philippines with 350,000, Thailand with 270,000, South Korea with 164,000, Bangladesh with 150,000, Sri Lanka with 60,000, Indonesia with 40,000, China with 10,000, and Malaysia with 2,000 workers.

Generally speaking, it can be said that this massive labor exodus both helped mitigate the problem of unemployment facing Asian countries, and at the same time contributed to an improvement in their international balance of payments. In the case of

Pakistan, for instance, foreign earnings from these workers between 1982 and 1983 compensated 96.7% of the country's trade deficit during the same period. Out of these foreign earnings, 83.0% came from the Middle East. In 1984 Thailand received $890 million in remittances from foreign workers, with $690 million of this coming from the Middle East, and this sum made up the country's third most important source of foreign exchange revenue after tourism ($1.21 billion) and rice exports ($1.1 billion) (see Ogawa, pp. 295–302).

In this way, the export of labor to the Middle East helped to mitigate the problems of unemployment and latent unemployment as well as to balance of payment deficits that have plagued these countries, and has thus acquired status as a means of helping their economies. The promotion of labor exports has thus become entrenched as national policy.

2 The Exporting Countries of Asia

In this section we will look at the Asian countries that export labor. They can be roughly divided into three categories: 1) Pakistan, the Philippines, and South Korea, for whom labor exports are important national policies; 2) China, Bangladesh, Indonesia, and Sri Lanka, which have some institutionalized measures and which place a relatively heavy weight on labor exports; and 3) Thailand, Malaysia, and India, where the governments do not promote migrant labor in any significant way. There are also some countries which act not only as labor exporters but as importers as well. The phenomenon experienced by these countries is generally termed 'step-wise migration,' and this will be dealt with in both this and in the next section.

The Gulf War had a major impact on migrant workers. Before the hostilities there were 2,360,000 foreign workers in the region, but in the space of just four months, 1,470,000 of them returned to their home countries (Ministry of Labor m, p. 48).

(a) Pakistan

Pakistan is one of Asia's major labor exporters, and at the beginning of the 1980's it is believed to have had nearly 2 million nationals working abroad. Even at the present it is estimated that roughly 10% of the country's labor force is employed abroad, the largest ratio for any labor exporting nation. Foreign work is so common that eight out of every ten men are said to hope to work abroad (Sasaki, p. 59).

For Pakistan, a 'migrant labor superpower,' labor exports form a central pillar of the economy. In FY1982/83 (from July to June throughout this section), remittances from workers abroad amounted to a staggering $2.89 billion, a sum equivalent to 110% of the country's total exports. In FY1985/86 this figure remained at a high level of $2.6 billion, or 88% of exports, but began to decline in FY1986/87, and in FY1988/89 dropped to below the $2 billion mark to $1.9 billion. Naturally, these figures only cover official remittances, and the existence of black markets leads us to surmise that the real figure was at least twice as large (Fukamachi, University of Tsukuba d, p. 124). Furthermore, the Gulf War brought with it a decrease of $150 million in remittances in 1990 alone (*Asahi Shimbun*, 21 September 1990).

Like other Asian labor exporters, Pakistan went through a three-stage experience. During the colonial period, many Pakistanis went to work in other English colonies, especially in Africa. In the 1950's, after Independence, the main destination changed as people began to find work as domestic servants in England, the former colonial master. In the 1970's, Western Europe and the United States became major destinations (Fukamachi; Sasaki, News #5 & #6).

As of 1982, there were a total of 570,000 Pakistanis residing in North America and Western Europe, divided between the following countries: 350,000 in the United Kingdom, 100,000 in the U.S., 50,000 in Canada, and 27,000 in West Germany (Yamanaka). The Pakistani government established a Migration Bureau in 1971 as a means of dealing with this situation, and labor exports became a matter of national policy.

In terms of the second phase, Pakistan was faster at the starting gate than other Asian countries, with the number of workers travelling to the Middle East increasing in the one-year period between 1978–79 from 40,000 to 140,000 people. The peak year for new departures was 1981, when roughly 170,000 workers left for overseas destinations (Table 4–1). In the early 1980's, it became more difficult for Pakistanis to gain admittance into Western Europe and the U.S., and because of this Canada and Australia gained popularity as new destinations (Fukamachi).

In order to cope with this enormous overseas population, the government in 1979 enacted a new law and a set of regulations concerning migration, and began to license labor dispatch companies. Under the new law, the Ministry of Labor was reorganized into the 'Ministry of Labor, Human Resources, and Overseas Pakistanis,' and the Immigration Bureau rechristened the 'Bureau of Immigration and Overseas Employment.' People finding jobs abroad were required to register with this bureau, and their departures were made conditional upon inspections concerning labor conditions at their chosen place of work. At the same time, an Overseas Employment Corporation was established under the government.

In the same year, the Overseas Pakistani Fund was established. Its purpose was to use remittances from workers abroad to deal with problems faced by the workers and by their families at home in Pakistan. The fund's uses include housing development, welfare, education and job training, as well as business promotion (Sasaki, p. 62; Documentation For Action Groups in Asia, p. 43).

The so-called 'Gift Scheme' was also set up as a means to entice workers to go abroad. Under this plan, people working abroad for a period of six months would become entitled to present their families or relatives with an automobile. For most Pakistanis purchasing a car is difficult, if not impossible, and this plan was therefore very attractive (Sasaki, News #6).

It is believed that in FY1982–83 somewhere between 1.7 and 2 million Pakistanis were working abroad, with 1.2–1.4 million in the Middle East (Fukamachi). This had a positive effect on the country, both in terms of mitigating balance of payment problems and relieving unemployment. In 1975 there were approximately 205,000 unemployed workers in the country, but with the departure of people to the Gulf region this number dropped to 140,000 or 150,000 (Ogawa, p. 300).

The Middle East boom was accompanied in Pakistan by what became known as the 'Dubai Syndrome.' There were three 'symptoms': first, the uneasiness brought about by the large loans the workers took out in their quests to go abroad; second, the uneasiness felt by their families, and especially their wives, while they were abroad; and third, the difficulties involved in rebuilding their lives upon returning to Pakistan (Fukamachi).

The third phase in Pakistan's involvement in labor exports began as the end of the oil boom and the increased competition from cheaper Chinese and Filipino labor led to decreases in the number of Pakistanis in the Middle East. In 1988, the number of new departures for the Gulf region fell to just 79,000. The number of workers in the Middle East remains high, however, with 1.2 million as of 1989, making the region the home to the second highest concentration of overseas Pakistanis, following Egypt (Sasaki, p. 59).

The stagnation of opportunities for work in the Middle East became a major problem for Pakistan, with its institutionalized structure of labor export, and moves quickly emerged to seek out new destinations.

In principle, all migrant workers are required to register at the Bureau of Immigration and Overseas Employment, but in reality many leave the country by underground routes. There are also, despite the requirement that dispatch companies be licensed, many unauthorized brokers.

There are roughly 300 companies working to send workers abroad, and it is said that the market price which they charge for getting a worker to Japan, including a one-way airfare and assistance in finding housing and jobs in Japan, can be as high as 30,000 rupees (¥220,000) or even 40,000 (¥290,000). For the United States, where visas are more difficult to obtain, the going rate is said to be 50,000–60,000 rupees (¥360,000-¥440,000). There are also many unscrupulous brokers who simply cheat people out of their money (Sasaki, News 5 and 6; Mainichi Shimbun a, p. 83).

Data from the beginning of the 1980's gives a description of these workers. First, 63.1%, or roughly two thirds, came from urban areas, versus 36.9% from rural regions. Second, 70% were married, and 66% of these married people had left their families behind in Pakistan. In terms of the money they sent home, most of it was earmarked for fees incurred for family ceremonies, purchases of foreign goods, and real estate investments (Yamanaka).

Many people came to work in Japan in that period, taking

advantage of the visa exemption agreement between the two countries. There are reports that large numbers of the people coming to Japan were from specific places in Pakistan. One industrial town of 600,000 people, about 60 kilometers from Lahore, the capital of Punjab State, has become known as 'Japan town.' It is said that 500 or even 1,000 people have recently came to Japan from this town alone. There are less than 10 brokers there. It is believed that this situation exists in other towns in the area (Mainichi Shimbun a, p. 83).

In January 1991, the visa exemption between Japan and Pakistan agreement was suspended, and a much more sedate mood now reigns in terms of overseas work in Japan. Meanwhile, it has recently become apparent that Japanese visas are being forged on a large scale (Sasaki, News #6; Fukamachi).

In the following paragraphs, we will introduce the data we gathered from visiting the family home of Amil, a Pakistani working in Japan driving a 4-ton truck. His family was living in a relatively large farming village about 150 kilometers north of Islamabad.

We entered the side entrance of the white wall that surrounded his house, and found his family and relatives waiting for us. What we found truly surprising was that they had no idea of what Amil was doing, and did not even know his address in Japan. The following day, they showed us around town and introduced us to their friends. The next surprise in store for us was the number of people who could speak Japanese. We discovered that approximately 25 people in the town had experienced working in Japan, out of a total population of some 2,000 people.

This exodus had been spurred by one man who heard, while trading rugs in the Philippines, about the opportunity of working in Japan using a *shugakusei* visa. The story of his discovery spread throughout the village, and soon his friends, and then their friends, were leaving in droves. It would be fair to say that nearly all of Amil's relatives had been to Japan. The villagers put their money together to buy an apartment in the suburbs of Tokyo, and the village network used this apartment as a sort of base camp which allowed the people to feel secure in Japan. The living conditions in the village were relatively high, especially for those who had family members in Japan.

(b) The Philippines

The Philippines, like Pakistan, has had a national policy of promoting labor exports. At the beginning of 1989, there were Filipinos working abroad in 132 foreign countries (*Asahi Shimbun*, 8 February 1989). It is said that they easily numbered above one million people, earning their country the title of a 'migrant superpower.'

According to ILO statistics, the number of Filipinos working abroad, including seafarers, rose from 36,000 in 1975 to 215,000 in 1980, 389,000 in 1985, 414,000 in 1986, 497,000 in 1987, 478,000 in 1988, and 523,000 in 1989. In 1989, there were a total of 115,000 Filipino seafarers abroad (Sasaki, p. 153).

The underlying causes for the promotion of overseas labor can be found in the country's worsening unemployment and balance of payment problems. As of January 1989, there were 1,960,000 fully unemployed people in the country (Yamamoto). The unemployment rate was 14.2% in April 1987, but this total would rise to 43% of the labor force if it included people working less than 40 hours a week.

Roughly 50% of these unemployed people were young, in the 15–24 age range. Furthermore, more than half were concentrated in the Metro Manila area (see Ministry of Labor f, pp. 85–89). It is quite clear that the policy of sending large groups of people to work abroad has worked to alleviate the unemployment situation.

If we turn next to the international balance of payments, we see that in 1987 the Philippines found itself in deep crisis, with accumulated foreign debts of $28 billion, or 24 times the national budget (Utsumi and Matsui, pp. 173–4). Remittances from workers abroad served a vital function in relieving this situation. In 1988, payments through legitimate banks amounted to $870 million (Yamamoto), and total payments including those through the black market can be assumed to have reached $2.5 billion. This figure represents roughly one third of the country's total export revenues of $7 billion during the same year (*Asahi Shimbun*, 8 February 1989). It is also estimated that the Gulf War was responsible for a nearly $200 million drop in these remittances (*Asahi Shimbun*, 21 September 1990).

Like other Asian countries, the Philippines experienced three phases in its labor exports. In terms of the years before the

Middle East boom, there was a long period between the early 1900's and the beginning of World War II in which large numbers of Filipino farmers went to the United States, the Philippines' colonial master, to work in Hawaii or California as agricultural laborers. In the period between the end of the War and the beginning of the Middle East boom, many went to the American colonies in Guam and Okinawa to work on reconstruction and construction, and others worked as civilian personnel in U.S. forces during the Korean and Vietnam wars.

After the 1965 revision of the U.S. Immigration Act, many sought work there in skilled professions, and others travelled to Western Europe to work as hotel employees, hospital workers, maids, nurses, and in other similar occupations. Furthermore, the rapid development of the international shipping industry during the 1960's prompted many to start working as seafarers. Many, as we saw in Section 2–5, were employed under poor conditions on Japanese flag-of-convenience ships. In this same period, nearly 2.8 million Filipinos left their country behind and went to live in the United States (Pacific Asia Resource Center a, b; Yamamoto; Catholic Institute for International Relations).

In the second phase, the major flow was, naturally, toward the Middle East. This growing movement following the oil shock reached its peak in 1983, when 380,000 people left the Philippines for that destination (Ogawa). This figure accounted for 85% of all Filipino overseas workers, and eclipsed the presence in all other Asian countries. Furthermore, 10,000 of these workers were sent under agreements made between the Philippine government's Overseas Employment Agency (POEA) and governments or government organizations of the six Middle East countries (Tezuka a, p. 123).

The POEA, the main government agency dealing with labor exports, was established precisely during this second phase. Earlier, in 1974, three bodies had been set up to promote labor exports: the Overseas Employment Development Commission, the Employment Service Bureau, and the National Seamen Commission (Sasaki, News #13). In 1982, then President Ferdinand Marcos unified the three groups as the Overseas Employment Bureau, an external organization of the Labor and Employment Ministry.

This agency received the following mandate: 1) to develop markets, establish employment placement offices, create increased opportunities for employment, and promote employment placement services; 2) its authorization/regulatory offices would set employment standards, and regulate the management of private labor brokering companies; and 3) its labor assistance and arbitration offices would offer services, both legal and welfare, to overseas workers and their families (Utsumi and Matsui, p. 173). The Agency was also given the mandate to offer 'entertainer' qualifications (Sasaki, News #2, is of particular interest).

Another agency, the Overseas Workers Welfare Agency, charges fees to employers and puts these into a fund for the welfare of workers (Sasaki, News #3).

The third stage began when the number of workers in the Middle East reached its peak, and continues up to the present. In 1988, a total of 250,000 workers newly departed for the Gulf (Yamamoto), much lower than the 380,000 who left during the peak year of 1983. The unemployment and foreign exchange situations, however, have not improved, and have even worsened. As a result, the government even in the period after the overthrow of Marcos and the takeover of the Aquino administration in 1986, has continued the policy, which was institutionalized during the second phase, of relying on a policy of labor exports. The focus now has been on finding alternative destinations.

In spite of the existence of the POEA, most of the work done assisting workers to go abroad has been carried out by private employment agencies. For instance, 97% of the workers going abroad at the beginning of 1989 did so with the help of private agencies. The number of private firms authorized by the POEA rose, from just 15 in 1975, to 1,023 in the peak year of 1983 (Yamamoto).

The maximum commission allowed under law for such services is 5,000 pesos, or ¥35,000, and this is the fee charged by the POEA when it acts as an intermediary. For private companies, however, the market rate is 10,000 to 30,000 pesos (¥70,000-¥210,000). People raise this money either through loans or, in the case of farmers, by selling their land, tools, or water buffaloes.

The Philippine government, under Presidential Decree No. 857, placed workers under the obligation to deposit a certain portion of their earnings into government banks. The portion varied according to occupation, but generally ranged from 50% to 80%, and those who failed to comply found themselves unable to renew their passports or work contracts. There was a movement during the Marcos era, primarily organized by migrant workers in Hong Kong, to have the decree abolished, and in response the punishment clause was removed. In addition, the government has taken between 1%–3% of the migrants' wages as taxes (Pacific Asia Resource Center a; Tatsuya Sato).

Incidentally, the Aquino regime changed the policy on registering private employment agencies, and by the beginning of the 1990's the number of authorized firms had fallen to roughly 700 (Sasaki, p. 164). At the same time, the government began to debate the idea of reinstituting the requirements that funds be sent home through government banks as a way of preventing tax evasion by migrant workers (*Asahi Shimbun*, 8 February 1989).

In 1988, the largest destinations for Filipino overseas workers were the Middle East (only the top six countries, including Libya), with 66.7%, followed by Japan, with 10.7%, Hong Kong, with 9.0%, Singapore, with 2.1%, and the United States with 1.4%. For the top-ranking Middle East countries, most of the workers continued to be men going to work in the construction sector (Yamamoto).

What stands out in the case of the Philippines is the importance of female overseas workers. In 1987, 47% of workers abroad (not counting seafarers) were women, working principally as maids, entertainers, and nurses. In Asia, in particular, roughly 97% of the Filipinos were women (60% were maids, and 37% entertainers) (Sasaki, News #3).

In 1989, 50,000 people went abroad to work as maids in Hong Kong (Sasaki, p. 180), in 1987, 17,000 left for Singapore, and 9,000 went to work in Saudi Arabia. In terms of entertainers, many were headed to Japan to work in the sex and entertainment industry. In 1987, 18,000 people left the country to work as nurses in Saudi Arabia (Yamamoto). Furthermore, in 1986 there were 162,000 Filipinas in Western Europe, working mostly as maids in households or in hotels, but with some working in the sex industry as well (Asia-Pacific Mission for Migrant Filipinos, p. 44). In addition, some 15,000 Filipinas are said to be working in Africa, mostly as schoolteachers (Utsumi and Matsui, p. 174).

Following the death of Filipina dancer Maricris Sison in Fukushima, in March 1992 the Philippine government decided to place restrictions on entertainers, requiring them to be at least 23 years old and to have at least one year's experience working in the business. The Japanese embassy, for its part, decided in August of the same year to not grant visas to people with less than two years' experience, but in spite of this there has not yet been any real decrease in the number of visas issued (*Nikkei Shimbun*, 28 August 1992).

Some of the special characteristics of Filipino overseas workers are that most are between 25 and 39 years old (most women are between 25 and 29), many have completed their secondary education (for women, a large number are university graduates), two-thirds come from the Metro Manila area, and roughly 70% were working before coming to Japan. Moreover, most of the money they send home is spent on durable consumer goods, especially electrical appliances, new houses, and on repaying debts (Kikuchi, p. 180).

In order to cope with the post-Middle East boom period, places such as Guam and Western Europe have become focuses of interest as potential destinations for overseas workers (Yamamoto), but there are very high expectations of Japan, and a great deal of effort has therefore gone into opening the gate to this country. In 1985, the POEA sent a joint government/business delegation to Japan, where they met with the Japanese Shipowners' Association, the Federation of Industrial Promoters, and other business organizations (Tatsuya Sato). In July 1987, when then-Foreign Minister Tadashi Kuranari visited the Philippines, he made an agreement with the Philippine government to set up a council to discuss the issue of migrant workers (Ishiyama, p. 194).

In September 1989, when the Philippines Minister of Labor and Employment visited Japan, he complained about the high unemployment rates in Japan's Asian neighbors, and appealed to the Japanese government to take positive steps to admit migrant labor. He also stressed the need for bilateral negotiations on the issue of periods of stay and numbers of trainees (*Nikkei Shimbun*, 30 September 1989).

In spite of this strong pressure on the issue of migrant labor, the percentage of visa applications accepted by the Japanese embassy in the Philippines has been on a downward trend. The percentage of visas refused (including those later retracted) rose from 0.5% in 1985 to 4.1% in 1986, 16.7% in 1987, and up to 21.3% in 1988. The main reason behind these rising figures was the tightening of screenings for the issuance of tourist and short-term business visas, an action which was taken with the intent of stopping the entry of migrant workers. Incidentally, the number of visas issued to Filipinos for marriages to Japanese nationals reached 4,503 in 1991, and continues to rise rapidly.

In the following section, we will describe the results of a visit to the Manila home of Andy, whose interview appears in Section 2–4.

It was just lunchtime when we reached his home in the well-known Manila slum of Tondo. We received a warm greeting. Not only his wife and three children, but many of their neighbors came out to welcome us. We could tell that Andy had told them to expect us, for when we arrived the table was already covered with a plethora of food, including lechon (roasted suckling pig, a specialty only eaten on ceremonial occasions).

Andy's children did not speak to us directly. First they whispered into their mother's ear, and then asked her to give us the questions. The reason for this was that the children could only speak Tagalog. When the mother said that, 'the children can't speak English,' it reminded us of how Andy had kept repeating, 'I want to give my children an education.'

Andy's wife told us that in the spring the second child, a boy, was going to start middle school. The money would come from the ¥100,000 that Andy was sending home every month. The mother said the eldest child, a girl, was also going to middle school in the same way.

She asked us many questions, the most frequently repeated one being, 'Does Andy have a girlfriend in Japan?' she kept telling us of how unfaithful Filipino men were, and that was apparently why she was asking the question. She also asked us, 'When is he going to come home from Japan?' They really seemed to be anxiously awaiting his return.

We were also able to talk to other people in the neighborhood. One of them was the sister of Rick, the man who was living with Andy in the three-mat room. Their home was just two houses away from Andy's. She told us that it was very fashionable in Tondo to go to work in Japan. In fact, she said that her own husband was planning, with the help of Andy and Rick, to go to Japan that April. He would arrive with a tourist visa, and the two others would arrange for his housing and his work.

There was also one local woman who said she had attended a language school in Tokyo. She told us she had married a Filipino she had met in Japan, and had returned to her home temporarily to give birth to a child. She said that once the child was born she would take it with her and go back to Japan.

We handed an electric pot to the family and some presents to the children, according to Andy's requests, and realized at that time that these goods were really what connected him to his family. The room was full of things – a television set, video player, big refrigerator, washing machine – that betrayed a lifestyle that one could not imagine by looking at the outside of the house. The wife hurriedly boiled some water with the new pot and made us some coffee. The children seemed hooked to the TV set.

As we left, they asked us to give a message to Andy. The message painfully expressed the feelings the family had about the absence of the father:

> Papa,
> We love you very much.
> Please don't come back to the Philippines.
> Because we don't have any money.
> (Of course, that's a joke).

(c) South Korea

South Korea is a very special case, in that it is both a member of the NIEs (Newly Industrializing Economies), and, like Pakistan, a country with a governmental policy of 'manpower exports,' or of systematically exporting labor.

Like other Asian countries, South Korea has experienced three phases in its manpower exports, starting with 1963. In that year, the government signed an agreement with West Germany to dispatch 247 miners there. A similar agreement was later signed for nurses and other medical workers. This was a period of high unemployment, many university graduates were having difficulty finding jobs, and in addition the country was experiencing a deep foreign reserves crisis.

During the first phase, the country's manpower exports were deeply tied to its involvement in the Vietnam War. Korean companies received contracts work for such as construction at U.S. bases in Guam and in other areas, and Korean workers were dispatched along with the projects. In 1966, when the war began in earnest, then-President Park Chung Hee sent 50,000 Korean soldiers to participate in the war, and dispatched civilians along with them to transport munitions and build barracks. The Korea Overseas Development Public Corporation (KODPC), a third sector venture set up for that purpose, is still active today.

Table 4–2 shows trends in South Korea's manpower exports. In 1966, more than 10,000 Korean workers were dispatched to South Vietnam, and more than 5,000 were sent there every year up until 1968. In the same period, workers employed by contracting companies were dispatched to a variety of places and were housed in labor camps (which seemed like military camps) far away from the local populations. This practice became a special characteristic of Korean workers (it is well documented in Hanabusa).

The second phase in Korea's labor exports began, like it did for other Asian countries, with the dispatch of workers to the Middle East. Table 4–2 shows that in 1974, the year immediately following the first oil shock, 395 people were sent to that region, but this number jumped to nearly 100,000 by 1979, just five years later. The number continued to increase after the second shock in that year, peaking at over 150,000 in 1982. It began to fall after 1983, but in 1986 was still over 40,000.

One special feature of Korean labor exports to the Middle East is that the workers accompanied Korean firms in the construction industry. Korean companies held an 8.6% share of the Middle East construction sector, the fifth largest among foreign countries, in the period from June 1975 to June 1976, but in the period between May 1977 and June 1979 had climbed to first place, with 21.4% of the total (Hirakawa).

During this period, Korean construction companies typically recruited their workers directly in the home country and then dispatched them to the Middle East. In 1983, for instance, 94.3% of all Korean workers in the region were employees of firms from their home country. Incidentally, Japanese construction companies in the region were also employing Korean workers. One of the major reasons behind this massive exodus of workers abroad is the fact that they could earn wages twice as high as those inside Korea, and in fact so many people went that it caused a labor shortage in their home country (Ogawa, p. 295).

Many of these workers were in their twenties or thirties, and regardless of whether they were single or married, signed con-

Table 4–2 Changes in South Korean manpower exports (1 person)

	Europe	Middle East	Asia	United States	Seafarers	Others	Total
1965	2,251	0	182 (93)	295	1,015	66	3,809
1966	1,520	0	10,418 (10,097)	24	978	7	12,947
1967	428	0	5,734 (5,328)	234	1,861	57	8,314
1968	94	0	6,472 (6,046)	682	1,307	73	8,628
1969	847	0	2,609 (2,131)	413	1,577	51	5,497
1970	3,022	0	1,864 (1,134)	914	2,874	108	8,782
1971	2,731	0	1,555 (355)	844	4,089	61	9,280
1972	1,728	0	1,548 (88)	736	6,199	109	10,320
1973	2,120	0	1,445 (8)	973	7,278	47	11,863
1974	2,416	395	2,697 (6)	608	8,403	19	14,538
1975	910	6,466	2,867 (1)	358	10,323	62	20,986
1976	379	21,269	1,765	526	13,098	155	37,192
1977	779	52,247	1,570	506	14,074	426	69,602
1978	97	81,987	903	676	18,169	156	101,988
1979	0	99,141	820	225	20,587	217	120,990
1980	3	120,535	4,004	154	21,649	91	146,436
1981	0	138,310	9,081	70	27,556	97	175,114
1982	288	151,583	12,597	857	31,252	278	196,855
1983	437	130,776	18,092	1,219	33,285	468	184,277
1984	378	100,765	16,350	805	34,067	308	152,673
1985	320	72,907	5,590	1,418	39,215	795	120,245
1986	338	44,753	4,882	2,093	42,751	458	95,275

Note: Figures in parentheses are exports to South Vietnam.

Source: Korean Labor Department.

tracts that put them out of the country for periods of one or two years. According to Hanabusa, 'Many of the worksites flew flags such as 'Hyundai Construction,' and bustled with Korean workers. These workers were, however, living far from their families. The local people of the Middle East, who speak different languages and have different customs, still whisper today that 'the Koreans seemed like soldiers who had changed into factory clothes.' In other words, it is fair to say that the system developed during the Vietnam War was still being used during the second phase in the Middle East' (Hanabusa).

Incidentally, there has been pressure in recent years for Japan to allow Korean construction companies to participate in the construction market here, including on projects like the Kansai International Airport. In July 1988, for example, the South Korean ambassador stated that 'There is a need for Japan to consider opening its construction market and to enthusiastically allow the influx of foreign workers' (*Nikkei Shimbun*, 6 September 1988). It seemed that the companies were expecting to recruit workers at home and to place them under the labor management practices outlined above. The Japanese Ministry of Construction, in response, agreed to begin granting licenses to Korean firms to participate in the Japanese market starting that year (Tezuka a, pp. 97–98). By the end of 1989, 11 companies had been licensed (*Nikkei Shimbun*, 22 December 1989).

Food and housing at the labor camps in the Middle East were normally provided by the companies, meaning that the workers could repatriate roughly 80% of their wages. There was, however, no obligation for them to send anything back at all. Table 4–3 compares remittances from overseas workers and balance of payments for the years 1977–1984. The table shows that the current balance began to fall into deficit in 1979, reaching $5.3 billion in 1980, and that starting in 1979, in contrast, the remittances from abroad climbed into the $1 billion range, and hit nearly $2 billion during the labor export peak year of 1982.

In other words, remittances from abroad played a major role in defusing the balance of payments crisis that South Korea faced between 1979 and the early 1980's. The revenue from construction contracts and from associated materials exports also contributed to easing the difficulties (Ogawa, p. 303).

These manpower exports to the Middle East, which had such an enormous effect, started declining after the drop in oil prices

Table 4–3 Changes in South Korea's balance of payments and remittances from overseas personnel ($ million)

	Remittances (A)	Current transactions	Export revenues (B)	Balance of trade (C)	A/B	A/C
1977	584.2	12.3	10,046	3,027	5.8	19.3
1978	769.8	1,085.2	12,711	4,450	6.1	17.3
1979	1,158.3	–4,151.7	15,055	4,826	7.7	24.0
1980	1,292.4	–5,320.7	17,505	5,368	7.4	24.1
1981	1,673.4	–4,646.0	21,254	6,598	7.9	25.3
1982	1,938.9	–2,649.6	21,853	7,476	8.9	25.9
1983	1,663.1	–1,606.0	24,445	7,178	6.8	23.2
1984	1,489.0	–1,371.3	29,245	7,316	5.1	20.4

Source: Kim and Choi, p. 33 (original data from South Korean Labor Department and Bank of Korea).

of 1983, falling to just 45,000 people in 1986. It is interesting to note, however, that the number of seafarers began to grow in this same period. Their numbers climbed steadily after reaching the 10,000 mark in 1975, and hit 43,000 in 1986, or roughly the same as the number of workers dispatched to the Middle East (Table 4–2). Incidentally, the number fell to 35,000 in 1989, and rising wages made it difficult for workers in the sector to find employment (*Tong-a Ilbo*, 28 May 1989). As a result, the overseas dispatch of seafarers was finally prohibited by the government in September 1990 (University of Tsukuba d, p. 100).

Traditionally, the main legal routes for Korean workers going abroad have been 1) to be hired directly by the employing companies; 2) to be recruited by labor dispatch companies; and 3) to go through the Korea Overseas Development Public Corporation (KODPC). The first route, as we have seen, has tended to be the most common. In regards to the second, there were seven such companies in 1990 (Sasaki, p. 228), but they will soon cease operations because of the country's entry into the ILO.

In terms of the third route, the KODPC, as mentioned earlier, was established in 1965 at the height of the Vietnam War, and in the period since then has dispatched at least 300,000 workers abroad. Roughly 70% of all workers who are not hired directly by a firm are sent through this one organization (Sasaki, p. 228). The KODPC's duties in terms of manpower exports include registering overseas employers, helping workers to select jobs, drawing up labor contracts between employers and employees, and training workers for dispatch.

In 1991, however, the KODPC was moved from the Labor Department to the Foreign Affairs Department, and was reborn as a new public corporation. It began to move away from manpower exports and toward accepting foreign trainees, dispatching specialists abroad, and to providing grants-in-aid (University of Tsukuba d, p. 101).

In this way South Korea, the honor student of the Asian NIEs, has found itself able to walk a very different path from other Asian countries during this third phase. When the construction boom that accompanied the 1985 Seoul Olympics cooled off, there was a temporary labor surplus, but generally speaking the decrease of overseas work has been absorbed inside the country, and in some sectors there have even been labor shortages. In addition, remittances from workers abroad are no longer the critical factor that they once were. At present, the government is trying to diversify host countries in an effort to maintain manpower exports, but in recent years there have been increasing calls for the government to review this policy.

The increasing numbers of Korean workers in the Kansai region, however, does not form part of the legal structure that we examined above. The decisions made by these workers to go to Japan have been personal ones, and lay outside of the official policy of manpower exports. As we indicated in the Introduction, the existence of resident Koreans in Japan makes it appear quite logical that this trend will continue in the future.

In the following few paragraphs, we will report on what we found when we visited the home of Chong Mu (whom we introduced in Section 2–3), the South Korean worker who was working in a mountain labor camp in Nara Prefecture.

As it turns out, we were lucky and Chong was home at the time because his visa had recently expired. As we left the city of Kyongju and moved into the countryside, the landscape turned to farmland. We rode in a bus for about 30 minutes, and then Chong met us with a tractor and drove us to his family home. His mother, wife, and his daughter, who was attending a commercial high school, were there to meet us. Chong had not worked since coming back, and was recovering from a stomach ailment he got in Japan.

The family lived in a one-story house with three rooms. The floor, which was made with 'ondol,' a traditional Korean floor heater, was warm. There were chickens and some dogs in the garden. Another Korean who accompanied us told us that this was a traditional Korean farmhouse. Chong's room was equipped with a television set as well as with a radio-tape cassette player that he must have bought in Japan.

Chong's family were part-time farmers, and most of their income came from his carpentry and plastering work, as well as the work he did in steelworking. They were currently planting 1,300 square meters of their own land and renting another 5,000 square meters for rice planting, though Chong told us that once his family had possessed 13,000 square meters of land. He said that 88 of the village's 114 families were full-time farmers, and that the rest, including his own, practiced part-time farming.

There was also, he said, a tangerine orange canning factory in the town, but the area was becoming increasingly depopulated. More and more young people were abandoning farming and streaming to the cities in search of work. One of the reasons for this was the difficulties that men in the villages faced in finding women willing to marry them. Chong's own son, in fact, was in Seoul at the time working as a chef in a hotel.

We asked him if he had received any inquiries about going to work in Japan since he had returned, and he answered that yes, he had. He felt, however, that he could not recommend young people to go there to work. It was dangerous, and the rewards were minimal, so he felt it was better for them to seek work in Korea.

He himself, however, was planning to go back to Japan in three weeks' time. It seemed the management of the old work camp wanted him to come back and work for them again, but he made it clear to us that he would go someplace else if he could get higher wages.

(d) China

In China, the term 'laowu shuchu' is used to refer to the national policy of exporting labor. According to the China Ministry of Foreign Trade and Economic Cooperation, 60,400 workers were working abroad under this policy in 1987, higher than the 54,372 during the period of January-May 1988 (Tezuka a, p. 103). The total number of people sent over the past 10 years has reached at least 300,000 (Tomoyuki Kojima).

The starting point for China's labor exports, as it was for other Asian countries, was the construction boom in the Middle East. The number, which was just 17,000 in 1981, had climbed to 47,000 by 1984 (Table 4–1), and thanks to the low wages demanded by Chinese workers' continues to increase today.

A turning point for overseas labor occurred, however, at the end of 1985, with the enactment of the 'Chinese Citizen Entrance and Exit Regulation.' Under this law, Chinese nationals could receive passports as long as they had the approval of their place of employment. In response to the new law, a growing number of people began to borrow and collect money in order to go abroad (Marukawa). At the same time, the government established a multitude of public (both national, provincial, and municipal) corporations to take direct responsibility for these labor exports.

The major destinations, in addition to the Middle East, have included Singapore and the former Soviet Union. The first major labor export to the Soviet Union came in October 1988, with a group of construction workers from Heilungchiang Province (Tezuka a, p. 104). In 1988, roughly 10,000 people from this province went abroad, by 1989 the number had climbed to 80,000, and in October 1990 the figure had reached 130,000 (*Nikkei Shimbun*, 8 January 1991).

The government's plans for 1992 were to send 105,000 people abroad, roughly 15% more than the figures for 1991, mainly to the Commonwealth of Independent States (CIS, or former Soviet Union), Hong Kong, and Vietnam (*Asahi Shimbun*, 10 March 1992). In addition, centers to help seafarers find jobs were set up in 10 coastal areas, and crew are being recruited for Taiwanese and other foreign-registered ships (Kiyoshi Ito).

In July 1988, Chinese Prime Minister Li Peng took the opportunity of then-Japanese Prime Minister Noboru Takeshita's visit to his country to push for an opening of the Japanese labor market to Chinese construction workers (*Nikkei Shimbun*, 8 September 1988), and this can be seen as an extension of the labor export policy. China's labor exports are not large at present, but it is believed that existing conditions will push China, like other Asian countries, to promote labor exports in the future.

It is said that 220 million of the 400 million workers in China's rural areas are surplus labor, and as a result there has been a mass migration from rural to urban areas, called '*mang liu*' (or 'blind rush') in Chinese. In China, people are not permitted to change their residence without official approval, so these people are not granted any of the rights given to residents of an area. In 1988, there were an estimated 1.6 million such people living in Peking, over 2 million in Shanghai, and in 1989 there were believed to be 50 or even 60 million throughout the country (Reito Kojima, pp. 66–7). The economic reforms and liberalization have increased the gaps between the coastal cities and the rural interior, and there are fears that the 'invisible rush' may pick up speed in the future.

In terms of the international balance of payments, China's external debt is growing rapidly. According to estimates from bodies such as the World Bank, China's external debts stood at $16.7 billion in 1985, and rose to $21.9 billion in 1986, $30.2 billion in 1987, and to $40.0 billion at the end of 1988 (Chinese government figures).

The Chinese government has maintained that it does not have a problem with debt payments, but export growth was sluggish in 1989, and this combined with a drop in tourism revenues has raised serious anxiety over the future balance of payments situation (*Nikkei Shimbun*, 14 September 1989). It is believed that the labor export policies will acquire increased significance as means to acquire foreign earnings and alleviate unemployment.

As one indication of this trend, the Chinese government in March 1991 sounded out Japan on the possibility of a major export of labor power to Japan. Specifically, it proposed to 1) create a single agency to deal with dispatching workers overseas; 2) dispatch workers as college students and as *shugakusei*; 3) establish, as a joint Sino-Japanese project, a center in China to give pre-training to workers; and 4) take responsibility for repatriating workers sent to Japan (*Nikkei Shimbun*, 17 March 1991).

With the advent of the labor export policy, many people, especially among the upper strata of Chinese society, have shown a strong interest in going abroad. People in that country have very little right to choose their own occupation, and the restrictions are particularly severe for university graduates. Going abroad is hence one of the few opportunities available for gaining a measure of freedom. The general dissatisfaction with the present system in China has also added steam to this trend. Another factor which cannot be overlooked is the widespread awareness that working abroad can be an economically advantageous experience.

We had the chance to visit one Japanese language school in Shanghai, and spoke to some of the students there. In the following few paragraphs we will discuss the results of our talk. The school was using classrooms in a Junior High School near Waitan, at the center of the city, and the classes took place in the evening after the students had finished work.

Zai Weida told us he had been studying Japanese on his own for 15 years, starting in 1973, when he was 20 years old. He attended the Kunming University of Technology for four years starting in 1967, where he studied metallurgy and design. After graduating he started working as a designer in a large factory in Shanghai, and was still working there at the time we met him. At one time he had served an invaluable role when the factory was introducing Japanese technology, and he had been asked to serve as interpreter for the Japanese technicians.

He told us that, 'The Chinese system is no good. Your income is always the same, no matter how hard you work and how much ability you have. There's no competition, so China has fallen behind. But I'm afraid the system won't change. To tell the truth, I'm not satisfied with my present work. It's called design, but there's no creativity at all involved. All I can do is to mechanically follow the instructions of the supervisors. Even if I can't get to Japan I will do whatever I can to change my workplace. The free competition in Japan is better. If I can get to Japan, I want to learn how to manage and compete there.'

Thus we can see that many Chinese people have a strong desire to go abroad, but it is very difficult for them to do so. To begin with, it is almost impossible to get permission to go abroad for tourism. Aspiring tourists must have both a guarantor in their place of visit and permission from their workplace, and in addition, the normally used people's yuan cannot, in principle, be converted to foreign currency. As a result, the only reasons Chinese can legally go abroad are for study, family visits, and for training.

The most popular foreign destinations are the United States, Canada, and Australia, and Japan is not actually a particularly popular one. The example of Tian Feng, who called out to us in

Japanese on the streets of Shanghai, is representative of the consciousness of people wishing to go abroad.

His Japanese was not very fluent, but his English was excellent. He told us he worked selling equipment designed by his father. His father was not allowed to sell products, so Tian drew up the contracts and signed them himself. This was in theory a job, but in reality he did not have much work.

He was an example of the traditional elite. In China, where only 4% of the population reach university, the intellectuals who graduate from these institutions tend to have great pride. When we said this, he answered that, 'That's absolutely true. They always look down on other people.' Over and over he told us about acquaintances and relatives of his who had high social status. He told us that five years earlier, when he was still in university, the U.S. ambassador had acknowledged his ability and invited him to go to America, but this was before liberalization and he had been too afraid to apply for an exit permit. He said that if the same thing happened today he would not hesitate.

He did not have any concrete plans to come to Japan at the time we met him, but made it very clear that if he did go the purpose would be 'to make money.' His real goal seemed to be the United States. We asked him, 'Why not Japan?' and he answered simply, 'Because it is too close to China.' He did add, however, that, 'Japanese men are dishonest and are fast talkers. I don't like them.'

It is believed that a great number of the Chinese who want to go to Japan or who already are in Japan either have, or had, plans to eventually go to the United States. The Consulting Company for Private Entry and Exit, which handles visa applications and gives advice to people in Shanghai who wish to study abroad, has more information about the U.S., Canada, and Australia, than it does about Japan. It is said that the reason for the scarcity of people from Peking among students in Japan is that they manage to go to the United States.

One reason for America's popularity is the possibility of getting permanent residency. Tian told us that many of the people who wanted to go abroad had at least some higher education, and fairly high social status. He said that they were dissatisfied with the present Communist system. In addition, the generation who experienced the Cultural Revolution seem to be afraid that with changes in policy they will lose their present status. For that reason, many hope to leave Japan and live permanently abroad. Many people go to Japan as *shugakusei* and after two years move on to the United States, Canada, Australia, or New Zealand instead of returning to China.

In the past, going to the U.S. as a college or language student was relatively easy, but the requirements have been stiffened, and it is now necessary to pass examinations to demonstrate proficiency in English and to have, in principle, at least a college education (Group Akakabu, p. 79; *Yomiuri Shimbun*, 12 October 1988). For this reason, there has been an increase in the flow of Chinese *shugakusei* to Japan, and in response to this, as we already pointed out in Chapter 1–3, the Japanese side has established restrictive controls.

In order to understand the effects of these measures, the case of Yuan Yizhi, whom we met in the previously-mentioned Japanese language school in Shanghai, will be helpful.

He paid a total of ¥85,000 through his brother, who was already in Japan, to a language school in Japan as an acceptance fee, but lost all the money when the school lost its qualification. Needless to say, this incident led him to give up most of his enthusiasm for going to Japan. He estimated that one-third of the people from Shanghai who wanted to study in Japan knew somebody there.

Incidentally, he graduated from a well-known transportation college, and said that whereas college graduates were serious students, many of the people who had only graduated from high school were just interested in making money. When we asked him how people exchanged people's yuan into foreign currencies, he said that when people had friends in Japan they would ask them to give them payments in Japanese yen, and in exchange would pay an equivalent amount, in people's yuan, to the acquaintance's family in China. Those who did not have such acquaintances used the black market.

The pattern of Chinese *shugakusei* going to Australia closely resembles that for Japan. Starting in 1986, the Australian government began to encourage foreign students to study English language there, and the number of Chinese students rose precipitously, to 15,000. There were many overstayers, and as a result the government tightened its controls at the end of August 1989, setting age and educational achievement requirements as well as requiring students to present the identity cards of potential employers before starting any job. As a result, it became extremely difficult for people to find their way to study in Australia (*Asahi Shimbun*, 31 October 1989).

The desire among people to leave China is particularly strong in Shanghai. As a result, one important feature of that city is the existence, which is lacking in other cities, of special agencies to assist people to go abroad. The first example of this, as noted above, was the Consulting Company for Private Entry and Exit, which was launched in July 1988 as a company to help individual travellers leave and enter the country.

In addition, there are tough controls against bringing foreign currency out of China, but the Consulting Company's parent company, the Shanghai Aijian Finance Trust & Investment Corp., received authorization from the Foreign Currency Control Bureau and the City of Shanghai to lend yen and dollars at a rate just slightly lower than those offered on the black market (*Asahi Shimbun*, 12 December 1988).

In the wake of the Tienanmen Incident, however, restrictions against foreign travel became harsher, and this had an effect on travel to Japan. Authorities feared that student activists might seek refuge abroad, and moved to tighten the issuing of passports (*Asahi Shimbun*, 8 September 1989). People leaving for the United States were now required to have exit permits in addition to visas (Kiyoshi Ito). Furthermore, In February 1990, the Chinese government set new regulations that people with degrees in higher education would not be allowed to go abroad to study with their own funds for a period of five years after graduating. In addition, going abroad to study with government funding became extremely difficult (*Ryugakusei Shimbun*, 1 April 1990). As a result of this, the number of people hoping to enter universities dropped drastically.

Trainees form an important part of the flow from China to Japan. As we saw in Chapter 1–2, Chinese were the largest group of trainees entering Japan in 1991, with a total of 10,668 people. Candidates for training programs, after receiving the permission of their workplaces, go through a variety of agencies which send them abroad.

One trainee in a construction company whom we interviewed told us that he received ¥40,000 per month as an allowance, ¥30,000 in cash for meals, and free housing. In addition, the company was paying ¥40,000 every month to the agency in China and ¥20,000 to the trainee's old workplace. The company had also paid for the trainee's airfare.

In this way, the agencies in China receive 20%–30% of the cost of the training from the accepting group in Japan, and the trainee's former place of work typically receives an additional amount. The former workplace usually uses this money to pay a salary to the family of the absent worker, and appropriates some amount for certain necessary expenses such as Japanese-language education. Sending trainees abroad thus directly contributes to foreign exchange earnings, and it can be said that the trainee system in Japan is a major target of China's policy of labor exports. Accordingly, there have been repeated attempts to use the trainee system to bring Chinese labor to Japan.

In addition to this, the landing in small boats of Chinese disguised as Vietnamese refugees became a major topic of debate in 1989. The reasons behind this can be found in the strong desire among Chinese to go abroad. In the period after May 29 of that year, a total of 22 boats landed (Yamagami f, pp. 28–29) with 3,478 people aboard (*Asahi Shimbun*, 21, 25 December 1989), and 2,844 of these passengers were determined to be Chinese (*Asahi Shimbun*, 24 July 1990). Most refugee boats land in Japan in the one-month period beginning in early August.

In response to this situation, the Japanese government decided on September 11 to take measures to deport all Chinese (including overseas Chinese from Vietnam) passengers as illegal entrants, and to introduce a screening system for Vietnamese to determine whether they were political or economic refugees (*Asahi Shimbun*, 11 September 1989). We will examine this policy further in Chapter 5–3. After these changes, the number of landings dropped to virtually zero. Chinese who come disguised as Vietnamese are now shipped home after receiving confirmation from their government. As of February 1991, 1,788 people had been deported, and 1,042 were still languishing in a detention camp (*Asahi Shimbun*, 2 February 1991).

Most of these refugee boats originated in Fujian Province. Not only does that region have a long history of sending out immigrants abroad, but it is also one of the major origins for *shugakusei* in Japan. As of the end of 1988, 35,000 of the passports issued by Shanghai City authorities for travel to Japan were given to residents of Shanghai, 10,000 were for residents of Fujian, and

1,000 to residents of Jiangsu Province (Group Akakabu, p. 75). It is clear that Fujian is an important source.

It is said that pre-college students in Japan can be roughly divided into four groups: those from Fujian's Fuqing Xian, Changlo Xian, and Fuzhou City, and those from Shanghai. In Fuqing Xian, one is surprised by the rich and newly-constructed stone mansions built by people returning from stints as *shugakusei* in Japan (*Asahi Shimbun*, 2 September 1989). In consequence, it is clear that one of the major motivations for the departure of refugee boats was the tightening of immigration restrictions on *shugakusei*. Incidentally, Fujian experienced a mass exodus of stowaways to Taiwan in the period following the tightening of Japanese regulations.

One of the major departure points for boats was in Fuqing Xian, but many of the boats also left from Changlo Xian and from Haitan Island in Pingtan Xian. Incidentally, Fuqing City is known as one of Fujian Provinces's major hometowns of overseas Chinese, and 60% of its people have relatives abroad. After the issue of boat people became a problem in Japan, authorities strengthened their enforcement activities in the region, and reports indicate that roughly 700 people have been arrested off the coast of the province on charges of illegally leaving the country (*Asahi Shimbun*, 1, 2, 6 September 1989).

No large organization existed to equip the refugee boats, so they were prepared one by one. In the following paragraphs we will look at one typical case, in which a group of people from Fujian happened to see on television a group of people from their own village entering Japan disguised as Vietnamese refugees. One group among them took the leadership and began to collect funds.

The few dozen people among them who had previously lived in Vietnam were not required to pay any fee, men going for the purpose of working paid 4,000 yuan each (¥200,000), and women paid between 2,000–4,000 yuan. With this money the organizers got their hands on a boat, forged Vietnamese birth certificates, and bought food. Most of the people raised the money by selling their land and borrowing money from their friends and relatives (*Asahi Shimbun*, 4, 25 October 1989).

In this way, overseas Chinese returning from Vietnam played a crucial role in these activities. Most of these 160,000 or so returnees had gone home to China starting in 1978, when relations between the two nations deteriorated (Kiyoshi Ito). There were in Fuqing City farms and factories which accommodated overseas Chinese, and many of the people working there had faced persecution in either Vietnam or Indonesia (*Asahi Shimbun*, 1 September 1989). The presence of these returnees was one of the conditions that led to the area being a starting point for departures.

This illegal entry has continued, though on a smaller scale. In March 1992, a boat tried to land on Hachijojima, where there is a smaller police presence than in the Kyushu and Okinawa area, but 13 of the 21 people aboard either drowned or became missing, and eight managed to reach the shore (one died later). In this case, a broker in Fujian acquired a Taiwanese fishing boat, and planned to have the passengers rendezvous with a group of Chinese already living in Japan (*Nikkei Shimbun*, 15 April 1992). Between January and July of 1992, there were eight other such incidents of illegal entry by groups, the largest when 61 people were seized in Muroto Cape in Shikoku on a fishing boat that left from Fujian Province (*Asahi Shimbun*, 29 July, 20 August 1992).

As we have seen, it is believed that there will be a continuing flow of Chinese disguised as Vietnamese refugees, but it is important to note that there are now people coming not as migrant laborers but rather as political refugees. On one boat that was seized on October 12, 1989, at least 10 people cited political persecution as their reason for fleeing, giving statements such as 'I participated in the student movement,' or 'Some of my relatives have been persecuted or even killed. I am fleeing persecution.' Many of the people on the boat spoke Mandarin Chinese, an indication that they were students, teachers, or other people with high education levels (*Asahi Shimbun*, 16 October 1989).

In addition, one woman who received a deportation order appealed for its withdrawal, stating that, 'I participated in the democratization movement and am a political refugee,' but in August 1991 she was forcibly repatriated. In April 1992, the Tokyo District High Court dismissed her appeal, giving as its reason that the plaintiff was not in Japan and could therefore not qualify for political refugee status (*Asahi Shimbun*, 14 April 1992).

(e) Bangladesh

In the following few sections, we will examine examples of countries in which national policy has given some degree of importance to labor exports. Bangladesh, the first country we will look at, did not start exporting labor to the Middle East (including Libya) as soon as other countries, but because of the country's unemployment problems this opportunity created a great deal of interest, and private foreign employment agencies blossomed.

In the midst of this boom, there were firms which promised to introduce workers to jobs in the Middle East, taking exhorbitant sums of money. Partially because of this, the government in 1976 established a Ministry of Labor and Manpower Employment Exchange Bureau, and began to introduce workers to overseas jobs and to train aspiring migrant workers. This was followed, in 1984, by the creation of the Foreign Employment Service Public Corporation (see Osada).

In the period following 1981, roughly 50,000–70,000 workers went abroad, mostly to the Middle East, but in the years 1989 and 1990 this number jumped to the 100,000 mark (Ministry of Labor m, p. 507). The main reason for this jump was that Bangladeshis demanded lower wages than workers from other countries.

In 1980–81 (from July to June, same for following figures) these workers sent $380 million in remittances, in 1986–87 this number rose to $730 million, and in 1987–88 it reached $790 million. For the same years, these remittances made up the following ratio of exports: 53.3%, 68.1%, and 64.0%, and it can therefore be said that labor constituted the country's primary export (see Osada). It has also been estimated that the Gulf War led to a $300 million drop in remittances (*Asahi Shimbun*, 21 September 1990).

As a result of these remittances, Bangladesh's balance of payments situation improved remarkably. Before this time, its large trade deficit had caused a shortage in current accounts, and a structure was in place that allowed this to be compensated to some degree by foreign assistance. The foreign remittances, however, coupled with an increase in aid, pushed the balance of payments into the black.

In terms of the ways in which the migrant workers spent their earnings, the so-called 'Dubai wala mansions' became well known. 'Dubai wala' refers to people who brought back money from Dubai, and the mansions they built were intended to be leased out to foreigners.

Much of the employment assistance carried out for overseas workers is done by private firms. The private companies control 40% of the market, government agencies less than 10%, and in the remaining cases the arrangements are made individually (see Osada).

Employment brokers in Bangladesh are much better organized than their counterparts in Pakistan. Many of the larger agencies have their own training facilities. One of the agencies sends laborers to work in construction projects in the Middle East carried out by South Korean companies, and the workers sent abroad by this agency are equipped with identical uniforms, hats, and name tags, and are then sent off to the airport.

One specific village, about 50 kilometers from Dhaka, is said to have sent '70% of all Bangladeshi migrant workers in Japan.' Approximately one person from every two or three families was working in Japan, and in one case a group of 16 people from two households were in Japan at the same time. There were also many 'Japanese houses,' big brick houses, under construction throughout the village, and they demonstrated the excitement of the villagers.

The mutual visa exemption agreement between Japan and Bangladesh was suspended, as was the agreement with Pakistan, in January 1989, but the enthusiasm for Japan remains strong (see Sasaki, News 8). Incidentally, in the two months following the cancellation of the agreement, the Japanese embassy issued 687 tourist visas, and the number of applicants has been rising since.

The potential emigration pressure that Bangladesh can exert was demonstrated in March 1989, when 10–20 million people suddenly applied for long-term residence in the United States (*Kokusai Jinryu*, June 1989, pp. 34–35).

We should also add that just before then-Prime Minister Toshiki Kaifu's visit to Bangladesh in May 1990, the President stated that he would request that the Japanese government consider the possibility of accepting a set number of workers on a yearly basis, thus showing the expectations held of Japan as a market for labor exports (*Nikkei Shimbun*, 30 April 1990).

(f) Indonesia

Indonesian labor exports to the Middle East began in earnest in 1978, and in the beginning were concentrated almost exclusively in Saudi Arabia. Most of these people worked as domestic servants, either as maids or chauffeurs. During the peak year of 1982, approximately 180,000 people went to the Middle East (Table 4–1), but by 1985–87 this number had dropped to 45,000. In 1989, for instance, it was said that 90% of all Indonesians in the Middle East were in Saudi Arabia, 80% were working as household servants, of which 60% were maids.

The Indonesian government agency in charge of sending workers abroad is the Overseas Employment Center, which falls under the Ministry of Labor. This Center supervises the country's approximately 50 foreign employment agencies. The companies are organized so that each one is responsible for a particular country, and they receive commissions not from the workers but rather from the employers.

In addition to this, there is also a considerable flow of undocumented migrant workers from Indonesia to Malaysia. There are said to be 150,000–200,000 such workers in East Malaysia (Sabah and Sarawak states), and 300,000–400,000 on peninsular Malaysia, where they work as construction or plantation workers. Most of the workers in East Malaysia came from Sulawesi or East Nusatenggara State. They enter with the help of brokers using wooden boats.

There are also undocumented Indonesian workers in small- and medium-size factories in Taiwan. The country's Fifth Five Year Plan which began in April 1989 set a goal of sending 500,000 workers overseas (see Sasaki, News #15, as well as Matsui, Fuke, and Kano, p. 173).

(g) Sri Lanka

There were very few Sri Lankan migrant workers abroad until 1978, when the country's restrictions on foreign travel were relaxed. In 1980, a law to regulate companies assisting workers to find employment abroad was promulgated, and in 1985 the Overseas Employment Bureau was established as an external organization of the Ministry of Labor. A Worker's Welfare Fund was also established, with contributions from workers' earnings, for the benefit of workers overseas. The OEB's responsibilities included licensing employment agencies, screening individual jobs to make sure they were being conducted under appropriate conditions, finding employment and conducting training for workers, and taking care of complaints involving, for instance, contract violations, exploitation, and accidents.

In the period around 1978, some 20,000 workers went abroad every year, but after the flow of workers to the Middle East increased starting in 1981, the number jumped to 57,000 a year. It is also believed that the number of workers abroad has not decreased significantly since the ebbing of the oil boom. Remittances from abroad have, as they have for other countries, contributed significantly to mitigating the country's international balance of payments. In 1984, these remittances totalled 7 billion rupees ($300 million), eqvivalent to 27.6% of total exports.

In contrast to other South Asian countries, which prohibit overseas workers from working as maids, roughly half of all Sri Lankan overseas workers are in this occupation, with conservative estimates putting the figure at least 40%, and more liberal ones placing it at over 50%. The main destination for the maids is the Middle East, but in recent years there have been sigificant flows to both Singapore and Hong Kong.

It is said that employment agencies have charged between 10,000 and 25,000 rupees (¥40,000–¥100,000), or roughly 3 to 10 times more than the legally-set fee, and several hundred agencies have had their licenses revoked. There are also, however, many unregistered firms. In spite of this, the role of the OEB has been estremely limited (see Sasaki, News #9; Documentation for Action Groups in Asia, pp. 64–65).

(h) Thailand

Thailand is an unusual example in that, despite the fact that it sends a large number of workers abroad, the government has virtually no policy to promote these exports. The country's first phase of labor exports mostly involved women going to work abroad. This flow first attracted attention in 1974, when women started going to work as maids or prostitutes in places such as West Germany, Switzerland, the Netherlands, and Scandinavia. Many went abroad to help their families' financial situation or to earn money to finance their marriages (Documentation for Action Groups in Asia, pp. 26–27).

The second phase, which involved a rapid increase of men travelling to the Middle East, began, as stated above, from 1980, and hit a peak in 1982, when more than 100,000 people left the country and headed for the Gulf.

In terms of the shift away from the Middle East during the third phase, we find that the number of people going to work abroad reached 67,000 in 1983, 73,000 in 1984, 70,000 in 1985, 86,000 in 1986, 86,000 in 1987, meaning that the number increased significantly after 1986, the year in which oil prices suddenly dropped. Even in 1987, 87.5% of departures were for the Gulf, showing that despite a slight drop in numbers the region was still as important as ever (Ministry of Labor f, pp. 129–130, original data from the Thai Ministry of the Interior, Bureau of Labor).

According to the Bank of Bangkok, there were, as of 1988, 301,000 Thai workers abroad. Of these workers, an overwhelming 76%, or 228,000, were in the Middle East, followed by Singapore with 31,000, Malaysia with 26,000, Brunei with 6,000, Japan with 5,000, Hong Kong with 2,500, with 3,000 in other places. A great majority, or 150,000, of those in the Middle East were in Saudi Arabia.

The number for 1987 was 313,000, meaning that the number dropped by some 12,000 people in the following year, and this decrease occurred principally in the Middle East, and especially in Saudi Arabia (Washio), which was trying to decrease its population of foreign workers by 600,000. Incidentally, it is said that a drop in wages in the Middle East is dampening the enthusiasm among workers to go work there (Japan Institute of Labor, p. 12).

We should point out here that the data from the Bank of Bangkok that there are 301,000 Thais outside the country is deficient in several aspects. First, it does not take female migrant workers into account. It is believed there are 100,000 such women spread around the world, most of them in Germany, Scandinavia, and other Western European countries which do not require visas, as well as in places like the Middle East, Taiwan, and Japan (Documentation for Action Groups in Asia, p. 20; *Asahi Shimbun*, 30 June 1989).

Second, as we mentioned earlier, there are significant numbers of undocumented male workers in Singapore, Taiwan, and Japan, but these people are not counted. Furthermore, there is a considerable number of Thai workers in Japan using the pretext of training. Some of these trainees have been sent by Thailand branches of Japanese companies, and some by organized Thai brokers who arrange connections with factories in Japan.

As a result, we can guess that the real number of Thai workers abroad is much larger than the Bank of Bangkok's estimate, probably reaching 400,000–500,000 people.

There is thus a considerable volume of labor flowing out of Thailand, and its effect on the country's international balance of payments cannot be ignored. In spite of this, one cannot say that the Thai government has taken steps to promote this activity, and in fact has limited its role to controlling and watching over employment agencies and to protecting the rights of its workers abroad. Specifically, this has meant cracking down on nefarious employment brokers and demanding that employment agencies train unskilled workers (Washio).

Thus, all of the assistance given to workers seeking overseas jobs is done by private agencies. The chairman of the Association of Foreign Employment Agencies, which has 300 member companies, stated that the strengthening of government regulations has led to rising commissions, and that the decreasing number of work destinations has worsened the financial situation of the agencies (Japan Institute of Labor).

The foreign earnings of Thai workers have typically been spent on housing, durable consumer items, and farm equipment. In Baan, Chiang Rai Province, an area well known for the many who have gone abroad to work as prostitutes, one can find many new homes, electric appliances, tractors, and farm trucks, all bought with money sent by workers abroad. In addition, many young men in the area have had great difficulties finding spouses (*Asahi Shimbun*, 30 June 1989).

Last, we will record the impressions we received during our visit to the home in Thailand of Sompong, the trainee we introduced in Chapter 1–2, who was working in a metal processing plant in northern Kanto.

His family home was located in a farming village several hours north from Bangkok by long-distance bus. The village was a cluster of a few dozen raised-floor houses. Sompong's wife, who had been told about our visit beforehand, gave us a very warm welcome. In one of the rooms there was a television set, radio, and new appliances including a refrigerator, and the home looked fairly rich. These items were most likely things bought with Sompong's earnings. Sompong's wife showed us a picture he had sent her from Japan, and when we left she gave us some hamburgers and bananas to take with us.

(i) Malaysia

The 100,000 Malaysians working in Singapore, including 24,000 who commute to work across the border, make up the major element of that country's labor exports. There are also undocumented workers in Taiwan (Sasaki, News #16). In addition, since 1989 there has been an increasing flow to Japan. Travel agencies are not compelled to be registered in Malaysia, and it is said that as a result brokering firms disguised as travel agencies have sent people to work in Japan in an organized fashion (*Nikkei Shimbun*, 19 May 1989).

(j) India

There are at present very few Indians in Japan. Considering the problems of poverty and the huge population pressure in that country, however, we cannot ignore the future possibilities for migrant labor exports.

Historically, Indians have shown much more of a tendency to settle abroad than to work as migrant laborers. There are currently 9 million Indians living permanently in 155 countries around the world, and 5 million of them have citizenship in these countries. Migrant labor from India only became an issue with, as for other Asian countries, the great demand for labor in the Middle East during the oil boom.

As we wrote in Section 1 of this chapter, the number of people leaving for the Middle East every year during the early 1980's was in the 200,000 range, but in the late 1980's this number dropped into the 100,000 range. Moreover, it is thought that remittances from overseas workers dropped by $500-$600 million because of the Gulf War (*Asahi Shimbun*, 21 September 1990).

One of the particular features of India's labor exports is the major role played by several thousand unlicensed employment agencies. One of the principal activities carried out by these firms is to send out large numbers of workers without passports or visas, and they reap exhorbitant profits from these workers. In order to deal with this situation, the government in 1983 passed an Immigration Law, which set up a licensing system for employment agencies and set procedures for protecting Indian workers abroad, but this did not have a significant effect.

One special feature of Indian migrant workers is that an unusually high number come from one specific area, Kerala State, a small region facing the Arabian Sea in the southern tip of the country. It accounts for more than half of all migrant workers leaving the country. As of 1989 there were 500,000–600,000 people from this one state in the Middle East, and it is believed that one out of ten households there has a family member working overseas. The major reason behind these statistics is the area's poverty, and its 26% unemployment rate.

Of these people from Kerala, 80% are under the age of 35, roughly half are unmarried, 25% have had at least some university education, up to 66% have had no previous work experience, many are Muslims, and there are virtually no women (see Sasaki, News #7; Documentation for Action Groups in Asia, pp. 48–61).

(k) Iran

Iranian government statistics put the country's inflation rate at 28% and unemployment at 20%–30%. In addition, up until April 1992 there was a mutual visa exemption agreement between this country and Japan, making Japan the only industrialized country which was easy to enter. As a result, among young Iranians a fierce 'Japan fever' began to spread. Many arrived at Narita airport, and paid several hundred dollars to brokers to find jobs (*Asahi Shimbun*, 19 November 1990).

3 Asia's Host Countries

Japan is not the only Asian host country for foreign workers. The countries and regions known as NIEs, namely Singapore, Hong Kong, Taiwan, and South Korea, have all become recipients, and other noteworthy destinations have included Malaysia and Brunei. In the following section we will look at the cases of these different countries.

(a) Singapore

Singapore is noteworthy for the strict supervision which it has imposed on the foreign workers it has admitted.

Singapore has never had a large working population, and in recent years the overwhelming tendency of young people to avoid manual labor has led to increasing concern over the country's labor shortage. For many years, however, Singapore has relied on foreign workers to fulfill its demand for so-called unskilled labor.

At the end of 1991, there were roughly 200,000 properly registered foreign workers, and it is said that there were several tens of thousands of undocumented workers as well. There were in addition, as we mentioned above, the 24,000 or so Malaysians commuting to work every day across the border into Singapore. This means that foreign workers constitute roughly 20% of the country's working population of 1,450,000.

The government has categorized suppliers of labor into 'traditional supply countries' and 'non-traditional supply countries,' and has basically given priority to the former category, which includes countries such as Malaysia, Hong Kong, Makao, China, and South Korea. All other countries fall into the 'non-traditional' category. With the exception of maids from Sri Lanka and other special cases, working permits have practically never been granted to people from South Asia.

In the next section, we will look at the question of which countries workers in different occupations have come from. At the present, the only businesses where the government permits foreigners to work are manufacturing, construction, the hotel industry, and domestic help, although there are also moves toward legalizing the retail sales business. For manufacturing, the major workforce consists of the more than 100,000 Malaysians working primarily in foreign-affiliated factories. Practically all of them are Chinese Malaysians. The construction industry employs roughly 30,000 workers, mostly from Thailand, the Philippines, China, and South Korea, though there are also some Taiwanese.

Maids were introduced principally as a way of encouraging Singaporean women to work. It is said that there are now 50,000 foreign domestic helpers, and that most are Filipinas, though there are also Sri Lankans and Indonesians.

Since 1982, the Singapore government has tried to improve the quality of its economy by ending its reliance on foreign workers. Specifically, in November 1988 it set the goal of reducing the ratio of foreigners in the employed workforce in any single company from 50% to 40%, and to raise the tax charged for employing foreigners in steps, reaching a peak in August 1990. As of the end of 1991, the ceilings set for the ratio of foreign workers in different industries were as follows: 75% in construction, 45% in manufacturing, 20% in services, with no ceiling set for maids.

Under the revised Immigration Control Act of April 1989, punishments were set for employers of undocumented workers, and caning and imprisonment were prescribed for workers overstaying by over 90 days. As a result of this, approximately 10,000 Thai undocumented workers surrendered and were deported in March, but because of the labor shortage, particularly in the construction industry, they were all issued new visas and permitted to go back to Singapore. As of July 1989, one Thai and nine Indian workers have received canings as sentences for overstaying.

Moreover, foreign domestic helpers are not only forbidden from marrying Singapore citizens, but they are not permitted to become pregnant while in the country, and are required to undergo monthly pregnancy examinations (the above information is from sources including Sasaki, News 1, 2, 4, 10, and 18; *Asahi Shimbun*, 20 April, 15 July 1989; Ministry of Labor f, pp. 416–418; Ministry of Labor m; Sugata; Yanobe; *Nikkei Shimbun*, 20 December 1989, 27 March 1990; *Bangkok Post*, 14 September 1991; and Japan Institute of Labor).

(b) Hong Kong

In 1988, as a way of relieving a labor shortage, the Hong Kong government decided to permit a small number of foreign workers to enter the territory to work at public construction projects (*Nikkei Shimbun*, 30 October 1989), and in May 1989 initiated an urgent 'Plan to Introduce 3,000 Skilled Foreign Workers.' Under the plan, workers could enter the territory for a non-extendable two-year period, and were prohibited from bringing their families along. By October of the same year, however, there had only been 273 applicants (mostly from mainland China) for visas (Sasaki, News 14). In 1991 the government planned to admit the following number of workers: 2,700 skilled mechanics, 10,000 manufacturing workers, and 2,000 people to work on projects related to the new airport (Ministry of Labor m).

In anticipation of the 1997 reversion, moreover, the government decided in September 1990 to relax labor regulations to permit Chinese citizens who had lived outside their country for at least two years to move to Hong Kong (*Nikkei Shimbun*, 26 November 1990).

Because of the social advances made by women in Hong Kong, there were, as of 1989, 50,000 Filipinas, 2,000 Thais, and smaller numbers of Sri Lankan and Indonesian women working as maids in the territory (Sasaki, News 14). In Hong Kong, as in other places, the fear of foreign workers settling down has led to strict policies. Foreign maids are repatriated immediately when dismissed by an employer, and even when they find a new employer they must go back to their home country and reapply for entry (Catholic Institute for International Relations, pp. 91–4).

In addition to this legal presence, it is believed that significant numbers of Chinese enter the territory illegally. Every year, between 27,000 and 30,000 Chinese citizens are deported from Hong Kong (*Asahi Shimbun*, 5 November 1989). As of the end of 1991, there were also an additional 14,000 people from Macao and China living in the territory by special permission (Ministry of Labor m). In one incident in March 1990, 30,000 illegal Chinese residents in Macao rioted demanding permanent residency (*Asahi Shimbun*, 30 March 1990).

Vietnamese refugees have also become a major social issue in Hong Kong. There were 58,800 refugees in the territory as of February 1992, most of them economic (*Asahi Shimbun*, 18 February 1992). The camps were highly overcrowded, and the living conditions deteriorating horrendously. In response, the government has encouraged the refugees to return home voluntarily, and in December 1989 carried out its first forced repatriation, sending a small number of economic refugees back (*Asahi Shimbun*, 6 February 1990).

(c) Taiwan

Up until 1990, Taiwan in principle did not permit the presence of foreign workers. The only exception to this rule was a specific portion of the construction industry, but in 1990 there were only 3,500 foreign workers, under special conditions, permitted in the country. Starting in 1991, however, the government began to take the first steps toward allowing the presence of foreign laborers, when the Labor Commission announced that foreigners would be permitted in the textiles, metals, machinery, power, and construction industries. A two-year limit was placed on this employment, as well as a stipulation that the employers make efforts at automating and modernizing their factories. In addition, a prohibition was instituted against foreigners making up more than one-third of the workforce in any factory or construction site. It was projected that there would be 15,000 such workers in 1991, and that the number would increase in the future.

A quota was also set up for admitting up to 1,200 foreigners to work on public works projects. These construction workers, however, had to have their fingerprints (for all ten fingers) and palmprints taken, and as a means to stop them from escaping were housed in barricaded dormitories and subjected to late night surprise roll calls.

These new measures formed a response both to the country's labor shortage and to the growing number of undocumented workers, which were said to number 60,000. In response to the growing presence, the government implemented a series of new policies between 1990 and 1991.

The first of these measures was to set an amnesty period for three months following February 1991, and overstayers leaving during this time would be exempted from paying income taxes and fines. New fines, however, were enacted against people leaving after this period. Only 22,000 people, however, took advantage of this offer. In response, the government instituted a new measure, this time requiring employers to register undocumented workers by April 30, and permitting them to employ the workers until July 14, provided that they deposited a sum of money equivalent to the amount needed to repatriate the workers. Moreover, a new bill, the Employment and Employment Services Act, which set punishments against both employers and workers, was presented. Undocumented workers would receive fines up to

$1,100, and employers prison sentences of up to three years and fines up to $11,000.

In spite of these efforts, it is believed that as of September 1991 there were approximately 20,000 undocumented workers in the country (for the above, see *Bangkok Post*, 6 April, 17 April, 23 June, 14 September, 1991; Nihon Hoso Kyokai Reporting Group, pp. 160-; Ministry of Labor m).

According to one report, there were 54,000 long-term overstayers (excluding mainland Chinese) in Taiwan as of January 1990. According to the list, there were 19,000 Malaysians, 9,000 Filipinos, 6,000 Thais, 5,000 Indonesians, with these four countries making up 70% of the total. Most of these undocumented workers were employed in the manufacturing, construction, and household maid industries (Ministry of Labor m, pp. 516–517).

In addition, it is said that several thousand people from mainland China were in Taiwan despite the government's policy of not accepting such people. They came into Taiwan either by getting passports in Southeast Asian countries or by being smuggled into the country (see Liu, *Nikkei Shimbun*, 30 October 1989). In March 1989, a major problem erupted when fishing boats loaded with Chinese from Fujian Province began to land in Taiwan, but the government was, through intensive patrolling, able to stem this tide (*Mainichi Shimbun*, 4 September 1989).

(d) South Korea

In South Korea, like in other NIEs countries, foreign workers have begun to have a presence, and as of 1989 it was believed that there were roughly 20,000 undocumented workers there (*Pusang Ilbo*, 22 May 1989). Other sources, however, put this figure closer to just 5,000 (*Nikkei Shimbun*, 31 December 1989). During the period between January and October 1990, 945 were apprehended as undocumented workers, more than twice the number for the entire previous year. Of these workers, 39% were Filipinos, 14% were Pakistanis, and 4% were Bangladeshis. Most were employed in 'unskilled' jobs (*Asahi Shimbun*, 26 November 1990). In addition, beginning with the mining industry (*Asahi Shimbun*, 7 March 1990), firms were given permission to hire foreign workers as long as they did not make up more than 1% of their Korean labor force (*Bangkok Post*, 14 September 1991). Also, more than 50,000 Chinese of Korean descent entered the country in 1991, and it is said that more than half became overstayers (Ministry of Labor m, p. 513).

(e) Malaysia

Malaysia has traditionally relied on foreign laborers to work in its plantations, but in the 1970's the plantations began to use overseas contract workers (OCWs) hired through the services of employment agencies. There was a major influx of both legal and undocumented workers, most from Indonesia, followed by Thailand, Myanmar, Sri Lanka, the Philippines, Cambodia, and Bangladesh. As of 1987, some 285,000 workers were employed in these plantations, but there was still a serious labor shortage.

As we mentioned in the previous section, a large number of Indonesians have come to Malaysia to work as undocumented workers in the plantation, construction, and informal sectors. Estimates of their number range widely from 200,000 to up to a million. It is also said that almost all of the country's 35,000 construction workers are Indonesians. In addition, there were some 7,000 foreign domestic helpers in the country as of 1989, the majority of them Filipinas (Sasaki, News 16). Kuwabara has estimated that there were 100,000–250,000 Filipinos, and 200,000–400,000 Indonesian workers (including families) in the country (Kuwabara, p. 70).

Malaysia has developed measures to provide amnesties to undocumented foreign workers. In August 1988, the state of Sabah instituted a program through which undocumented workers who surfaced within a set period would be able, after returning to their home countries, to come back to Malaysia without any punishment if they received a valid visa document. The deadline was extended several times, and by the end of February 1989, 61,000 people had taken advantage of the offer. On the peninsula, the government offered a program in January 1989 in which employers merely had to register their workers to receive labor permits, but because of stipulations that, for instance, the employers would have to bear the cost of repatriating the workers, only 30,000 people were eventually registered (Sasaki, News #15, #16).

Furthermore, the Malaysian government announced that starting in January 1992, it would permit undocumented workers in the plantation, construction, and domestic help sectors to legally stay in the country for a maximum period of five years, provided that the employer paid a special tax (*Bangkok Post*, 14 September 1991).

(f) Brunei

In closing this section, we would like to make some mention of Brunei, which is a special case among host countries. Brunei, which gained independence in 1984, is a small country at the northern tip of Sumatra, with a population of just 250,000, but its vast oil and natural gas resources have made it extremely rich.

In addition to the country's Chinese immigrant permanent residents, there were as of 1986 a total of 34,000 foreign workers, making up 36% of the total labor population. Foreigners made up 65% of the workforce in agriculture, forestry, and fisheries, 75% of service workers, and, incredibly, more than 90% of the construction workforce. There are no employment agencies. Companies that require workers apply to the Ministry of Justice for an 'allotment,' and hire the workers themselves. Workers are permitted to stay for a period of two or three years; the visa is renewable, but they must return home to receive an extension. These workers come from such places as Malaysia, Indonesia, and the Philippines (Sasaki, News #18).

In this way, some Asian countries such as Malaysia, as well as Taiwan and Korea, are in a step-wise migration phase, as they continue to export labor but at the same time are accepting foreign workers.

4 Latin America

The deep economic crisis facing the countries of Latin America has been the main factor behind the large influx of Nikkeijin coming to work in Japan. Many of their home countries have experienced 4-digit inflation rates.

In Brazil, inflation stood at 366.0% in 1987, at 933.6% in 1988, and reached a disastrous 1,764.9% in 1989. GDP growth, by contrast, fell from 3.6% in 1987 to minus 0.3% in 1988, and grew again at a slow rate of 3.6% in 1989. Per capita income growth was 1.4% in 1987, but fell to –2.3% the following year. Furthermore, the country's foreign debt reached $112 billion, and domestic debt amounted to nearly 40% of GDP. This situation deteriorated even further in March 1990, when the new president Fernando Collor abrubtly cut the money supply by one-third. The economy stagnated and unemployment began to soar (Akagi). By the end of 1990, there were 850,000 unemployed people within the city of Sao Paolo, and the national unemployment rate stood at a high level of 29%. About 70 million people, or half the population, faced malnutrition (*Nikkei Shimbun*, 18 November 1990). The low-income segments of the Nikkei population were hit especially hard (Akagi).

As of 1991, there were at least 630,000 Brazilians working overseas in the core capitalist countries, with roughly 330,000 in the United States, 150,000 in Japan, and the rest distributed throughout Western Europe (Watanabe and Mitsuyama, pp. 10–).

At present a significant portion of the Nikkei population is working overseas. There are two major estimates of the Nikkei population in Brazil, one placing the figure somewhere over 500,000, and the other placing it at over 1,200,000. The former, based on documents from the Immigration Department of the Ministry of Foreign Affairs' Consular Section, counted the number in 1986 of first generation Nikkeijin who had taken Brazilian citizenship, as well as second, third, and higher-generation Nikkeijin, and found that there were 520,000 such people. In addition, it found that as of 1989 there were approximately 109,000 Japanese citizens living in that country (Ministry of Foreign Affairs a). In contrast to these estimates, a survey of the population of Nikkeijin in Brazil conducted by the Japan-Brazil Cultural Study Center found that, as of 1988, there were roughly 1,280,000 people in Brazil with some Japanese blood (Japan-Brazil Cultural Study Center a). Thus, the number of Nikkei Brazilians working overseas would be a little less than 20% according to the first estimate, and 10% according to the second.

Other Latin American countries with a significant Nikkei population include Peru, with approximately 80,000, Argentina with 30,000, Bolivia with 6,000, and Paraguay with 7,000 (JICA, p. 69). It is thus clear that the number of Nikkeijin from Peru and Argentina who are working in Japan make up significant amounts of those populations.

We can thus see that the ability of these communities to provide labor power in Japan has already reached a limit. According to the Japanese consulate in Sao Paolo, it is unlikely that more than another 100,000 Nikkeijin will seek to go to Japan. One major employment broker is quoted as saying that, 'All the young and energetic people have already gone to Japan. The only job left for us now is to comb the countryside' (*Asahi Shimbun*, 2 August 1990). Recently, even college-educated people and middle-level managers have rushed to find work abroad (*Nikkei Shimbun*, 7 September 1990).

One of the results of the rapid development of this mass migration has been to place a question mark in front of the very existence of the Nikkei communities which once existed in those countries. There have been numerous examples of farming communities losing the ability to conduct the athletic meets and festivals that had earlier become established custom (*Nikkei Shimbun*, 4 April 1990). Many Japanese language schools have also been forced to close because of teachers going to work in Japan (Akagi). One powerful Nikkeijin-run bank in Sao Paolo was seriously hindered in its ability to conduct business when nearly 300 of its employees went to Japan (*Nikkei Shimbun*, 7 September 1990).

In the following few paragraphs, we will introduce the results of an interview survey we conducted in a farming area in the suburbs of Sao Paolo. Moji das Cruzes is a suburban farming village some 50 kilometers east of the city, and it has roughly 4,000 or 5,000 Nikkei families. One of the settlements, District A, had 68 families, with approximately 350 people, practically all of them engaged in farming.

We were told that the first person to go work in Japan had left three years earlier, but had not told anybody and when he returned the neighbors did not even realize what had happened. In recent years this situation had changed, though, and because of the popularity of it people who did not go were asked, half in jest, questions like, 'Are you sick?' or 'Are you a coward?'. At the time we were there, 39 people from 16 families were in Japan. This number included seven heads of household, five mothers, and five young couples.

Many of the people who went to work in Japan were having financial difficulties on their farms, and in recent years many people went repeatedly. We asked several former migrant workers or families of current migrant workers why they had gone, and the answers including such hopes as renovating their houses and getting the money to send their children to school. Some of the young people said they wanted to see Japan, and some of the first generation people said they wanted to go back there while they were alive. Incidentally, many of the people who have gone to Japan from the area have been students.

Eventually, police began to focus their attention on the booming employment agencies. The Brazilian federal police conducted two sweeps, in November and December 1990, against Nikkeijin-owned travel and employment agencies. The November raids were based on the suspicion that the agencies were providing employment assistance to migrant workers without the permission of the Ministry of Labor, and that this was illegal (Fujisaki, pp. 136–139). There are opinions, however, that under the Brazilian penal code it is not illegal to give assistance to people migrating permanently or to give assistance when the person made the choice to migrate independently (Yamashita, p. 188).

The December campaign went beyond the mere question of violations of laws such as the Labor Dispatch Law. It is said that behind the raids was a campaign conducted by one radio station emphasizing that 'limiting recruitment for migrant labor to just Nikkeijin amounts to racial discrimination,' and that such discrimination was prohibited under the Brazilian constitution (Fujisaki, pp. 234–236).

We discussed the Brazilian labor brokers earlier in Chapter 1–1, and we should also mention that in Peru there exists a species of malicious, mainly Nikkeijin brokers. For a sum of $5,000, these people prepare forged documents to get false Nikkeijin into Japan, but in many cases the victims have been caught when they tried to convert their visas to permanent residencies (*Chunichi Shimbun*, 27 May 1992).

We will now briefly review what we learned in this chapter. The migrant workers come principally from Third World countries, and these countries are suffering under deteriorating economic conditions. Concretely speaking, balance of payments crises have led to increasing foreign debt burdens, and this process has been accompanied by growing populations of unemployed people.

Labor exports have become an inescapable part of Asian countries' economic structures, since they constitute an effective way of coping with this situation. Many of these countries in fact could not survive without their exports of migrant labor. The development of this structure was triggered, principally, by the labor exports to the Middle East during the oil shock period. In addition, the NIEs countries of Asia have all become acceptors of foreign labor, and this has added a complicating factor to the problem of foreign workers.

Migrant labor to Japan from Latin America has mostly consisted of Nikkeijin. Two issues that have arisen from this are first, the destruction of the Nikkei communities in Latin America, and two, the mounting criticism that only allowing Nikkeijin to work in the country constitutes a form of racial discrimination.

5 Beyond the Closed Door/Open Door Debate

1 The Closed Door/Open Door Debate

There has already been a great deal of debate in Japan on the subject of foreign workers. On May 12 and 13, 1989, the NHK (Japan Broadcasting Corporation) television network ran a two-part program entitled 'Explosive Debate on Foreign Workers: Should We Open or Close the Door?' and this program was greeted with strong reactions. At that time, thus, foreign workers had already become an issue of national debate. Nevertheless, the debate, until now, as demonstrated by the title of the program, has largely been divided into support for either an open or closed door policy.

The main point stressed by proponents of the closed door policy is the idea, based on the Western European experience, that the acceptance of foreign workers brings intractable problems to the societies in the host countries, and that measures must be taken soon, in the early stages of the process, to prevent the influx of workers into the country.

In the Western countries, migrant workers were incorporated into the lowest layers of society, and problems such as unemployment, school truancy, juvenile delinquency, and city ghettoization concentrated here. In addition, these groups became the scapegoats for the West's relative fall in the world, and thus became targets of convenience for right-wing groups.

Proponents of this view argue not only that the same situation will inevitably occur in Japan, but also warn that the influx of foreign workers may pose a threat to the purity of Japanese culture (see Nishio for a representative articulation of this view).

The proponents of an open door policy can generally be divided into two major strands, although there are also those (see Ishikawa, for instance) who argue that it is precisely their policy which can refine the country's culture.

The first of these strands argues that in order for Japan to fulfill its responsibilities in an era of internationalization it is important not only to liberalize exchanges of goods and money, but also the flow of people. They base their assertions on the fact that other countries have expectations that Japan will carry out this policy.

The second strand emerges from the more practical needs of the business community. In recent years the Japanese economy has experienced worsening labor shortages in specific fields, and businesses reaching the limits of rationalization have seen the introduction of foreign workers as a way of mitigating the problem.

The shared government view on the issue can be seen in the May 1988 Five Year Economic Plan, which was adopted by the Cabinet, and which stated that 'For the moment, our position is that foreigners with specialist techniques or skills should, in as far as possible, be allowed into the country' (Economic Planning Agency b, p. 29). In June of the same year, the Employment Measures Basic Plan, which was also passed by the Cabinet, stated that, 'As far as so-called unskilled laborers are concerned, this problem should be dealt with using appropriate prudence' (Ministry of Labor d, p. 22). At the Cabinet Forum on the Problem of Foreign Workers, which first met in December 1989, many of the opinions expressed looked favorably at the possibility of admitting trainees, but were very cautious on the idea of allowing unskilled workers.

In December 1992, however, the Provisional Council for the Promotion of Administrative Reform released a report entitled 'Second Report on Administrative Reform, Promoting Internationalization and Improving Quality of Life,' which recommended cracking down on employment agencies and employers who were benefiting unlawfully from foreign labor. To accomplish this, it suggested more strictly enforcing the laws against promoting illegal labor. It also recommended replacing the current trainee system with a new 'Technical On-the-Job Training System' to provide skills and techniques useful both to the trainees back in their home countries and to their home countries' socio-economic development. Under this new proposal, a skill assessment would be conducted at the end of the training period, and those reaching certain standards would be given permission to do on-the-job training for a set period (Provisional Council for the Promotion of Administrative Reform).

In response to this report, the Cabinet passed a resolution in December ordering the strengthening of controls against promoting illegal labor, and proposing the possibility of establishing a new system for training. Essentially, the government itself, under the guise of 'training' and 'on-the-job training,' began little by little to open the country's doors to foreign labor.

There have been debates on this issue within the different ministries and agencies, but the well-known territorial disputes between different groups have thrown the process into confusion. There are, however, two major sides: the Ministry of Justice, which is responsible for immigration policy, and the Ministry of Labor have tended to support the closed door policy; whereas the Ministry of Foreign Affairs and a few other agencies have tended toward the open door policy.

We will now examine these different opinions in slightly more detail, beginning with the Ministry of Justice, through a report released in March 1989 by its 'Committee to Consider the Issue of Entry by Foreign Workers' (Chairman: Shozaburo Kimura, Professor at Tokyo University) (Ministry of Justice h). On the issue of unskilled laborers, the report pointed out that there was not yet a national consensus on the subject, and that, in addition, the opinions expressed at the committee were divided. The majority believed that unskilled workers would have to be gradually accepted, though conditionally, but there were strong counter opinions as well.

In May 1992, the Ministry released its 'Basic Plan on Immigration Control,' which upheld the previous line, though it did make concessions to the report of the Administrative Reform Council and the Cabinet decisions by recommending urgent deliberations on the feasibility of establishing a system to allow trainees to work under the same conditions as Japanese workers for a set period of time following the completion of their training (*Kokusai Jinryu*, May 1992, p. 32).

At the Ministry of Labor, the Study Group on Foreign Workers' Affairs (Chairman: Kazuo Koike, Director of the Kyoto University Research Institute of Economics) issued a report in March 1988 which represented the first voice from that ministry on this issue (Ministry of Labor c). The report recommended the adoption of positive measures to allow foreigners to work in professional and technical occupations as well as in administrative posts, but supported the continuation of the previous government policy of not allowing unskilled workers. In fact, the group worked out a policy to strengthen their expulsion.

The main feature of interest in this report was its recommendation for setting up an 'employment permit system.' Under this proposal, firms wanting to employ foreign workers would have to apply for a permit (with a time limit) beforehand, and firms neglecting to do so would face punitive sanctions.

The Ministry of Labor's Conference for Research on Foreign Workers' Affairs (Chairman: Jiro Enjoji, Advisor to the Nihon Keizai Shimbun, Inc., a leading economic newspaper company) released an opinion paper in December 1988 (Ministry of Labor e) which also generally adhered to this basic policy. Because of strong opposition from the Ministry of Justice and the business world, however, the idea of an employment permit system was effectively deferred.

In addition, the Ministry of Labor has plans to introduce a 'reporting system on employment of foreigners,' under which the ministry would, starting in FY1993, require employers to submit an annual report on working conditions at their workplaces (*Nikkei Shimbun*, 7 August 1992). It is believed that this idea derives from the same idea as the employment permit system.

Another body within the Ministry of Labor, the Employment Stability Bureau chief's private advisory committee known as the Study Committee on Effects of Foreign Workers on the Labor Market (Chairman: Koichiro Yamaguchi, Professor at Sophia University), issued a report in January 1991 finding that the acceptance of foreign workers not only did not have any positive effect on economic development and employment creation in the developing countries, but that even when the workers were accepted in labor shortage-plagued occupational fields, they tended to move to other areas with better working conditions, and in addition incurred large social costs in such diverse areas as education, job training, housing, and health and welfare. As a whole, the document saw the possibility of accepting workers in very negative terms (Ministry of Labor k).

In June 1992, a panel of experts from this same study group released a report calculating projected revenue increases to both national and local governments from taxes and social security payments from foreign workers, and compared these to projected costs incurred by these bodies for administrative costs and social welfare benefits. They found that the costs would far outweigh the revenues. The group made its calculations on the assumption that 500,000 workers would enter the country, and compared the revenues and costs for a series of periods: in the first, the migrant workers would live alone; in the second, they would live along with their spouses; and in the third, they would have one child of school age each. The group found that the costs would outweigh the benefits by ¥246.0 billion, ¥341.4 billion, and ¥4,114.5 billion in the different periods, adding up to a net loss of ¥4,209.9 billion. Because of these huge projected costs, the report gave a very cautious appraisal of the prospects of accepting unskilled foreign workers (Ministry of Labor n).

In March 1992, the International Labor Section of the Labor Ministry's secretariat issued a *1992 White Paper on Overseas Labor*, finding that migrant labor did not necessarily alleviate unemployment in the countries of origin, that it aggravated gaps between migrant workers and other people in those countries, and that it had a detrimental effect on the family lives of the workers. The report cited demerits in the host countries as well: labor productivity improvements become precarious, the labor market was stratified, wage rises were slowed, and social costs were increased (Ministry of Labor m).

As we have seen, thus, the Ministry of Labor has generally taken the closed door side of the issue, but in the summer of 1992 it finally, on the basis of the Provisional Council report and the cabinet decision, firmed up a policy of creating a 'technical intern training program' and accepted the idea of a partial opening. Incidentally, the Ministry of Construction is unequivocably opposed to any participation by unskilled foreign workers in the construction labor market.

Turning to the agencies that have tended to take the open door side, the Ministry of Foreign Affairs (MFA) has proposed that Japan as an economic superpower has certain responsibilities it must bear, and that some consideration needs to be given to the possibility of opening the country to unskilled labor. The MFA has also made proposals that trainees be accepted under bilateral agreements according to which the trainees would receive wages and be covered by labor laws and ordinances (*Nikkei Shimbun*, 19 May 1989). It also established a Foreigners Section in May 1989 to take charge of the problem of human rights violations against foreigners in Japan. The Ministry of Agriculture, Forestry and Fisheries and the Ministry of Transportation have also shown positive attitudes toward the acceptance of foreign workers as a means of regaining Japanese competitiveness in deep-sea fishing and international merchant shipping.

The first government agency to give approval to the idea of accepting unskilled foreign workers, though indirectly, was the Economic Planning Agency (EPA). In April 1989, the EPA Study and Research Committee on the Effects of International Movements of Labor Power on Local Labor Markets (Chairman: Haruo Shimada, Professor at Keio University) issued a report (Economic Planning Agency c) setting out the four following relatively feasible choices for future policy: 1) a laissez-faire system; 2) a closed door policy; 3) a controlled flow of migrant labor; or 4) the promotion of integration.

The system envisaged in the 'controlled flow' model is the acceptance of workers, but coupled with the creation of a government agency to supervise the process, and the exertion of thorough-going control in terms of numbers, periods of stay, and occupational fields. The 'integration' model envisages a system under which foreigners are not subjected to isolation or discrimination, but are accepted as members of the overall community, though it does not imply their 'Japanization.'

The report found that as a fundamental long-term strategy the integration model would be most appropriate, but that it was necessary to consider using the controlled flow model as a temporary emergency measure.

Turning next to the Ministry of International Trade and Industry (MITI), we find that in May 1990 a report was released by the Forum on Industrial Labor Problems (Chairman: Fukutaro Watanabe, Professor at Gakushuin University), a private advisory group to the ministry's Industrial Policy Section chief (Ministry of International Trade and Industry b), which found that an increase in the presence of undocumented workers in the country would slow the process of rationalization in labor-intensive industries and have a negative effect on the employment conditions of workers in the country. As a result, it recommended stiffening penalties against employers of undocumented workers. In addition, it recommended increasing the number of trainees to some 50,000 per year, and giving more opportunities for medium- and small-sized businesses to take advantage of the program.

The positions of the different government agencies outlined above may differ in nuance, but they are united in their opposition, in principle, to allowing the entrance of unskilled workers. We must qualify this, however, by pointing out that there is a general consensus among the agencies on the partial opening, which we mentioned earlier, represented by the admission of large numbers of Nikkeijin workers and by the introduction of the trainee status.

We will now turn to the business world. Of the four major business organizations, Nikkeiren (the Japan Federation of Employers' Associations) alone has taken up the government's unified position and shown a cautious attitude toward the acceptance of unskilled workers. Up to about the fall of 1988, however, it is fair to say that this position was generally shared among the different organizations.

The Business Policy Forum Japan (*Kigyo Katsuryoku Kenkyujo*), for instance, a group made up of representatives from electrical power, steel, and electrical appliance manufacturers, issued a proposal in July 1988 not to accept, at least in the short run, unskilled laborers into their businesses (Business Policy Forum Japan). Similarly, the Kansai Employers' Association (*Kansai Keieisha Kyokai*) released a proposal in July 1988 stating that, 'There should be no change to the present policy of not admitting unskilled laborers into the country' (Kansai Employers' Association a). This policy was maintained in a September 1989 report released by the same organization (Kansai Employers' Association b).

In addition, a mid-term opinion paper on the acceptance of foreign workers released by the Tokyo Chamber of Commerce and Industry (*Tokyo Shoko Kaigisho*) in September 1988 recommended a much larger acceptance of people with specialist expertize, skills or knowledge, but decided to continue to deliberate, cautiously, on the question of whether or not to accept unskilled workers (Tokyo Chamber of Commerce and Industry a).

Eventually, however, voices nearer to the open door policy side of the argument began to emerge. In December 1988, the National Committee for Developing Economic Foundations for the 21st Century (*21-Seiki Keizai Kiban Kaihatsu Kokumin Kaigi*), (Chairman: Mikio Sumiya, Professor Emeritus at Tokyo University), a private think-tank, issued a proposal that the acceptance of foreign workers not be limited to people with specialist skills or knowledge, but that unskilled workers be accepted in a positive way as well. The major reasons given for this proposal were both the necessity to respond to the growing requests, especially among Asian countries, for Japan to open its doors, as well as estimates that Japan would have a labor shortage of some 2.7 million workers by the year 2000 (National Committee for Developing Economic Foundations for the 21st Century).

In January 1989, the Kansai Association of Corporate Executives (*Kansai Keizai Doyukai*) became the first business association to make a proposal that foreign workers without specialist skills or knowledge be, with certain conditions, admitted into the country. Specifically, it proposed the establishment of a 'dispatch center' which would hold a monopoly on the dispatch of foreign workers to prospective employers, and, in addition, a condition that the workers would be repatriated at the end of their work period. The dispatch center would be given responsibility for ensuring that the treatment given to foreign workers was at least on par with that of their Japanese counterparts (Kansai Association of Corporate Executives).

The year 1990 marked the beginning of a series of calls for the acceptance of unskilled workers. First, an April 1990 report by the Kansai Economic Federation (*Kansai Keizai Rengokai*) called, as a concrete program to implement the entrance of unskilled workers, for the establishment of a labor licensing system to allow entry within limited occupations, localities, and periods of stay (Kansai Economic Federation). In May 1990, the Japan Food Service Association, a business association of restaurants, compiled a proposal that up to 600,000 foreigners, making up 1% of the labor population, be allowed to work in the country provided they were single and were rotated every two or three years (Japan Food Service Association).

At the same time, the business world was giving increasing importance to amending the trainee system in order to accept workers. We earlier introduced the position taken by Nikkeiren, and will now consider the attitudes of the three other major business organizations. The Japan Association of Corporate Executives (*Keizai Doyukai*), an extremely powerful group, suggested in March 1989 that the an 'on-the-job apprentice program system' be established as a way to admit unskilled workers. Specifically, it proposed a system through which the workers would study Japanese in their home countries, then be introduced by a coordinating organization to a business firm where they would work as apprentices, and then after one or two years would be sent back to their home countries (Japan Association of Corporate Executives a).

The same association released a second report in June 1992, reaffirming this plan and proposing the creation of a 'new apprenticeship program' and an 'international rotation system.' According this plan, the 'apprenticeship' system would be established in addition to the current 'trainee' status, and workers in this plan would receive wages and be covered by labor laws. Classroom education would take up just one to three months of the program, with the rest being spent on on-the-job training. Moreover, a 'reserve fund' system (where the workers would receive their payments upon return to their home countries) would be created to ensure their return. Japan would create an international rotation organization, and the home countries would organize Japan centers (Japan Association of Corporate Executives c).

Keidanren (Federation of Economic Organizations) released a proposal in May 1992 opposing the current state of affairs in which the issue of undocumented unskilled workers was effectively being left untouched, and proposing the creation of a new trainee-accepting system which would serve to transfer technology in a smooth way (Federation of Economic Organizations).

If we turn to the Japan Chamber of Commerce and Industry (*Nihon Shoko Kaigisho*), we find that one of its regional organizations, the Tokyo Chamber of Commerce and Industry, called in December 1989 for the creation of a 'foreign worker skill formation program.' Under this proposal, workers would be allowed to work in general labor fields, a new organization would be established to act between the center and the local regions, and on the basis of bilateral agreements workers without families would be accepted to work for a period of up to 24 months (Tokyo Chamber of Commerce and Industry c). The group repeated this proposal in a July 1990 request made to the government (Tokyo Chamber of Commerce and Industry d).

In addition, the Nagoya Chamber of Commerce and Industry, in a July 1990 opinion paper, suggested that foreigners be permitted, after finishing a period of training, to work for a maximum of two two-year periods, and that a government organization be established to take overall responsibility for the training and employment of foreigners (Nagoya Chamber of Commerce and Industry).

The Japan Association of Corporate Executives released a proposal in July 1990 titled 'Living in Harmony with Foreigners,' which suggested making Japan more livable for legal foreign residents (Japan Association of Corporate Executives b). The Tochigi Prefecture Association of Corporate Executives, incidentally, made its own suggestion in November 1989 that foreign workers be allowed to work using trainee status for periods of up to two years, and that this be implemented according to bilateral agreements between the governments (Tochigi Prefecture Association of Corporate Executives).

Thus, many business associations, like the government agencies, have begun calling for the introduction of foreign workers as trainees or on the basis of similar schemes.

Turning to labor unions, we find that the Japanese Trade Union Confederation (RENGO), Japan's largest trade union federation, in its April 1990 'Demands and Recommendations in Areas Related to Policies and Institutions,' suggested that foreigners without specialist skills or knowledge not be accepted, that undocumented workers as well as brokers and employers promoting illegal labor be prosecuted, and that the undocumented workers be deported immediately. This has been the traditional stance of the labor world (Japanese Trade Union Confederation).

In contrast to this, RENGO's Research Institute for Advancement of Living standards (RIALS), a think-tank associated with the confederation, released a report in October 1990 which showed some tendency toward the open door side of the issue. Specifically, it stated that frameworks and rules needed to be drawn up from a mid- and long-term perspective concerning the admission of foreign workers into the labor market, instead of allowing it to open piece by piece and to include illegal workers. The report proposed that consideration be given to creating quotas in both numbers and occupations, establishing an employment permit system, providing social security benefits, and giving voting rights to foreigners in local governments (Rengo's Research Institute for Advancement of Living standards).

The National Federation of Construction Workers' Unions (*Zenken Soren*), which organizes carpenters, masons, and owners of small contractors, has since its regular general assembly in the fall of 1987 been opposed to the acceptance of any foreign workers. The reason for this strong opposition is the fear that the admission of foreigners may further depress wages and working conditions for Japanese workers. Furthermore, in March 1989 the

Japan Confederation of Ship Building and Engineering Workers' Unions (*Zosenjuki Roren*) became possibly the first industrial union to tell its management counterparts that it was opposed to the employment of foreigners as general workers. Thus, the general trend among labor unions has been to take the closed door side of the issue.

In contrast, however, the National Confederation of Trade Unions (*Zenroren*), another national center, has favored the acceptance of foreign workers, albeit with restrictions on numbers (Shinano Mainichi Shimbun b, p. 51). Furthermore, the National Union of General Workers (*Ippan Roso*), which is made up of workers in small- and medium-sized enterprises, became in January 1992 the first Rengo-affiliated union to support the conditional acceptance of unskilled workers (*Yomiuri Shimbun*, 13 March 1992). The National Machinery and Metal Workers' Union of Japan (*Zenkinzoku*) also came out in favor of agreement standards which would allow the acceptance of foreign workers (*Asahi Shimbun*, 19 February 1992).

In June 1990, the Social and Economic Congress of Japan (*Shakai Keizai Kokumin Kaigi*) (Chairman: Shuzo Inaba), a think-tank, released its 1990 White Paper entitled *The Situation of the Labor Shortage and the Problem of Foreign Workers*, emphasizing that efforts needed to be made to promote employment for women and older people, and that it was inappropriate to open an easy path for foreign workers to enter Japan (Social and Economic Congress of Japan).

In closing this section we will take a brief look at the position of the different political parties. The Liberal Democratic Party (LDP)'s Special Committee on the Problem of Foreign Workers has veered toward the open door side of the debate by considering the question of accepting unskilled foreign workers (*Nikkei Shimbun*, 8 February 1992). The Komei Party, for its part, became the first party to come out clearly in favor of the acceptance of foreign workers (*Nikkei Shimbun*, 24 August 1992). As far as the Social Democratic Party of Japan (SDPJ) is concerned, it is difficult to find any unified position at all. The positions of other parties include the Democratic Socialist Party (DSP)'s calls for 'strict punishment for illegal labor and an enlargement of the trainee framework,' and the Japan Communist Party's calls for 'the preparation of treaties to allow a principled acceptance of unskilled workers' (*Asahi Shimbun*, 2 February 1990).

2 Trends in Public Opinion

We will now look at the question of how the general public in Japan sees the issue of foreign workers. We will attempt to look at the various public opinion polls that have been conducted, and will use their results to formulate an outline of trends in public opinion. First, we will look at the four following large-scale surveys which took the entire Japanese nation as their universe populations: one by the Economic Planning Agency (EPA), two by the Prime Minister's Office, and one by *Asahi Shimbun*, comparing and analyzing their results.

The EPA's survey was conducted by mail in October 1987, with 3,000 people of at least 20 years of age as subjects. It attained a response rate of 27.9% (Economic Planning Agency a).

The first survey conducted by the Prime Minister's Office was done in February 1988, with questions directed to 10,000 people of at least 20 years of age, with a response rate of 76.5% (Prime Minister's Office a). The second was conducted in November to December 1990 according to the same method, but with 5,000 subjects, and with a response rate of 78.6% (Prime Minister's Office b).

The *Asahi Shimbun* survey was carried out in October 1989, by interview, on 3,000 eligible voters, with a response rate of 79% (*Asahi Shimbun*, 6 November 1989).

First, we will examine trends in people's attitudes on the basic question of whether or not to allow foreign workers into Japan. In the EPA survey, 63% of respondents said they favored the acceptance of foreign workers in general (not limited to unskilled laborers) with 'some conditions,' 11.0% said they favored the acceptance with 'no restrictions,' 4.8% were opposed under any circumstances, and 21.2% of responses were either 'undecided' or the response was unclear. In other words, three-fourths of respondents were in favor of some acceptance.

Respondents who indicated that they supported acceptance with 'some conditions,' however, gave the following occupations as areas in which they thought foreign workers should be permitted to work (with multiple responses permitted): 4.4% said 'unskilled manual labor,' and 23.9% said, 'any occupation,' showing that there was still a relatively negative attitude toward permitting the entrance of unskilled workers.

In the first Prime Minister's Office survey, 51.9% of respondents said that 'unskilled laborers should be allowed to work within certain restrictions,' 24.2% said, 'the present policy of not permitting unskilled laborers to work should be maintained,' and 23.8% answered, 'undecided,' indicating that half of the respondents favored acceptance. In the second survey, however, the number of people responding 'unskilled laborers should be allowed to work within certain restrictions' rose to 56.5%, with 14.9% answering that 'they should be allowed to work as Japanese, without any special limitations,' 14.1% that 'the present policy of not permitting unskilled laborers to work should be maintained,' and 14.4%, 'other or undecided,' indicating that more than 70% favored acceptance.

In the *Asahi Shimbun* survey, 56% of respondents, when asked about future policy toward unskilled laborers, responded that 'they should be accepted with conditions,' 33% said, 'the policy of not accepting them should be continued,' and 11% answered, 'other or undecided.'

These surveys show that the percentage of people favoring acceptance is somewhere between 50% and 70%, and that in recent years the number of people giving answers such as 'undecided' has decreased.

Next, we will examine popular attitudes toward undocumented workers. The first survey, conducted by the EPA, did not include any questions on this subject. In the Prime Minister's Office surveys, the respondents were asked about appropriate responses to undocumented workers, and they gave the following answers (for the first, then second, survey): 'They should only be prosecuted heavily in cases when they are working with organized crime, prostitution, or in other malicious undertakings,' 40.7% and 40.6%; 'In as far as they are acting illegally they should be deported in accordance with the law,' 37.0% and 33.6%; and, 'Japan is suffering from a labor shortage, and they should not be prosecuted if they are working in fields where there is a shortage,' 7.3% and 11.4%. This shows that between the two surveys there was a relative decrease in support for deportation and an increase in support for a laissez-faire policy.

In the *Asahi Shimbun* survey, 45% of respondents said that 'the law should be changed to allow undocumented workers to work legally,' 34% said, 'undocumented workers should be firmly persecuted according to the law,' 16% said, 'the problem should be overlooked if they are not involved in malicious activities,' and 10% responded 'other or undecided.' Again, more people supported legalization than did expulsion.

The *Asahi Shimbun* and Prime Minister's Office surveys show, similarly, that roughly half of the population is willing to let undocumented workers stay in the country, and that roughly one-third is in favor of strict prosecution to stop them.

In addition, the *Asahi Shimbun* survey provided data on the correlation between views on the acceptance of foreign workers and attitudes toward undocumented workers. The results showed that only 36% of all respondents were supporters of both the acceptance of foreign workers and the legalization of undocumented workers, and just 21% were opponents of both acceptance and of legalization, meaning that there was not a necessary connection between the two. Many Japanese see these two problems as separate issues.

The Prime Minister's Office surveys queried respondents about their thoughts on the increasing number of undocumented workers. In response, 45.4% in the first, and 55.0% in the second, answered, 'It is not a good thing, but it cannot be helped,' 39.0% in the first and 32.1% in the second answered, 'It is not a good thing,' with 15.2% in the first and 13.0% in the second giving the answer of 'other or undecided.' Thus, the number of people responding that it could not be helped increased between the two surveys and became a majority opinion.

In the EPA survey, respondents were asked to indicate whether or not they agreed with four statements. For the first, 'I am concerned that employment opportunities will be taken away from Japanese citizens,' 41.2% agreed, answering either, 'I completely agree,' or 'I somewhat agree.' For the second statement, 'Public safety will be worsened by the presence of foreign workers,' the figure was 40.7%; for the third, 'The presence of foreign workers will add dynamism to Japanese society,' 26.2%; and for the last, 'It is Japan's duty to accept workers from developing countries,' it was 23.1%.

In the Prime Minister's Office survey, respondents were asked their reasons for choosing either 'It is no good' or 'It cannot be helped' in reference to the presence of undocumented workers. The five highest reasons given in the first survey were (with multiple responses allowed) 'The earnings of these workers will allow their families to live,' 'Their human rights will be violated as they are forced into jobs such as prostitution, and they will become a hotbed of crime,' 'Public security and the social climate will worsen,' 'Those people consent to come and work,' and 'It is only natural for people to come here in search of higher wages.' In the second survey, the five highest responses were, 'The earnings of these workers will allow their families to live,' 'Their activities are in violation of Japanese law,' 'Their work helps to relieve the labor shortage for Japanese companies,' and 'Public security and the social climate will worsen.' The second survey showed much more concern for two issues – illegality and the labor shortage – than did the first.

In the *Asahi Shimbun* survey, when respondents were asked what they thought about foreign workers, 29% responded 'They help to relieve the labor shortage,' 16% that 'They provide inexpensive labor power,' 14% that 'It is the responsibility of developed countries to accept them,' 13% that 'They ruin public security and the social climate,' 12% that 'We are forcing them to perform disagreeable work,' and 16% that 'They are pulling down the wages and working conditions of Japanese workers,' with 10% responding 'other or undecided.' The major awareness seemed to focus on the labor shortage and the contributions that foreign workers could make to alleviating the problem.

In summary of these surveys, we can say first of all that all show a certain level of fear of crime and of the deterioration of public security and the social climate. In the second Prime Minister's Office survey, also, 47.9% of respondents agreed with the statement that, 'Their work helps to relieve the labor shortage for Japanese companies,' and a similar 45% in the *Asahi Shimbun* survey responded either that 'They help to relieve the labor shortage' or 'They provide inexpensive labor power.' Both the EPA and *Asahi Shimbun* surveys also both showed deep-rooted support for the idea of an 'obligation to accept workers.'

Next, we will look at the conditions Japanese would like to place on the acceptance of foreign workers. In the Prime Minister's Office surveys, people who had answered that, 'Unskilled workers should be allowed to work within certain conditions' were asked what conditions they would place on this employment. With multiple answers accepted, 43.0% in the first and 48.2% in the second survey responded, 'They should be permitted to remain for a set period, and should not be allowed beyond that period'; 34.8% and 23.4% responded, 'Only responsible bodies such as national and local governments should be permitted to hire them'; 14.7% and 20.1% said, 'Only the workers themselves should be accepted, and they should not be allowed to bring their families'; 17.8% and 17.9% said, 'They should be given permission to work in specified occupations, and should not be permitted to change jobs'; and 10.3% and 7.7% said, 'Limits should be placed according to the nationality of the workers,' with 15.1% and 8.1% responding 'other or undecided.' This shows that there has been increasing support for limits on periods of stay and against bringing families.

In the *Asahi Shimbun* survey, when respondents were asked to select one restriction they wished to place on entry or employment, 27% said, 'The employment period should be restricted,' 25% said, 'There should be restrictions on the companies or government offices at which they are permitted to work,' and 22% said, 'Their numbers should be restricted,' with these three choices each occupying more than 20% of respondents. Other answers included 'No special restrictions need be applied,' with 11%, 'Dependent families should not be permitted to accompany them,' with 5%, and 'Other or undecided,' with 10%. Thus, in all three of these surveys time limits were the top choice. Moreover, the problem of bringing families, which has become a major issue in Western Europe and the United States, does not seem to have yet become a major concern.

Incidentally, the *Asahi Shimbun* survey also asked respondents, 'How would you feel about foreign workers becoming your neighbors?' In response, 47% answered, 'I would want to help them to become accustomed to society,' 20% said, 'I would avoid socializing with them as much as possible,' 11% said, 'I would look at it as a good chance to experience foreign culture,' 10% said, 'I would wish they would move somewhere else,' with 12% responding 'Other or undecided,' meaning that 58% had positive feelings about the possibility, almost double the 30% who had negative feelings.

In the previous paragraphs we compared the results of these four surveys. The strongest impression that emerges is that there is a strong desire among Japanese to treat foreign workers well. The Japanese tend to consider the welfare of the families that the workers have left behind in their home countries, and seem to want to help them if they find themselves as neighbors.

In the period between February and March 1992, the Tokyo Metropolitan Government conducted a 'Public Opinion Survey on Internationalization' on 3,000 people living in the city (conducted by random sampling, by interview, with 2,115 respondents). Of the respondents, 10.2% said, 'It is a good thing that the number of foreign workers is increasing,' 40.8% said, 'I am not concerned one way or the other,' 9.4% said, 'I am upset about it,' with 39.4% responding, 'I do not think it is a very good thing,' meaning that the group with positive feelings, who made up 51.% of the total, slightly outnumbered the 48.9% who had more negative feelings (0.1% gave no answer) (Tokyo Metropolitan Government n). If we contrast this survey to the four nationwide ones mentioned above, we notice that 1) there were practically no non-answers, and 2) that the number of people with positive feelings has fallen so that it is now almost on par with those with negative ones. These results bear close watching as this was a quite recent survey.

A considerable number of surveys have been conducted on the views of businesses and managers regarding the question of foreign workers. In the following paragraphs, we will introduce the results of some of these surveys.

In April 1988, the Tokyo Chamber of Commerce conducted a survey by mail targetting 5,000 of its member firms, and achieved a response rate of 22.6%. In response to a question on the advisability of accepting foreign workers, including unskilled ones, 59.3% of the respondents said, 'Regulations should be relaxed, and larger numbers should be accepted than under current policy,' 36.7% said, 'Current restrictions are appropriate,' and 3.9% said, 'Regulations should be strengthened, and fewer numbers accepted.' Thus, almost 60% of the firms favored a relaxation of regulations. When asked which regulations they thought should be relaxed, 40.6% said that unskilled workers should also be permitted to work (Tokyo Chamber of Commerce b).

The Osaka Chamber of Commerce, for its part, conducted two separate surveys of its membership. The first, in August 1988, involved questionnaires sent out to 2,252 companies with headquarters in Osaka Prefecture, and achieved a response rate of 37.5%. The second, in February 1990, involved questionnaires sent out to 2,762 firms, mostly headquartered in Osaka City, though it included some in either Kyoto Prefecture or Hyogo Prefecture, and achieved a response rate of 33.0%.

In the 1990 survey, the companies were asked what they thought of the increasing number of foreigners including unskilled workers, and the most popular responses were: 'It is acceptable if a system for accepting them is established,' with 36.6%, 'It is inevitable,' with 28.1%, 'The number should be kept as low as possible,' with 18.0%, 'It is a good idea,' with 7.7%, with 9.7% giving, 'Undecided or no answer.' The 1988 survey showed similar results, as nearly 60% of the firms surveyed were hoping for a change in the Immigration Control Act which restricts the number of foreigners.

Of the firms surveyed, 11.1% were employing foreign workers at the time. Of those which were not, 8.9% said 'We want to hire foreign workers immediately,' 5.1% said, 'We would like to hire foreign workers one or two years from now,' 28.5% said, 'We have plans to hire foreign workers in the future,' 28.1% said, 'We do not have such plans,' and 29.4% gave, 'Undecided or no answer.' In the 1988 survey, 30% of the firms gave answers of either 'We want to hire foreign workers immediately' or 'We have plans to hire foreign workers in the future,' showing that there has been a great increase in the number of companies wishing to employ foreigners. This desire was stronger among firms with fewer than 1,000 employees than it was for larger ones, and was strong in manufacturing industries, especially in machinery, metals, textiles and clothing, as well as in the food and service industries (Osaka Chamber of Commerce a, b).

It is thus interesting to note that attitudes toward unskilled labor vary according to industry and to the size of firms. The survey conducted by the Shinagawa Ward Labor Administration Office in Tokyo which we introduced in Chapter 1–2 can provide insights into this phenomenon.

In terms of scale, a high level of 28.4% of the firms with at least 1,000 employees were opposed to the introduction of unskilled laborers, whereas among companies with between 10 and 29 employees 78.0% were in favor – in fact, 23.3% favored their unconditional acceptance. In terms of industry, 20.0% of respondents in the construction, transportation, and communications fields were unconditionally in favor. In some industries, support for conditional acceptance was strong. For instance, 65.9% of respondents in service industries, and 59.4% in the wholesale/ retail and restaurant industry, were in favor of this option. The firms that were most enthusiastic about hiring unskilled workers if they were accepted included those with between 10 and 29 employees, as well as those in the construction, financial and insurance, and manufacturing sectors (Tokyo Metropolitan Government h).

There are also surveys in existence which document the views of small- and medium-sized firms. The Small and Medium Enterprise Agency conducted in December 1988 a 'Fact-Finding Survey on Labor Problems,' and in December 1989 a 'Fact-Finding Survey on Employment Problems.' Small and medium enterprises in this context means corporations capitalized at less than ¥100 million or with fewer than 300 employees, or private companies with fewer than 300 employees (the definition also covers wholesalers capitalized at less than ¥30 million or with fewer than 100 employees, or retail and service businesses capitalized at less than ¥10 million or with fewer than 50 employees).

In the 1988 survey, 56.8% of firms responded that, 'We are not currently employing foreign workers, and do not see the need to do so,' 15.8% said, 'We are not currently employing foreign workers, but feel the need to do so,' 25.6% said, 'We are not currently employing foreign workers, and are not sure whether there is a need,' and 1.9% responded, 'We are currently employing foreign workers.' By the time of the 1989 survey, three of these categories had grown: now 70.2% said, 'We are not currently employing foreign workers, and do not see the need to do so,' 26.8% said, 'We are not currently employing foreign workers, but feel the need to do so,' and 3.2% responded, 'We are currently employing foreign workers.'

It seems that this shift was caused by the fact that one category included in the 1988 list, 'We are not currently employing foreign workers, and are not sure whether there is a need,' was removed from the choices. When asked why they needed foreign workers, the most popular responses were (with multiples responses permitted), 'Because the labor shortage is serious,' with 80.5%, 'Because we can acquire cheap labor,' with 32.6%, and 'Because they are willing to do work that Japanese avoid,' with 28.1% (Small and Medium Enterprise Agency b, Chapter 2–2).

Additional information on smaller companies can be found in a survey released in October 1991 by the National Association of Shinkin Banks. The survey was targetted at 15,000 small- and medium-sized companies who did business with credit unions, and achieved a valid response rate of 96.6%. When asked whether it would be beneficial for the Japanese economy and society to accept foreign workers, 8.2% answered, 'Strongly agree,' 41.9% said, 'Basically agree,' 16.9% said, 'Basically disagree,' 5.0% said, 'Strongly disagree,' with 25.5% answering, 'Undecided.' Thus, more than half of respondents expressed agreement, but there was also a large group who were undecided (National Association of Shinkin Banks).

Another such survey was conducted in October 1988 by the Tokyo Federation of Corporate Taxpayers Associations (*Tokyo Hojinkai Rengokai*), with questionnaires mailed to the management of 700 small- and medium-sized member corporations (capitalized at under ¥100 million) with major offices in the Tokyo metropolitan region (including the Tama region), and with a valid response rate of 53%. Of the respondents, 60.4% said that the acceptance of foreign workers was 'Sometimes inevitable,' a figure almost double the 32.2% who answered that it was 'Not a good thing' (Tokyo Federation of Corporate Taxpayers Associations).

We can get a glimpse of how companies' attitudes are shaped depending on whether or not they employ foreign workers from surveys conducted by the Ministry of Justice. In November 1988, the ministry's Immigration Bureau sent out questionnaires to 1,144 firms selected from among major corporations listed in the First Section of the Tokyo Stock Exchange, and to 1,856 other firms who were employing foreign workers. The Bureau received valid responses from 624 of the major corporations, and from 1,270 of the other firms. Of the major companies, 75.5% had at least 1,000 employees, whereas 69.8% of the firms using foreign workers had less than 500 workers.

If we look at the results for the First Section firms, we find that 45.4% were either enthusiastic about the introduction of foreign workers or were willing to support a conditional acceptance, but that they were slightly overshadowed by the 50.0% who opposed the introduction. For the companies which were employing foreign workers, however, 50.7% of the managers found themselves in the open-door category, and although the difference is not striking the percentages were reversed compared to the former group.

In addition, when asked about appropriate punishments for employers using undocumented workers, 18.3% of the respondents in the First Section category stated that, 'They should be strictly prosecuted,' 69.4% that, 'We must take circumstances into account, but those involved in malicious hiring must be punished directly,' 7.7% that 'It is enough to prosecute them as abetting violations of the Immigration Act when overstayers or people working without authorization are found, as is currently done,' 1.5% that 'There is no particular need to prosecute,' with 9.5% not answering. Surprisingly, almost 90% of the respondents favored harsher punishment.

In contrast, a mere 25.2% of firms employing foreign workers said, 'They should be strictly prosecuted,' whereas 53.9% said that, 'We must take circumstances into account, but those involved in malicious hiring must be punished directly,' accounting for just under 80% of the total, a much lower figure than that given by the First Section firms (Ministry of Justice g).

In terms of restaurants, the Japan Food Service Association conducted a survey of its members in September 1989, and received 182 responses. Of the respondents, 15.9% said, 'Foreign workers should be introduced with enthusiasm,' 59.3% said 'They should be accepted, but with conditions,' meaning that three-fourths of these firms were supportive of acceptance (Japan Food Service Association).

In terms of attitudes on the acceptance of trainees, we can refer to the Ministry of Labor survey which we introduced in Chapter 1–2. When asked about the acceptance of publicly-sponsored trainees, 64.1% of respondents said, 'The numbers should be increased in the future,' 19.4% said, 'The numbers should remain at current levels,' and 12.5% said, 'Other,' with 4.1% not answering. When these firms were asked if they would accept trainees, 36.0% said, 'We would like to, but do not have sufficient equipment or know-how to make this possible,' 19.2%, 'We would not,' 18.2%, 'We would if we were asked to,' 8.3%, 'We are positively considering it,' 14.9%, 'Do not know,' with 3.3% giving no answer. Thus, more than 60% of firms said they would accept trainees (Ministry of Labor j).

In addition, the four prefectures in the capital region have all conducted company surveys. A 1989 survey done by Chiba Prefecture found that 4.8% of firms were employing foreign workers, 21.2% (including those employing foreigners) said that they 'Want to hire foreign workers', 43.4% that they, 'Do not want to hire foreign workers', with 32.9% responding, 'Undecided' (Chiba Prefecture). In 1990, Saitama Prefecture conducted a survey, and found that 6.3% of firms were employing foreigners, 6.4% (including the first group) said they had, 'Plans to employ foreign workers,' 4.9% said they were 'Considering the possibility,' 27.8% said they had 'Interest in the possibility,' and 41.0% had 'No plans to hire foreign workers,' with 19.9% 'Undecided or no answer' (Saitama Prefecture).

In the same year, Kanagawa Prefecture conducted its own survey, finding that 9.6% of firms said they were 'Currently employing foreign workers,' 41.7% that they 'Would like to hire foreign workers in the future,' and 41.9% that they saw 'No need to hire foreign workers,' with 6.2% responding 'Undecided' (Tezuka, Komai et al., pp. 316–). Finally, Ibaraki Prefecture found in a 1992 survey that 9.2% of firms were employing foreigners, 10.4% said that they 'Would like to hire foreign workers in the future,' 46.8% that they had 'No plans to hire foreign workers,' 32.9% that they had 'Not thought about the idea,' with 0.7% of the responses listed as 'Unknown' (Ibaraki Prefecture).

For the next series of surveys, we will limit ourselves to simply introducing the distribution of those in favor and against an open-door policy. In 1990, the Daido Mutual Life Insurance Co. conducted a survey on 1,000 company managements throughout the country, and found that 70.7% said that 'Foreign workers should be accepted,' against 11.8% that 'Foreign workers should not be admitted,' with 10.7% responding, 'Undecided' (Daido Mutual Life Insurance Co.). In the 1989 survey by the Tokyo Metropolitan Institute for Labor which we described in the Introduction, 29.9% of respondents were strongly in favor of acceptance, 39.2% mildly in favor, and 17.9% opposed (Tokyo Metropolitan Government k, Figure 1–18).

In 1989, the Tokyo Tomin Bank conducted a survey of company managements who did business with them, and found that 76.8% were in favor of accepting the employment of foreign workers, and 9.4% opposed (Tokyo Tomin Bank). The Yokohama Chamber of Commerce did its own survey in the same year, finding 49.9% in favor, 34.8% supporting a maintenance of current policy, and 2.7% opposing (Yokohama Chamber of Commerce). A similar survey by the Tochigi Prefecture Association of Corporate Executives found 63.8% in favor, and 36.2%

either opposing or being cautious on the issue (Tochigi Prefecture Association of Corporate Executives). In 1990, the Nagano Prefectural Employers' Association did a survey and found that 16.2% of respondents were in favor of accepting unskilled foreign workers, 68.8% thought it was inevitable, and 14.3% were opposed (Nagano Prefectural Employers' Association).

We have thus looked at surveys targeted at either companies or managements, and have seen that the tendency to support a policy change to accept so-called unskilled workers seems to be growing. This tendency is particularly strong among the managers of small businesses.

Next, we will look at the evaluations given of foreign employees by their employers. In the previously mentioned survey by the Tokyo Metropolitan Institute of Labor, 54.3% of firms said that their workers' attendance was 'good,' a solid 49.8% rated their working attitude as 'good,' 27.8% rated their worksmanship favorably, and 25.1% called their working style 'brisk.' In terms of negative evaluations, the highest was in working style, where 10.3% of respondents gave them a rating of 'sluggish,' and for the other questions were only in the 5% range (Tokyo Metropolitan Government k, Figure 1–16).

The Tokyo Association of Shinkin Banks conducted its own survey in February 1990 of 10,319 small- and medium-sized firms that did business with its members (by poste restante mail), achieving a response rate of 43.6%. It found that of the 419 companies that had employed foreign workers, 11.2% said they were 'satisfied' with their work, 29.6% were 'somewhat satisfied,' 20.5% 'could not say one way or the other,' 18.6% were 'somewhat unsatisfied,' 15.5% were 'unsatisfied,' and 4.5% gave no response. In other words, roughly 40% were satisfied, as opposed to 30% who were dissatisfied, meaning that there was a higher level of dissatisfaction than that shown by the Tokyo Metropolitan Government's survey. If we divide the results by sector, we find that satisfaction was high in wholesales, manufacturing, and construction, and low in areas such as retailing and service (Tokyo Association of Shinkin Banks). In a 1988 survey by Kawasaki City, 36.4% of firms that were employing foreign workers were supportive, saying that they 'worked diligently and hard' (Kawasaki City).

There is a very interesting survey conducted by the International Federation of Chemical and General Workers' Unions,

Japanese Affiliates Federation (*Nihon Kagaku Energy Rodo Kumiai Kyogikai*) (which groups unions in areas such as electric power, chemicals, synthetic fibers, rubber, pulp, and gas) which examined the attitudes of Japanese workers toward this issue. Questionnaires were distributed to 6,500 union members in September 1987, and 84.1% responded (International Federation of Chemical, Energy, and General Workers' Unions, Japanese Affiliates Federation).

When asked whether they would 'support the acceptance of foreign workers if they were necessary,' 33% said, 'Yes,' 24% said, 'It would be unavoidable,' and 20% said, 'No,' with 23% of the answers listed as 'Don' t know or unclear.' In addition, the responses were classified by occupation, and there were marked differences between blue- and white-collar workers. Among blue-collar workers, 38.8% responded either 'in favor' or 'unavoidable,' compared to an almost equal number, 33.3%, who responded, 'opposed,' but for other occupations the figures were 68.0% compared to 11.9%, meaning that the blue-collar workers expressed a much stronger opposition to foreign workers.

This strength of opposition is a common feature in Western Europe and the United States. People engaged in research were most accepting, with 73.2% responding either 'in favor' or 'unavoidable,' and just 10.4% saying they were 'opposed.'

A survey conducted by the University of Tsukuba in 1989 with the cooperation of municipalities provides some interesting insights into the attitudes of local residents. One of the sections involved questionnaires mailed to all the representatives of town associations and self-governing associations in four wards of Tokyo: Shinjuku, Toshima, Shibuya, and Itabashi. When town leaders of Toshima Ward were asked whether they had received complaints from local residents with regard to foreigners, 59.6% answered, 'Yes,' and 33.3% 'No,' which was very different from respondents in the other three wards, where negative replies outnumbered positive ones. When asked about the nature of these complaints (with multiple responses accepted), the highest three answers were 'The way they put out garbage,' with 53.5%, 'The way they speak in loud voices,' with 31.3%, and 'Trouble with lease contracts,' with 26.3% (University of Tsukuba c).

This suggests the possibility of increasing antipathy from residents in mixed residential areas. We saw this earlier in the results of the survey conducted by Okuda et al. which we introduced in

Chapter 3. A total of 105 Japanese people living in Toshima Ward in Tokyo were asked to tell of rumors or talk they had heard of concerning foreigners (with multiple answers possible), and they cited 88 instances, including 15 cases of 'Trouble concerning rent or their use of apartments,' 14 'Rumors concerning shoplifting or other crimes,' 10 'Not obeying local rules concerning for instance putting out garbage,' 10 'Rumors of creating disturbances in the neighborhood by having parties late at night,' 10 'Rumors of them having bad attitudes and not keeping promises,' as well as 29 other complaints (Okuda and Tajima a, p. 151).

We can gain additional insights from a survey conducted by the Council for Public Policy (*Kokyo Seisaku Chosakai*) on residents in areas where many foreigners were living. It was carried out between February and March, 1990, in six cities or areas within five regions – Tokyo, Saitama, Chiba, Kanagawa, and Gunma. Questions were asked of a total of 1,600 people at least 20 years old, 100 each selected randomly by ten local police stations chosen because the police thought that many foreigners lived in the area, as well as from six other stations in zones with low foreign population densities.

When asked whether the presence of foreigners in their neighborhoods caused them any uneasiness, 40.2% responded, 'Yes, but it is a vague feeling,' 33.4% said, 'I do not,' and 3.3% said, 'I feel very uneasy,' with 23.1% listed as 'No answer.' The level of unease tended to rise as people lived closer to foreigners. The largest specific causes of unease were (with multiple answers accepted) first, worries over increasing crime, second, the fear felt by women walking alone late at night, and third, unaccountable fears.

This survey also included direct interviews with foreign workers. A total of 116 foreigners were interviewed in the period of February-March 1990, with five to seven people selected by random sampling from the jurisdictions of the local police stations noted above. When asked about their relationships with Japanese, 52.6% said, 'I do not have any,' 26.7% responded either, 'I greet people on the street,' or 'I have small talk with people on the street,' 19.0% said either, 'We visit each others' houses,' or 'They are kind enough that I can ask them for advice,' with 1.7% giving 'No answer' (Council for Public Policy, Chapters 3–4). This demonstrates that social exchanges between foreign workers and other residents in their neighborhoods were very sparse.

In addition, in November 1991 the Tokyo Metropolitan Government conducted a 'Public Opinion Poll on Urban Life' (by interviews, selected by random sampling, with 2,106 valid responses) on 3,000 residents of the city, and 8.2% of respondents said 'I would like to associate with foreigners,' 26.6% said they would 'like to have such acquaintances if possible,' 27.7% said they 'would not feel like having such acquaintances,' with 30.3% saying, 'I would definitely not like to have such acquaintances,' meaning that 58.0%, a larger group than the 34.8% saying they did want to have such relationships, said they did not (Tokyo Metropolitan Government m).

In relation to this, in the summer of 1990 a series of rumors began to spread through the south-eastern part of Saitama Prefecture and into parts of neighboring Chiba Prefecture that Japanese women were being attacked by foreigners. Police authorities tried to quell the rumors by stating that they were groundless, but some town associations ended up putting warning signs on their bulletin boards, and sales of burglar alarms were reported up (*Asahi Shimbun*, 28 November 1990). A similar rumor spread through Koganei, Kokubunji and Tachikawa, three cities in or near Tokyo and along the JR Chuo Line, in the summer of 1992. This time, the rumor was that 'gangs of Iranians are raping Japanese housewives' (*Asahi Shimbun*, 4 July 1992).

The effects brought about by the increasing social exchanges with foreigners can be seen through data collected by Miyazawa et al. This group conducted a survey in 1989, looking at the consciousness of residents, as well as people commuting to and people attending school in, two cities in Saitama Prefecture, Kawaguchi and Warabi, since these two areas present Japanese citizens with many opportunities for meeting foreigners. When asked about their feelings toward undocumented workers, 44.0% of the 214 respondents said they felt antipathy, a much larger group than the 23.8% who said they felt empathy. Out of 32 residents who had actually experienced social exchanges with foreigners, 45.1% expressed empathy versus only 35.5% who expressed antipathy, meaning that the figures were reversed (Keio University, pp. 74–75).

Incidentally, there has been some information in recent years that employers of Chinese workers have begun to express complaints about their workers. One manager of a soba restaurant in Higashi Ikebukuro said bluntly that, 'We cannot have people working here who do not speak Japanese. Chinese people seem to think that they deserve to be paid just for being here' (*Asahi Journal*, 20 October 1989).

Furthermore, a group of employers in Tokyo's Kabuki-cho district were asked about their opinions of Chinese. One restaurant owner said, 'They do not take orders, but just sit around watching television. When I warn them they walk outside in a huff.' Another said that, 'We have received increasing complaints about delivery orders not coming, even though the delivery person left the store long before. There have been problems with mistaken orders and with orders being delivered to the wrong addresses.' One owner of a game center said that, 'My workers used to come back and tell me there was not enough money in their pay envelopes even though I counted to make sure the figure was correct' (*Naitai Leisure*, 22 September 1989).

3 Resident Koreans and Refugees

In Japan, an influx of foreign workers in some ways existed even before World War II, in the form of people brought from the Japanese colony on the Korean Peninsula. Many of the people who ended up in Japan during this period continue to live in Japan as what are known as 'Zainichi,' or 'resident Koreans' (in Japanese the terms for people of North Korean and South Korean origin are different, but we will use the single word 'resident Koreans,' only making the distinction where necessary). The issue of the treatment these people have received in Japan and the question of how they have hoped to live are very important in considering the future of the foreigners who will inevitably enter Japan from now on.

There is in fact an enormous amount of material available on resident Koreans in Japan, and in this section we will simply examine a small amount of this material which has relevance to the situation of foreigners who will inevitably end up in Japan in the future.

According to Suh, the movement of Koreans to Japan up until

1945 can be divided into four general periods (Suh). The first covers the ten years following the annexation of the peninsula in 1910, and involved mainly an import of cheap colonial labor. Some 30,000 people came to Japan during this time. The second period covers the ten years including the global depression which began in the late 1920's. During this time, the total number of Koreans living in Japan rose to roughly 300,000.

During the third period, which covers the time between 1931 and 1938, when Japan initiated its invasion of China, the number of Koreans rose to 800,000. The fourth period runs between 1939 and 1945, a time when labor shortages brought about by the start of the Pacific War were relieved by an import of Korean slave labor. Somewhere between 720,000 and 1,260,000 people were forcibly brought to Japan in this way. In all, over 2,300,000 Koreans were living in Japan at the end of the War in 1945. In addition, between 50,000 and 70,000 Korean women were forced to become 'comfort women,' or sex slaves, for the Japanese forces on the battlefields of China and Southeast Asia, and at the end of the war they were simply abandoned.

During the first to third periods, most of the Koreans were employed as construction workers, miners, and diggers, with others employed as factory workers in small- and medium-sized enterprises (Kim Chandong, p. 227). In addition, they experienced discrimination in terms of wages, which were roughly one half of those given to Japanese workers (Suh, p. 8).

According to certain documents, the labor conditions faced by conscripted Koreans were, '1) lower wages than their Japanese counterparts; 2) longer hours than other workers; and 3) dangerous, dirty and difficult work' (Park b, Vol. 2, p. 971).

During the fourth period, the time of labor conscription, the Koreans were forced to work as miners, as well as construction, steel, and agricultural workers (for references on conscripted workers, see Park a, pp. 49–). In this way, with the exception of mining, we find that the pattern in which men worked at low wages in '3D' jobs in areas such as construction and small- and medium-sized manufacturers, and the exploitation of women, shows similarity with the way in which foreign workers are treated today.

In 1945, with the end of the War, the Korean Peninsula was liberated from Japanese control, and in a short period of time more than 1,500,000 Koreans returned to their home country.

Roughly 500,000 others, however, who had already been in Japan for some time and had built up a basis for livelihood, ended up staying, in part because of the political uncertainty and high inflation in their homeland and because of the difficulties of repatriating the property they had accumulated (Oonuma, p. 150).

At the time, the Japanese government took the stance that all people in its former colonies would be granted Japanese citizenship until the time of the signing of a peace treaty to end the state of war. According to the 1945 House of Representatives Election Law, however, these people were not given voting rights or made eligible for public office. The last Imperial Edict, the 1947 Imperial Edict on Foreign Registration, signed by Emperor Hirohito, which was issued and put into effect the day before the enactment of the new Constitution, stated that 'Until further notice the inhabitants of the former Japanese colonies will be considered foreigners,' that they would be required to register as foreign residents, and that people failing to do so could be subject to deportation. This effectively deprived people from former colonies who had settled in Japan of the right to choose their nationality.

This Imperial Edict was in reality a public security measure aimed at protecting the social order by establishing a system to control resident Koreans and Taiwanese Chinese in Japan (see Oonuma, Part 1, Chapter 3). In later years, the Japanese policy toward foreigners outside of those from the former colonies has continued to have a tinge of public security measures.

The special features used to describe these measures have included strict surveillance accompanied by disregard or a light regard for human rights, as well as coercive assimilationist policies, with expulsion seen as the final penalty for those refusing to accept it. In this way a harsh structure of discrimination toward foreigners in general has emerged, and it has functioned most strictly against resident Koreans.

The 1952 Immigration Control Act was enacted as Japan regained its independence with the signing of the San Francisco Peace Treaty. In the same year, a circular by the director general of the Justice Ministry Civil Affairs Bureau gave instructions that, 'All Koreans and Taiwanese, including those residing in Japan, are henceforth no longer Japanese citizens,' placing them firmly under the jurisdiction of the Immigration Act. The pillars erected to deal with them were the 1950 revision of the Japanese Nationality Act, which made paternal blood descent the basis for nationality, the 1951 enforcement of the Immigration Control Ordinance, and the 1952 Foreign Registration Act which was based on revisions of the Foreigner Registration Ordinance.

The resident Koreans who were denied citizenship by Japan acquired the following fundamental statuses: those with family registries in the Republic of Korea (South Korea) became citizens of that country, and those with blood ties in the Democratic People's Republic of Korea (North Korea) were granted citizenship there. At present, there are roughly twice as many people with South Korean as with North Korean citizenship, and their numbers are increasing (Institute of Social and Educational Affairs of Korean Residents of Japan, Part 1, p. 90).

Under the terms of the 'Agreement on Legal Status and Treatment of Nationals of the Republic of Korea Residing in Japan,' which was created on the basis of the 1965 treaties signed between Japan and South Korea, applicants who had South Korean citizenship were given a special 'treaty-based permanent residency.' In addition, with the 1981 enactment of the Immigration Control and Refugee Recognition Act, which was based on a revision of the Immigration and Emigration Control Ordinance, many others, most of whom held North Korean citizenship, became eligible for a similar 'special permanent residency.' In terms of the requirements for deportation, however, those with the 'treaty-based permanent residency' gained a stronger position.

The 1952 Foreigner Registration Act, which was passed with the objective of controlling foreigers, established a fingerprinting system and put foreigers under the obligation to carry an alien registration and to show it to authorities upon demand. Offenders would be subject to punishment, including imprisonment.

Under this law, all foreigners were required to register as aliens within 90 days of entering or within 60 days of being born within the country. This foreign registration certificate contains a great deal of information, including occupation, and the name and address of the workplace. In addition, people over the age of 16 staying for at least one year were required to give their fingerprints, and were also required to apply for a new certificate every five years. Those failing to comply with these requirements could be penalized with up to one year in jail or a fine of up to ¥200,000.

Because the forced taking of fingerprints has been seen as a violation of human rights, many foreigners have refused to comply with the procedure. In 1985, for instance, 42 boys and girls who had just reached the age of 16 refused to have their fingerprints taken (Suh, p. 66).

According to Ministry of Justice data, only 25 countries around the world require foreigners to give fingerprints, and all of these with the exception of the United States, Spain, and Portugal, are either Latin American or Asian countries. All of these, however, with the exception of the U.S., have the same requirements of their own citizens (Tanaka b, p. 92). According to Oonuma, in the U.S. this procedure is not carried out in practice except in the case of immigrants and permanent residents. Oonuma pointed out, therefore, that the concept of fingerprinting not only lacks universal acceptance, but it is doubtful whether there is any necessity to identify people and whether it is even an effective means of reducing falsified registrations (Oonuma, pp. 279–). In essence, it is being forced on people in spite of the fact that it is a meaningless procedure.

In addition to this, the rights of resident Koreans to enter and leave the country have been violated by a system which requires them to apply for re-entry permits. Under this system, the Ministry of Justice has the right to permit or reject these applications. If a person is refused such a permit and leaves the country, he or she is in essence subjected to deportation, and as a result people who are refused re-entry permits find themselves unable to leave Japan. This system has also placed tremendous restrictions on overseas travel by resident Koreans (Yun). In addition, the refusal of re-entry permits has sometimes been used as a sanction against fingerprint refusers.

In January 1991, at the time of then-Prime Minister Toshiki Kaifu's visit to South Korea, the governments exchanged protocols on the question of clarifying the legal status and improving the treatment of resident South Koreans in Japan. As a result, some of the discriminatory legal practices outlined above were mitigated to some extent. A Special Law on the Emigration and Immigration of People Who Lost Their Japanese Citizenship as a Result of Peace Treaties with Japan was submitted to the National Diet, under which all such people would be treated as 'Special Permanent Residents.' In addition, deportations were limited to people who had committed heavy crimes such as sedition, and this represented a step forward in the granting of permanent residency. The maximum period that a person could stay outside Japan with a valid re-entry permit was also extended from two to five years.

There were changes in the fingerprinting regulations as well. The government placed a revised Foreigners Registration Act before the Diet in April 1992, and under this revision mandatory fingerprinting was suspended for resident Koreans and other permanent residents, and in its place they were required to register their photograph, signature, and family status. The penalty for refusing to sign was also lightened to a simple fine. For non-permanent residents staying for a period of at least one year, however, neither the fingerprinting requirement nor the obligation to carry an alien registration certificate were lifted, and the problems hence still exist.

Resident Koreans in Japan have, however, experienced many other forms of racial discrimination. One of the most serious problems they face in everyday life is housing discrimination. In the prewar period, landlords in Osaka totally refused to rent to Koreans. In one particularly obnoxious example, a sign in front of a house for rent was reported to say 'We do not rent to dogs or Koreans.' Koreans occasionally passed themselves off as Japanese to find housing, but would find themselves evicted as soon as their identities became known. They could rent places too disagreeable for Japanese, but even then they were required to have a Japanese guarantor, stable employment, and a certificate that they had been employed for at least one year (Kim Chandong, p. 65).

Housing discrimination remains widespread today. There are still blatant examples, including instances of 'Japanese citizenship' or 'resident card' (which foreigners do not have) being required for renting (Coalition Against Racism, p. 153), or of real estate agencies displaying signs indicating that 'foreigners are not accepted' in front of their stores.

Employment discrimination also remains extremely serious. In 1984, a 'Fact-Finding Survey on Foreigners Living in Kanagawa Prefecture' was conducted on resident Koreans and Chinese at least 20 years of age, with 1,028 responses received. In this survey, 36.2% of respondents said they had experienced some form of employment discrimination.

The most common specific forms which this racism took was

either discrimination in hiring or refusals to hire because of nationality, but there were also instances of people being fired or having their initial hiring cancelled, of being harrassed during interviews or after getting a job, being refused assistance or introductions to jobs by school counselling services or by teachers, being forced to hide their nationality, or either choosing to or being forced to use a Japanese name (Kinbara, Ishida et al., pp. 30–).

One of the major areas of difficulty in terms of employment discrimination concerns the right to public service. The Government Officials Act does not contain any clear reference to nationality, but at the level of the central government the regulations of the National Personnel Authority have served to deprive non-Japanese of this right, and at the level of local governments bureaucratic 'guidelines' have enforced this policy. The only basis for it is a 1953 document from the first secretary of the Ministry of Justice's Legal Systems Bureau, stating that, 'It is a natural legal principle for civil servants that, as they exercise state power and participate in the formation of the state will, that they be required to hold Japanese nationality.'

An increasing number of local governments, however, beginning with Amagasaki City in 1974, have moved to abolish the citizenship requirement for public employees. All of the cities, towns, and villages in Hyogo Prefecture, with the exception of Kobe City, all in Osaka Prefecture, with the exception of the city of Osaka itself, and all 27 cities in the capital metropolis have now abolished the requirement for all occupations. In April 1992, Osaka City became the first ordinance-designated city to open the way for non-nationals to perform university graduate-level clerical work in their offices, and it was later followed by the cities of Kobe, Yokohama, and Kawasaki (*Nikkei Shimbun*, 21 April, 17 May 1992). Kawanishi City in Hyogo Prefecture set another trend by becoming the first city to employ a foreigner in a management position (*Asahi Shimbun*, 22 April 1992). Then, in 1986 the Ministry of Home Affairs issued a directive allowing the employment of foreign nationals as nurses. In this way, the movement of foreigners into local government jobs is progressing, though slowly. Foreigners have also been granted permission, as a result of a series of efforts, to be employed as workers for the public telephone company (now privatized as NTT), as students of the governmental Legal Training and Research Institute, and as post office delivery personnel, but these are the exceptions to the rule.

In terms of teaching, foreigners gained access to employment at state and other public universities in 1982. In the same year, however, the Ministry of Education issued a directive that forbid non-nationals from working at public elementary, junior high, and senior high schools (see Nakai). As of 1988, there were just 33 non-Japanese working as teachers in four cities or prefectures, including Tokyo, and in two ordinance-designated cities, and two working as full-time instructors in Nagano Prefecture.

On the basis of the aforementioned exchange of diplomatic memoranda, however, the Ministry of Education granted foreigners the same rights as Japanese to take the tests required for elementary, junior high, and senior high teachers, and at the same time instructed local education boards to hire successful applicants as full-time instructors. Unlike regular teachers, however, full-time instructors cannot become head teachers, principals, or vice-principals. The salaries are also different (see *Asahi Shimbun*, 23 March 1991). As a result of this, 12 out of 19 local governments who were employing foreigners as regular teachers found themselves forced to demote these employees to the status of full-time instructors. Seven local bodies, however, including Tokyo, Kanagawa Prefecture, Kawasaki City, and Yokohama City, are currently looking into ways of keeping foreigners as regular teachers (*Sankei Shimbun*, 14 June 1992).

Hiring discrimination in private companies is also serious. In 1970, a resident Korean who had been told by Hitachi that he would be hired was subsequently refused employment with the excuse that he could not produce a copy of his family register (which only Japanese possess). He sued the company, claiming that using family registries as a reason for non-hiring amounted to racial discrimination, and the court decision in 1974 almost completely upheld his claim (Nakai, pp. 81–). In the years since this decision, the door has increasingly been opened for foreigners to work in work-site operations and low-rank office work in private companies, but subtle discrimination still exists.

In terms of social security and welfare, most citizenship-based restrictions, including those concerning eligibility for public housing, housing loans, national health insurance, the national pension system, and child allowances, have been gradually abolished starting with the ratification of the Universal Declaration of

Human Rights in 1979 and especially with Japan's accession to the Convention Relating to the Status of Refugees in 1981. Foreigners are still legally outside of the purview of livelihood assistance, however, and they have only been granted benefits as 'charitable measures.'

Incidentally, resident Koreans in Japan do not, needless to say, have voting rights or eligibility for office at either the national or the local level. Not only this, but they do not have the right to membership in district welfare commissions, boards of education, or human rights commissions, and thus have no direct way to express their rights as residents. This has been to the great disadvantage of these permanent residents (Coalition Against Racism, Parts 3, 4).

Japanese people also tend to hold deep-rooted prejudices against resident Koreans. For instance, 1989 saw a rash of incidents of bullying against Korean children and students triggered by the 'Pachinko Scandal,' in which pachinko game parlors were found to be funneling profits to North Korea. According to a survey by Chongryun, the main association of North Korean residents in Japan, as of November of that year there were 48 incidents involving 64 people of verbal harrassment, kicking, and punching against Koreans (*Asahi Shimbun*, 19 November 1989).

Table 5–1 presents the the common points found in three surveys which we conducted on the subject or attitudes of racial prejudice among Japanese. The first was carried out in 1974, with 190 interviews of residents of Tokyo, the second in 1976, with 224 interviews of residents of Naha, in Okinawa, and the third in 1987, with 339 interviews of residents of Sapporo, in Hokkaido, with all subjects selected randomly from people at least 20 years of age.

The table shows, first, the percentage of respondents in the surveys who indicated that they would like to become friends with members of different racial groups, and second, the percentage who said they would not mind if a brother, sister, son, or daughter, married a member of the different groups (the Tokyo residents were asked if they would marry one themselves). As a result, the columns do not add up to 100%.

The results show that prejudice toward Koreans in terms of 'friendship' has improved considerably over time, but that in terms of 'marriage' it has not. The numbers show that whites have continued to hold the most favorable position, but that

Table 5–1 Social distance between Japanese and other races

'Would you agree to becoming intimate friends with a person of the following group?' (%)			
	1974 (Tokyo residents)	1986 (Naha residents)	1987 (Sapporo residents)
White	43	56	55
Black	39	41	44
Korean	36	46	53
Filipino[1]	38	44	x
'Would you agree to one of your family members marrying a person of the following group?'[2] (%)			
	1974 (Tokyo residents)	1986 (Naha residents)	1987 (Sapporo residents)
White	21	18	22
Black	12	9	14
Korean	13	14	17
Filipino	14	14	x

x: Question not asked

[1] In the Tokyo residents' survey, it was asked for Indonesians.

[2] In the Tokyo residents' survey, respondents were asked whether they themselves would marry the following people.

Source: For Tokyo residents: Komai a; for Naha residents: University of Tsukuba a; for Sapporo residents: University of Tsukuba b.

where once Koreans and blacks were almost even, Koreans have now taken a higher position. Still, just roughly half of the respondents said they would become friends with Koreans, and slightly under 20% said they would not mind if one married into their family, indicating the level of prejudice which exists among Japanese people.

Efforts among resident Koreans to develop an 'ethnic education' have faced severe handicaps. This education began to emerge spontaneously in the Korean community in the period after 1945, with children being taught Korean language and history. In response, Ministry of Education issued a 1948 directive stating that these children should go to Japanese schools, and that it would not accept the establishment of non-regular schools to educate children of school age. The government then took measures to close down these schools, and in one incident in the Kobe area one person was killed and more than 1,700 arrested after police were mobilized (Park c, p. 184).

Starting in the late 1950's there was a revival of school building in the Korean community, and at present there are 66 kindergartens, 83 primary schools, 56 middle schools, 12 high schools, in addition to a Korean university. With the exception of two schools in Osaka, however, they are classified as 'miscellaneous schools,' meaning that they are not eligible for government private school subsidies and that their pupils cannot receive student discounts for railway passes. In addition, only a limited number of public universities allow graduates of these high schools to take their entrance examinations (Coalition Against Racism, pp. 131-; All Japan Prefectural and Municipal Workers' Union, pp. 59–). Less than 20,000 of the roughly 120,000 resident North Koreans of school age are presently attending Korean schools (Institute of Social and Educational Affairs of Korean Residents of Japan, Vol. 1, p. 91). The remaining at least 100,000 are studying in Japanese schools, but even in areas of high concentrations of resident Koreans 'ethnic education' is only provided through the autonomous efforts of individual teachers.

Roughly 90% of resident Koreans are either second or third generation, meaning that they were born in Japan (Park c, p. 523). According to a 1986 survey conducted by the Ministry of Justice (with 2,413 responses), 92% of respondents said they hoped to continue to live in Japan (*Mainichi Shimbun*, 6 September 1986).

In the midst of this situation, Kim Sukbun's book *'Zainichi' no Shiso*, or 'The Idea of "Resident Koreanism," ' gained the sympathy of many Koreans in the younger generation. The main point of this book was that resident Koreans no longer had any ties to either North or South Korea, and that they needed to change their perspective to one based on the recognition that their destiny was to remain in Japan. In other words, he said that when people went beyond the indictment of racism in Japan and began to act autonomously, they would have to consider themselves 'resident Koreans,' and their 'relationship to their home countries and to the question of the reunification of the peninsula would have to be looked at from a "resident Korean" perspective' (Kim Sukbun).

A similar call for a 'third path' has encouraged the idea that Koreans would live permanently in Japan, but without losing their ethnic identity. It called on Japanese society to neither try to drive away or assimilate the resident Koreans, but to eliminate the different forms of discrimination that existed and grant them civil rights (Kim Dongmyung).

The ideas of 'resident Koreanism' or the 'third path' seem to be calls for Koreans not to adopt Japanese nationality, but to choose to live in Japan as permanent foreign residents. What this indicates is that many resident Koreans feel strong resistance to the idea of becoming Japanese. In the aforementioned Ministry of Justice survey, just one-third of respondents said they hoped to become Japanese. Furthermore, the association of resident South Koreans in Japan conducted a survey of its own (with 2,000 members as subjects), and found that just 19% hoped to become naturalized (*Mainichi Shimbun*, 6 September 1986). As of the end of 1988, there were in Japan a total of 145,000 naturalized Japanese citizens of Korean ancestry (*Kalabaw*, No. 14, 15 November 1989).

One of the major reasons for this is that the Japanese government requires these naturalized citizens to completely abandon their identity as Koreans and to assimilate into Japanese society without resistance. They are forced, for instance, by the 'guidance' of authorities, to give up their original names and take Japanese ones, despite the fact that there is no clause in the Japanese Nationality Act requiring this (Oonuma, p. 266).

In addition, they are forced to undergo investigations into their life history, including in extreme cases having authorities look into how much garlic they use in their daily cooking (Koreans were once known as garlic lovers, whereas Japanese were not). There have also been instances of applicants being turned down because inspectors came to their houses and found women wearing traditional Korean dresses known as *chimachogori* (Iinuma, pp. 108, 222).

It is undeniable, however, that a slowly increasing number of resident Koreans are adopting Japanese nationality. In 1984, the Japanese Nationality Act was amended to follow patri-matrilinear rather than patrilinear lineage. As a result of this amendment, the children of Japanese women married to resident Koreans became eligible for Japanese nationality, causing an increase in naturalizations (Institute of Social and Educational Affairs of Korean Residents of Japan, Vol. 1, p. 64). Incidentally, in recent years nearly 60% of resident Koreans getting married have done so with Japanese partners, and this number has been roughly equal for men and women (Oonuma, p. 271). As of the end of

1989, there were 600,795 resident Koreans in Japan with permanent residency status (Tanaka b, p. 43), clearly lower than the figure of roughly 700,000 given in the past.

In 1989, a group of three people who had been forced to change their names to Japanese ones sued for the return of their original names, and the court upheld their claim (*Asahi Shimbun*, 7 October 1989), perhaps opening the path for people to become Japanese nationals without losing their identity as ethnic Koreans.

In a similar vein, during the summer of 1992 election campaign for the House of Councillors, a political party was formed by third-generation resident Koreans in order to campaign for voting rights. The registration for the group, called 'Voting Rights for Resident Foreigners '92 (Zainichi-to),' was accepted by the Osaka Election Administration Commission, and conducted a signature campaign during the campaing period asking for election rights for foreigners (*Yomiuri Shimbun*, 2 June 1992).

In closing this section, we would like to touch upon the issue of refugees, where the closed door ideology has been particularly strong. The first major event for Japan involving refugees was the 1884 'Kim Oh Kyon Incident,' where a man defected to Japan an attempt to have the Japanese government try to overthrow the Korean government. Later, the government adopted a position of not accepting any refugees (Japan Federation of Bar Associations, p. 203). In the 1960's, the government received petitions for refugee status from both North and South Koreans who were involved in the Reunification Movement, and from independence activists from Taiwan, but it refused all of these requests (Fukihara, p. 111).

A major change in this situation occurred with the emergence of boat people from Indochina. The first group of nine arrived in Japan in 1975 after being rescued by a Danish ship. The number increased rapidly after this, but their right to settle in Japan was only recognized after a 1978 Cabinet understanding. Subsequently this decision came to include exchange students and others from the three Indochinese countries who were in the country prior to 1975, Indochinese refugees who were staying temporarily in other Asian countries, and people who had left Vietnam legally to meet their families abroad.

The Japanese government long showed reluctance to sign the 1951 Convention Relating to the Status of Refugees as well as the 1967 Protocol to the treaty. In 1979, an International Conference on Indochinese Refugees was held in order to find ways to deal with the large number of people escaping from the region, and at this conference the largest population resettlement plan since World War II was adopted. Following this, and as a result of international pressure, the National Diet ratified both the Treaty and the Protocol in 1981, and the government signed them in the following year.

Because of the Japanese government's reluctance to accept refugees, the refugees themselves ended up being subdivided into three categories: boat people treated as temporary refugees, long-term Indochinese refugees who were granted special status, and 'treaty refugees' who were granted refugee status on the basis of the Immigration Control Act (Ministry of Justice e).

Temporary refugees refers to those who were accepted temporarily in Japan until such time as they could be granted permanent status either in Japan or in a third country. By December 1989 there were a total of 12,797 temporary refugees in Japan, including people born in the country, and 2,643 of them had settled in this country (Honma, p. 148).

There were a total of 6,398 long-term refugees as of January 1990 (for numbers, see *Nikkei Shimbun*, 21 April 1990), a much lower figure than the upper limit of 10,000 set in the 1985 Cabinet understanding. As of April 1988, other countries which had allowed large numbers of Indochinese refugees to settle included the United States, with 720,000, Canada with 120,000, Australia with 120,000, France with 110,000, West Germany with 24,000, the United Kingdom with 18,000, and Hong Kong with 10,000 (see Fukihara, p. 21). By international standards, therefore, Japan has accepted only very limited numbers of refugees.

The Japanese government has continued to hold its very negative stance on accepting refugees even after acceding to the Convention Relating to the Status of Refugees. By May 1990, it had accepted just 192 people on the basis of the Treaty (Honma, pp. 151–152). Of these 192 refugees, 156 were from Indochina, 23 from Iran, 9 from Afganistan, and 4 were from other countries, though not a single one came from Africa (Japan Federation of Bar Associations, p. 205). The standards for acceptance have been extremely harsh, and only two out of 150 cases which the Legal Aid Society (*Horitsu Fujo Kyokai*) handled over a six-year peirod eventually received recognition (Kazuo Ito). In April 1992, also, three Myanmarese who said they had participated in the democratization movement were finally granted recognition (*Asahi Shimbun*, 23 April 1992).

Recent years have seen such incidents as the 'run-around refugees,' where three refugees from Afganistan who arrived in Pakistan were subsequently forced to move around between Kuala Lumpur, Tokyo, and Karachi. This is illustrative of current attitudes toward refugees. In another event, the 1989 'Chinese refugee hijacking incident,' a Chinese hijacker applied for political asylum in Japan, saying that he had been involved in the Tienanmen Incident, but the government handed him over to Chinese authorities (Defense Lawyers Group in the Zhang Zhenhai Incident).

Increasingly, refugees from Indochina have been economic rather than political. In order to deal with this, an International Conference on Indochinese Refugees was held in 1989 with the participation of 77 countries. The participants agreed that boat people would, on the basis of the Treaty, be subjected to screenings to determine their status, and that those rejected under the screenings would be repatriated without being given the chance to seek settlement in a third country (Yamagami d). This meant that economic refugees, even those from Indochina, would not be allowed to settle. The Japanese government took the opportunity of a large-scale influx of Chinese disguised as Indochinese boat people in 1989 to implement the terms of this agreement and begin refusing settlement to economic refugees.

The employment situation of settled refugees cannot be said to be good. According to the Foundation for the Welfare and Education of the Asian People Refugee Resettlement Assistance Headquarters, which assists Indochinese refugees to settle in Japan, only 36 of the 2,558 refugees who are employed are working for companies with at least 1,000 employees (*Asahi Shimbun*, 3 November 1988). Moreover, more than 50% of all refugees who have been introduced to jobs by resettlement promotion centers in the different regions have quit these jobs, an indication of the poor labor conditions (Fukihara, pp. 56–7).

Incidentally, as of 1988 only 35 settled refugees had become Japanese nationals (*Asahi Shimbun*, 25 August 1989). As is the case for resident Koreans, these people have been either half-coerced or 'guided' into taking Japanese surnames, and authorities have recommended them to marry Japanese nationals (Fukihara, p. 62).

4 The Theory of Unavoidability

As we saw in Section 1 of this Chapter, the choice that has most often been put forward is that between an open door or closed door policy, but we do not feel that either of these are appropriate.

One of the major ideas presented in support of the open-door policy is usually that there is a growing tendency toward a liberalization of trade for goods and money, and that it is therefore necessary to liberalize the trade in people. This neglects the fact, however, that given unequal terms of trade and unbalanced development on a global scale, liberalizing trade in people will only mean that Third World countries will find themselves robbed not only of goods and money, but of people as well.

This is because the open-door policy is based on the economic rationale of labor demand in the core capitalist countries, and what it is in reality demanded is low-wage labor to act as a regulating valve for the economies in these core countries. It is true, of course, that Third World countries have already experienced an exploitation of their people in the form of multinational corporations from the core, but the export of labor has only served to intensify this tendency.

In its current form, the open-door policy seeks labor, but the fear that the settling of workers may give rise to problems within Japanese society have led to calls for 'limited employment,' meaning the placement of limitations on periods of stay as well as requiring workers to come without their families, as ways of ensuring that they return to their home countries once they have completed their allotted work. The government has, with a view toward fulfilling these conditions and allowing entry, albeit in a step-by-step and orderly way, started a partial opening of the labor market using Nikkeijin as well as the pretext of training. The government has judged that trainees come under an acceptable level of supervision during their stays in Japan, and justify their presence by the nice-sounding idea that their training helps the transfer of skills to Third World countries.

Aside from the question of whether these people are really trainees or not, the idea of conditional employment presents significant problems from the perspective of Third World countries. The idea behind this is to hire people for the two or three most productive years of their lives and then to basically discard them. In addition, and they can easily be expelled when there is an economic downturn in Japan. Japan was not, however, burdened with raising and educating them, and it is not Japan that will have to take care of them when they grow old. We cannot shut our eyes to the logic that places on the exporting countries the burden of reproducing labor which helps to bring greater profits to the core countries.

In addition, the policy of conditional employment is based on the premise that workers come alone. This is quite inhumane, as it means separating people from their families and loved ones for long periods of time. This practice has been recognized internationally as a violation of human rights, and this point has been made clear by international treaties. It needs to be impressed upon readers that the phenomenon of '*tanshin funin*,' where Japanese workers sent on assignments move to the new location without their families, shows the strange preference given to corporations in this society.

We should also not neglect the damage inflicted on families and communities by these policies. The absence of men places a heavy burden on their wives and children. Workers going abroad tend to come from certain concentrated regions, and the conduct of social life in these areas is impeded.

We have thus seen the problems created specifically by policies of 'conditional employment,' but the exploitation of workers creates a myriad of problems regardless of whether the employment is time-conditional or not. First of all, highly-qualified people tend to go abroad as migrant workers, meaning that the local societies are deprived of people who can make real contributions to their development. The export of labor carries, to a greater or lesser degree, the characteristics of a brain drain. According to MITI statistics, a high percentage, between 27.0% and 46.0%, of foreign employees of companies in Kanagawa, Saitama, and Gunma prefectures, are university graduates. Most of these people, moreover, are working in manufacturing factories (Ministry of International Trade and Industry b, p. 34).

Another significant problem is the emergence, on a large scale, of societies which become structurally dependent on labor exports and therefore unable to survive without them. The problems of balances of payments and of unemployment are results of the unbalanced terms of trade and unequal development, and not only does the large-scale export of migrant labor fail to resolve these problems, but in addition it hinders the process of true development.

We need to take special note of the largest instance of labor export in the history of world, namely that of slaves from Africa, and to the fact that the result of this was a long-term stagnation of that continent, the damage from which it has yet to recover. In Japan, too, the increasing isolation and collapse of societies in mountain villages and isolated islands began with the transfer of labor power in the form of migrant labor. The exploitation of Third World people may well repeat, on an Asian or even a global scale, this tragedy.

The problems brought about by this open door policy are not limited to the exporting countries of the Third World, but are incurred at the recipient end as well. We can learn from the Western European and American experiences the difficulties of a policy of conditional employment. Many of the migrant workers there who were supposed to return to their home countries failed to do so, instead bringing their families to their host countries to settle. There is therefore a possibility that a policy premised on importing labor during boom times and expelling it during recessions is bound to fail. In other words, any discussion of open door policies needs to begin with the assumption that the workers introduced into the country will eventually settle.

The strong point of the arguments used by proponents of the open door policy is that foreigners can make a solid contribution toward an opening of Japan's hermetic culture. We would like to point out, however, that it is difficult to see how people who are treated as nothing more than a source of cheap labor can be expected to act as bearers of culture. People who are treated as cheap labor become simultaneously objects of exploitation and of sympathy and pity. In this situation equality, which is a requisite for cultural exchange, is simply not present.

Not only this, but there is a strong possibility, as can be seen in the case of resident Koreans, that foreign workers will become subject to prejudice. The existence of social and economic discrimination is a reality, and prejudice serves as a mechanism to justify it. The discrimination in which Asian people are only paid the wages usually given to part-timers or are only employed in '3-D' jobs serves, as we saw in Section 2 of this chapter, to strengthen the prejudice against these people.

In a 1989 survey, 82 foreigners living in Tokyo's Shinjuku Ward were asked if they had been subjected to discrimination or prejudice by Japanese people, and 23% responded, 'Often,' 59% 'Sometimes,' and 15%, 'Almost never.' Some 80% therefore indicated that they had felt it at some time. Incidentally, 71% of the respondents were either exchange students or *shugakusei* (Tokyo Metropolitan Government b).

In 1988, Tokyo's Minato Ward conducted another survey of 810 foreign residents (by random selection, by mail, with a response rate of 40.5%). Among the Chinese respondents, 52% said they 'Sometimes' experienced prejudice or discrimination, with 10% answering 'Often.' For Filipinos the similar ratios were 56% and 5% (Tokyo Metropolitan Government a). This shows that foreigners are generally objects of prejudice, and are not generally seen as people who can make cultural contributions.

The exclusionistic nature of immigration control administration in Japan only serves to aggravate this tendency. As we examined in some detail in the case of resident Koreans, there is no legal framework in Japan to provide a sufficient protection of human rights to allow foreigners to settle in this country. Foreigners are seen either as objects to be expelled and controlled, or to be forcefully assimilated into Japanese society, and there are few signs of the will to end racism and the ideal of promoting culture that are present in Western Europe and the United States. It is easy to understand what treatment foreign workers receive in such a society.

Furthermore, because foreign workers inevitably come to work as low-waged laborers, there is a possibility of a class division developing among ethnic lines between the foreigners, who work with their bodies in either '3D' jobs or in the sex industry, and Japanese who work in intellectual jobs and keep their hands clean. In its extreme form, this structure has the potential to develop into a new form of slavery. It is believed that the kinds of serious problems that plague the European and U.S. societies emerged fundamentally from the existence of this type of structure.

Another ground of departure for proponents of the open door policy is the expectation that Japan's population will begin to decline in the future because of low fertility rates, and that foreign workers will be necessary to offset the resulting absolute long-term labor shortage. In response, we would like to point out that population and fertility rates can be increased or stabilized with appropriate measures. Regardless of this, however, we need to pay attention to the fact that Western Europe has seen decreasing fertility rates among the immigrants themselves, and thus faces a situation where new immigrants have to be found again and again. The social costs of this process are very high (Ministry of Labor m, p. 549).

There are significant problems with the closed door policy as well. First of all, in actuality a great wave of foreign workers has already flowed into Japan, and has been structurally incorporated, making it in reality physically impossible to close off Japan. If a closed door policy is imposed against undocumented workers, new workers will simply emerge behind masks of legality.

In addition, such facts as Nikkeijin being conveniently treated as Japanese even though many of them, with the exception of those of the first generation, are foreigners in every way, from language to thinking patterns, as well as the way in which workers are brought in using the guise of training, shows symbolically that in practice the idea of a closed door policy is already bankrupt.

Moreover, the social costs of forcefully expelling undocumented workers would be extremely high. In concrete terms, it would be difficult to conceive of the 1,930 Immigration Bureau employees (as of 1992), or of its 668 border guards, somehow expelling the more than 280,000 undocumented workers.

In addition, as we saw in Chapter 2, a significant number of companies have already had some experience employing undocumented foreign workers, and many are the small and weak companies that make up society's lower strata. Putting a stamp of illegality on this huge number of companies would treat such widespread corporate behavior as criminal. From the generally-accepted viewpoint of society in general, this behavior should be permitted rather than condemned.

Any strong policy taken to try to stop an inevitable flow of foreign workers into the country will unavoidably develop strains. We can point, as an example of this, to the increasing anti-Japanese sentiment among Asian people that has accompanied stricter controls on the issuing of visas.

The general pattern for foreign workers is to enter Japan on tourist visas and then stay on, and as a result the issuing of such visas has become very strict. Thais, for instance, must have a Japanese guarantor in order to receive even a tourist visa, which makes it nearly impossible for ordinary Thai citizens to visit Japan. Screening for other visa types are also extremely harsh. This is bound to draw strong anti-Japanese sentiments from among Asian people.

Not only this, but oppressive measures to apprehend foreign workers will no doubt worsen the impression these people themselves have of Japan. These people, who are considered of high quality and who form the mainstream of their own societies, will come to be considered as criminals in Japan, and it is said that their impressions of immigration officials are particularly negative. If we look at this situation in the long run, and consider the numbers involved, this can only prove to be a major minus for Japan.

Policy Proposal

In closing this book, we would like to make a policy proposal, from the viewpoint of 'unavoidability,' for dealing with foreign workers. We have divided it into three sections: the first composed of urgent proposals that ought to be implemented immediately; the second a middle-term program to be implemented in the next few years; and the third a long-term plan.

For the immediate term, we should: 1) protect the human rights of the 600,000 or more foreign workers now living in the country; 2) have municipal governments strengthen their systems for coping with the presence of these workers; 3) conduct a comprehensive review of the revised Immigration Act; 4) review the trainee category, which has been used as a first step to opening Japan's door to foreign workers; 5) conduct a review of immigration policy, which has been extremely harsh; and 6) offer Japanese language education in Third World countries. We will now examine these proposals in further detail.

We face the urgent task of protecting the human rights of undocumented workers. The obligation given to public servants under the Immigration Act to report the presence of undocumented workers has been a major obstacle for efforts to rescue people from confinement, forced prostitution, and the increasing occurances of workplace accidents, non-payments of wages, sudden dismissals, and extremely low wages. In order to provide protection for the human rights of foreign workers at the national and local levels, public servants must be freed from the obligation to report their presence.

In August 1988, the Tokyo Legal Affairs Bureau of the Ministry of Justice established a special agency for human rights consultations geared toward foreigners. In order to make such consultations practical, the bureau announced that it would keep all information confidential, in effect skirting around the disclosure obligation. The logic behind this decision was that 'The duty to protect private information takes precedence in situations involving the protection of human rights' (Tokyo Federation of Bar Associations, p. 39, 130). As of 1991, four district legal affairs bureaus had established such counselling services with interpreters (Management and Coordination Agency, p. 248).

In November 1989, also, the Labor Ministry established 'Foreign Worker's Consultation Corners' at its Labor Standards Bureaus in Tokyo, Kanagawa, Aichi, and Osaka. In January 1988, it issued a ministerial directive ordering that 'Information [concerning undocumented workers] shall not be disclosed when this information interferes with existing labor administration' (Japan Occupational Safety and Health Resource Center a). The ministry issued a similar directive in November 1989 when it established the special corners at its four labor standards bureaus (*Asahi Shimbun*, 1 December 1989).

By 1991, similar consultation corners had been established in a total of 12 prefectures. According to a survey conducted by the Management and Coordination Agency, between 1988 and 1991 there were only 116 cases in 16 prefectures of labor-related agencies reporting the presence of undocumented workers, and in five prefectures the agencies made no reports at all during the period (Management and Coordination Agency, p. 5). This number was unexpectedly low.

The Tokyo Metropolitan Government then announced that it would not report the illegal employment of foreign workers to immigration officials. In addition to the 'Foreigner's Consultation Corners,' the metropolitan government provides labor-related counselling services at its Bureau of Labor and Economic Affairs as well as in its labor administration offices in Shinagawa, Chuo, and Shibuya (*Asahi Shimbun*, 4 October 1989). These examples are noteworthy in that they represent instances where organizations have, as a means of ensuring the fulfillment of their functions, refused to comply with the duty to disclose the presence of undocumented workers.

The problems that foreign workers face can be loosely divided into employment, medical, housing, and educational questions. In terms of work, the generalized practice of concealing workplace accidents has become a major issue. Putting an end to the duty of public servants to disclose the presence of illegal labor, along with efforts to enlighten employers and workers alike, can be a means to bring the number of successful claims for worker's compensation insurance closer to the number of accidents taking place. We also urgently need to create a system to ensure that workers are paid their proper wages, regardless of whether they are documented or not.

Under the present system, unemployment insurance is only applicable to permanent residents and to other foreigners with no work restrictions. During the present recession, however, unemployment among foreigners has become a problem too clear to ignore, and unemployment insurance rules must be changed to include even undocumented workers. In view of the virtual lack of any system at present to introduce foreigners to employment, we should create a system which would even include undocumented workers. In addition, efforts must be made to enforce the Employment Security Act and the Man-Power Dispatching Business Act in order to root out the activities of brokers which affect all foreign workers, and especially the dark activities of the employment agencies that work with Nikkeijin.

In the area of medical care, too, there are a multitude of problems. First, overstayers are not able to register for any health programs at all. For other workers, who are eligible for the National Health Insurance plan, the strict conditions and premiums make entry impossible. For this reason, foreign workers face heavy financial burdens when they fall sick or are injured. They thus hesitate before going to see doctors.

The provision of emergency medical care to foreign workers is another area of considerable worry. As we saw in Chapter 3–3, the Ministry of Health and Welfare issued a directive forbidding the use of livelihood public assistance for the emergency medical treatment of overstayers and illegal entrants. This is a violation of the fundamental right of people to life, and must be changed immediately.

Information on medical institutions as well as medical data forms for use during examinations should also be provided in different languages.

The pension system is another area with significant inadequacies. It consists of old-age pensions, as well as disability and survivor pensions, for which benefits go to either the individual or the individual's family when he or she is disabled or dies. The first type includes the national pension plan as well as one for corporate employees and mutual aid programs, which are based on the individual's income.

This system is closed to foreign workers without alien registration cards, but even among registered foreigners very few have coverage. The major obstacle to their joining is the fear that their monthly payments may essentially come to nought. In order to receive payments from the national pension system, one has to have made payments for at least 25 years, and individuals must reach the age of 65 (actually it is still 60 but will soon change). Foreigners have begun to settle in Japan, however, and we will eventually see the emergence of a population of aged foreigners. To cope with this we need to set a fundamental policy to deal with their entry into pension systems.

Housing is another major problem for foreigners, who must deal with the dual problems of discrimination on the one hand and high rents on the other. Efforts are therefore needed to enlighten and provide guidance to landlords and real estate agents not to discriminate against them. In addition, there is a need to radically expand the amount of public housing to which foreigners have access. If we consider the fact that many foreign workers are concentrated in cheap wooden housing, we should consider the possibility of preserving and rehabilitating this type of lodging. We should be very careful about efforts to redevelop these areas.

The gradual settling of foreigners in Japan has brought with it the problem of education for their children. We must provide good information to foreign residents concerning entry into nursery schools, kindergardens, and elementary and junior high schools, and must strengthen Japanese-language education for foreign children in these institutions.

In spite of an increasing number of marriages between Japanese nationals and foreign workers, immigration officials have not always granted visas to people in these situations, and there have been many cases of married people, some even with children, being deported. All people have the fundamental human right to live with their families, and people married to Japanese should therefore be granted resident status.

On top of this, foreigners lose their residency status when they are divorced. Divorce rates for marriages between Filipinas and Japanese men run at roughly 70% (All Japan Prefectural and Municipal Workers' Union, p. 92). For many of these divorcees the basis of their livelihoods is already in Japan, and forcing them to return to their home countries causes them many hardships. In addition, foreigners with Japanese children do not receive any residency status as parents, so if they are divorced from their spouse they are forced to choice between returning alone to their home country or taking their children with them. This situation must be remedied immediately.

As we can see, the government policy toward foreigners has preserved many aspets of monoracialism, and is far from a policy which upholds human rights. The task of getting rid of the contradictions of this attitude has, as a result, fallen on the shoulders of NGOs, or private support organizations, and local self-governing bodies. Some representative support organizations include Kalabaw no Kai in Yokohama, ALS no Kai in Nagoya, and the HELP Women's Shelter and CALL Network in Tokyo. Organizations like these with significant track records should be given rights and institutional status as organizations able to represent the interests of foreign workers.

We will turn next to the question of local governments, which are charged under the Local Government Law with protecting the residents, including foreigners, within their jurisdictions. In practice, however, local governments are mandated to carry out many of the policies of the national government, but even within this framework there is considerable scope for them to find ingenious ways to provide assistance to their foreign residents.

There is also room for local governments to intervene in resolving disputes between Japanese residents and foreign workers in such areas as proper garbage disposal and noise.

Some of the private support groups have proposed that local governments create a 'foreigners' human rights ombudsman' system. This would allow them to deal simply and promptly with cases and complaints of specific human rights violations, and to make recommendations on how to improve the situation in general (CALL Network, p. 169).

One of the major significances of the revised Immigration Control Act which went into effect in June 1990 was that it partially opened the door to two groups of legal foreign workers, namely Nikkeijin and trainees. With regards to the Nikkeijin, it must be pointed out that the idea of allowing people with Japanese blood to work legally and forbidding those without this blood is problematic as an example of racism based on monoethnicism. As we saw in Chapter 4–4, this racism has already become a subject of controversy in Brazil, and in the future will surely emerge as an important indicator of the true nature of Japanese society.

With regards to trainees, this visa category has the potential of becoming a major future route for accepting foreign workers into Japan. Under the revised Immigration Control Act, the acceptance of trainees, which was previously restricted to major corporations, has been opened to small- and medium-sized enterprises, and is clearly in some ways simply a measure to alleviate the labor shortage. For many companies, however, the trainee system has been used as an excuse to fraudulently employ foreign workers, and even from an ethical standpoint this should not be allowed to continue. This is a betrayal of the expectations of those who come to Japan hoping to receive training, and carries with it a huge number of problems, including the issue of unfair compensation.

In order to deal with this situation, the government has drawn a sharp line between the concepts of training and employment, and has decided to allow special trainees to seek work after the end of their training. Regardless of these changes, however, the nature of the trainee system remains unchanged: a measure for the legal introduction of manageable low-wage labor. Furthermore, the supposed benefit, in which the training helps to transfer skills, in reality helps the activities of Japanese companies in Third World countries by nurturing a core workforce, and has been seen as a way of spreading the Japanese technological system throughout the world. In the midst of the current economic recession, in addition, there is no need to increase the number of foreign workers seeking employment here.

We have serious doubts over the wisdom of the fines levied against employers under the revised law, since a great number of companies have already had the experience of employing undocumented foreign workers. First, we should point to the social appropriateness of making the behavior of so many companies illegal, and second, the lack of consideration for the situations of the small- and medium-sized companies at the bottom of the subcontracting structure, who have been forced to rely on foreign labor. In addition, levying heavy fines against employers will only drive the presence of undocumented workers further underground, increase the roles of unscrupulous brokers, and this will make the task of protecting the human rights of the workers that much more difficult. The increasingly severe regulations against working outside of authorized status may have a serious impact on college students and *shugakusei*, since they are already in a weak position. Many of these students, who were properly admitted into Japan, arrived to face the fact that it is impossible to survive working just four hours per day. Strictly applying the four-hour limit has, literally, the potential to drive these people to starvation.

As we pointed out in the previous section, the excessively harsh attitude taken by the Immigration Bureau, which has focused solely on driving out undocumented workers, generally carries the demerit of increasing anti-Japanese sentiments. Complete exclusion is, moreover, has in reality been made impossible by the economic gaps that have emerged from unequal development.

We can see from the high demand for Japanese language education that there is a great need to provide such instruction, though not for profit, to people in the other countries of Asia. This will help to drive out the malicious companies that sell such 'education' in Japan. In addition, there is a need to establish a unified Japanese language competency test (like TOEFL for English) to test potential students before they come to Japan.

We will now proceed to the medium-term plan. Not only is it impossible to expel the people working now as overstayers or working outside of their authorized status, or even to completely stop the further flow of such people into the country, but we must begin with the premise that the flow of legal workers will also unavoidably increase in the coming years. Trying to stop this flow will only serve to increase human rights violations against undocumented workers, and carries in addition the demerit that it will be socially very costly.

As we have already seen, the settling in of foreign workers has already begun in Japan, as it has in Europe, and can be grasped from the increasing number of people coming more than once, the settling in of Filipinas, the tendency for Chinese college students and *shugakusei* to stay for long periods or overstay, and for Nikkeijin to migrate permanently with their families.

In the past, Japan under its ideology of 'monoethnicism' constantly discriminated against and drove away foreigners. The presence of foreign workers and resident Koreans and Chinese, as well as the existence of the Ainu people, increases the need for creating a multicultural society. As a medium-term plan, therefore, we need to both structurally incorporate these long-term settlers into Japanese society, and develop policies to protect their human rights. With regards to this idea, Oonuma's proposal to create a new category of 'settled foreign residents' should be instructive (Oonuma, p. 353).

As the first part of such a medium-term plan, illegal residents in Japan should be granted amnesty. A significant number of such people have already lived in Japan for many years, and they have continued to live and work under the threat of discovery. In order to protect their human rights, we need to consider how to give assistance to people who have been staying for longer than some certain period. The requirement can be that the person have stayed for a long time and that deportation would have grave consequences for them or their families. No limitations should be placed on the employment or residency of people who are granted amnesty (Kanto Federation of Bar Associations, p. 156).

A second step in the medium-term plan should be for Japan to sign the International Convention on the Elimination of All Forms of Racial Discrimination. As we have seen, this treaty, along with the Convention on the Elimination of All Forms of Discrimination Against Women, and the Convention on the Rights of the Child, is one of the pillars of human rights protection. It has the greatest number of signatories of all the human rights treaties, and it prohibits employment and housing discrimination, as well as racial hatred and violence (see Kim Donghoon a). In Japan, in particular, housing discrimination against foreign workers has reached a point where it must be seriously addressed, and there has been an increasing incidence of discrimination based on racial prejudice. They must be censured under the law as criminal actions.

As a third part of the medium-term plan, Japan should sign the International Convention on the Protection of the Rights of All Migrant Workers and Members of Their Families. This Treaty focuses on labor conditions, social security, and cultural autonomy, and gives attention to the needs of undocumented workers and their families. The Japanese government has shown absolutely no inclination to ratify the treaty, although it possesses significance as an international standard on the problem of migrant workers. The government should promptly ratify it.

Partly because of the national government's reluctant attitude toward these two treaties, some support organizations have urged local governments to enact an 'ordinance on the rights of foreigners.' This ordinance seeks to create an environment in which violations of the fundamental human rights of foreigners will not occur, and to create local communities in which it will be possible to swiftly stop the emergence of such violations (CALL Network, p. 161).

A fourth part of the medium-term plan should be an effort to do away with general discrimination against foreigners who have settled in Japan. Japan's policies toward foreigners began as public security measures against resident Koreans, and there are thus many points that need improvement. As we pointed out in Chapter 5–3, 1) the contents of alien registration must be simplified; 2) foreigners should not be required to carry their alien registration cards at all times and produce them on demand; 3) the re-entry permit system must be fundamentally reviewed; 4) opportunities for foreigners to work as public servants must be increased; 5) voting and election rights should be granted at the local government level; 6) foreigners should be permitted to become members of local welfare commissions, boards of education, and commissions for the protection of fundamental human rights; and 7) foreigners should be granted the right to make residents' petitions.

The fifth part of the medium-term plan is a revision of the Japanese Nationality Act. A second generation of foreign workers is already emerging. In other countries it has been found that relatively few of these workers choose to become naturalized nationals, and even among second- and third-generation resident Koreans the number of applicants is fairly low. Regardless of this reality, the freedom of settled foreigners to choose their nationality needs to be broadly protected. It would therefore be beneficial to amend the Nationality Act to give priority, as is the practice in France and the United States, to the place of birth. In addition, some thought should be given to the idea of recognizing dual nationalities.

In relation to this, we must point out that Japan has not accepted a sufficient number of Treaty refugees. A special effort should be made, in the spirit of the U.N. Convention Relating to the Status of Refugees, to accept especially political refugees from neighboring countries.

A sixth part of the medium-term plan should be to respect the cultures brought by foreign workers from their home countries. We must learn from the experiments of 'multiculturalism' in the U.S. and 'the rights of the other' in France, and develop the conditions to change Japanese society into a multi-ethnic one made up of a variety of cultures.

In order to achieve this, first and foremost we must promote ethnic education. The ethnic education that was built by the self-reliant efforts of resident Koreans is not recognized as 'proper' education under the School Education Act. Recognizing Korean schools can be a first step in creating a multi-ethnic society, and this should be followed by promotion and assistance to schools for other ethnic groups. Teaching these childrens' native languages will become a major task for these schools.

The current guidance provided to people who want to acquire Japanese citizenship is not acceptable, as it is strongly based on the concept of monoethnicity. An incredible lack of respect for human rights can be seen in the requests that people discard their original names and take Japanese ones, and even assimilate into Japanese society at the level of everyday living.

As a long-term policy, we need to build societies, both in the exporting countries and in host countries like Japan, which do not rely on the existence of migrant labor. We also need to work to stop the emergence of political refugees, and to reach global accords on the international migration of peoples. We should point out in this regard that during the Uruguay Round of the General Agreement on Trade and Tariffs (GATT), Third World nations pressed for the export of unskilled labor to be included within the framework of services, but the core capitalist countries opposed this proposal, and as a result, the chairman's draft relegated negotiations concerning migrant workers to bilateral agreements. What this proposal showed is that there is approval among elites in the Third World of the degree to which societies are dependent on migrant labor.

Migrant labor brings great sacrifice not only to the exporting countries, but to the laborers themselves and to their families, and can only be described as an 'plunder of human beings.' In spite of this, however, migrant labor is being promoted as a way to reverse balance of payments problems and to relieve unemployment pressures. The background to this is of course the international capitalist order that has forced unequal terms of trade upon the Third World, and on the basis of which an enormous plunder of wealth has taken place. The result of this has been unbalanced development, and migrant labor has moved from the periphery or semi-periphery toward the semi-periphery or core regions.

A much different strategy from current models will have to be pursued in order to build a Third World which is not dependent on migrant labor. Monoculture cropping has been given priority as a means of producing cash crops, and Third World agriculture has thus been incorporated into the unequal international trading mechanism. This has produced an impoverishment of farming villages and rampant landlessness. Migrant labor and urban migration has become universal, creating an unusual concentration of population and increasing numbers of unemployed and semi-employed people in the Third World's gigantic cities.

In addition, Japanese companies have advanced into the Third World in search of low wages, but Japan has maintained control over finance and management as well as a great lead in high technology. This has led to the creation of a new vertical international division of labor. Thus Japan with its economic surplus has committed a great plunder, and the results can be seen in the worsening of Third World debt. The international balance of payments crisis in the Third World is thus structural.

Finding a real solution to the problem of foreign workers will require improving this situation in the source countries. As one means to accomplish this, we need to conduct a thorough-going review of Japan's official development assistance (ODA). In 1986–1987, an average of 20.0% of loan assistance given by member countries of the OECD's Development Assistance Committee (DAC) was spent on economic intrastructure projects, whereas for Japan this ratio was 51.1%. These projects included electric power plants, roads, harbors, and airports.

Another outstanding feature of Japanese ODA is the relatively enormous portion which is in the form of loans. Grant ratio figures (which indicate how much of a country's assistance is grants) for 1988–1989 show that just 43.2% of Japanese ODA was in grants, compared to a ratio of 97.8% for the United States and 100.0% for Sweden (Ministry of Foreign Affairs b).

Japan's ODA, with this emphasis on building infrastructure, only serves to increase the development of cash cropping and of a vertical international division of labor. In addition, the emphasis on loan aid worsens balance of payments problems since it obliges the recipient countries to repay both interest and principle. It is therefore believed that current ODA patterns place additional pressure on Third World countries to send out migrant workers.

Next, we will consider how to stop the dependency that Japan as a host country has on migrant labor. As we have seen, the employers who have come to rely upon foreign workers tend to be those from small- and medium-sized companies at the bottom of Japan's complex subcontracting industrial structure. The demands from their parent companies to meet order schedules and cut unit costs have caused labor conditions in their businesses to decline, and they have found it simply impossible to hire young Japanese workers.

In other words, as long as a complex structure exists in which parent companies can increase their profits at the expense of their subcontractors, the strong demand for foreign workers willing to work for low wages will not disappear. Accordingly, in order to build a society which does not depend on foreign workers, we must fundamentally alter Japan's industrial structure.

Another important means of protecting our own environment will be to stabilize Japan's population, which can be done by enacting appropriate measures to maintain the birth rate. Instead of focusing solely on economic growth and then importing foreign workers to alleviate a labor shortage, we must establish a pattern with stable population and labor power which does not emphasize the building of a structure of economic growth.

As a second part of a long-term policy, we need to consider ways to stop the emergence of political refugees. It is believed that the United States and Western Europe have reached a point where it will be very difficult for them to continue the allopathic method of simply accepting more refugees. Many refugees come from the socialist countries and other autocratic political systems. We should therefore refrain from actions which will perpetuate such regimes.

Finally, there is a need for an international agreement on the global migration of populations. If we look at the problem from the point of view of 'unavoidability,' we find that it will be impossible for the host countries to solve it by themselves. This agreement will have to include issues such as how to stamp out international broker organizations, prevent the emergence of undocumented workers in their home countries, and protect them in the host countries, in addition to some serious debate at the global level on the effects of our current dependency on migrant labor.

In any case, the acceptance into Japan and cohabitation with foreigners, not as cheap labor but as equal and respected human beings, will have increasing significance for Japan in its place within international society. In order not to stray from the new path we are following toward the creation of a multicultural society, we must, above all, start from the point of respecting the human rights of the foreign workers who will unavoidably enter, work, and live, in Japan.

References

A Newspapers, magazines, newsletters

Asahi Shimbun
Mainichi Shimbun
Nikkei Shimbun (*Nihon Keizai Shimbun*)
Yomiuri Shimbun
Asahi Journal
Bangkok Post
Chubu Yomiuri Shimbun
Chunichi Shimbun
Gekkan Kensetsu
International Entertainment Association News
Naitai Leisure
Nihon Biru Shimbun
Ryugakusei Shimbun
Pusang Ilbo
Sankei Shimbun
Shimotsuke Shimbun
The Daily Engineering and Construction Industry News
The Daily Yomiuri
The Japan Times
Tong-a Ilbo

B Support organization newsletters

Kalabaw: Kalabaw no Kai, Sanwa Bussan Biru 701, 3–11–2 Matsukage-cho, Naka-ku, Yokohama-shi, Kanagawa-ken

CALL Network: Workers and Citizens Association for Solidarity with Our Friends Who Are Working and Studying in Japan, Kawada Bldg., 2–3–4 Koishikawa, Bunkyo-ku, Tokyo-to

Migrant: ALS no Kai, Migrant Editor, c/o Fukushinkan, 2–6–29 Aoi, Higashi-ku, Nagoya-shi

C Valuable source of information (magazine)

Kokusai Jinryu (International Population Flows), Immigration Association, 4F Tachibana Shoten Bldg., Kanda Ogawa-machi, Chiyoda-ku, Tokyo-to

D References in Japanese language

Administrative Management and Financial Affairs Research Institute (Gyozaisei Sogo Kenyujo) ed., *Gaikokujin rodosha no jinken*, [The human rights of foreign workers] (Otsuki Shoten 1990).

Administrative Management Research Center (Gyosei Kanri Kenkyu Center), *Kokusaika jidai to jichitai – arata na gyosei chitsujo no keisei e mukete* [The age of internationalization and local governments – toward the creation of a new administrative system], (March 1991).

Akagi, Kazunari, 'Naze karera wa Nihon wo mezasu no ka – Brazil Nikkeijin dekasegi to Nikkei shakai no genjo,' [Why do they come to Japan? Brazilian Nikkeijin migrant workers and the situation of Nikkei society]' in *Kokusai Jinryu*, July 1990.

All Japan Prefectural and Municipal Workers' Union (Jichiro), Research Institute on Local Governance, Central Promotion Committee, *Gaikokujin wa jumin desu* [Foreigners are residents] (October 1991).

ALS no Kai, ed., *Lapin jiken no kokuhatsu* [An indictment of the Lapin incident] (Tsuge Shobo 1990).

Aoyama, Morio, 'Tenka no daidokoro wo sasaeru gaikokujin rodoshatachi' [The foreign workers who support our kitchens], in *CALL*, No. 1, 30 July 1990.

Asahi Shimbun, *Anata no tonari ni – rupo sakoku Nippon no 'Gaikokujin'* [Living next door – report on the foreigners in a closed Japan] (Asahi Shimbunsha 1991).

Ashita, June 1992.

Association for Overseas Technical Scholarship (Kaigai Gijutsusha Kenshu Kyokai), *Goriyono tebiki* [Handbook for users] (1988 version).

Association for the Promotion of Japanese Language Education a: Association for the Promotion of Japanese Language Education (Gaikokujin Shugakusei Ukeire Kikan Kyogikai), *Kaiho*, Issues 1 and 3 (March, July 1987).

Association for the Promotion of Japanese Language Education b: Association for the Promotion of Japanese Language Education (Gaikokujin Shugakusei Ukeire Kikan Kyogikai), 'Enquete ni yoru gaikokujin shugakusei jijo' [The situation of foreign shugakusei seen through questionnaires], in *Kokusai Jinryu*, June 1989.

Azuma, Saburo, ' "Kakuremino" to shite no Nihongo gakko' [Japanese language schools as cloaks], in *Shinchihei*, September 1986.

Business Policy Forum Japan (Kigyo Katsuryoku Kenkyujo), *Gaikokujin rodosha ukeireni kansuru teigen* [Proposal concerning the acceptance of foreign workers] (July 1988).

CALL Network, *Anatano machino gaikokujin* [The foreigners in your town] (Daiichi Shorin 1991).

Chiba Prefecture, Bureau of Labor Administration Affairs, Commerce and Labor Department, *Gaikokujin koyo jittai chosa hokokusho* [Report of survey on the employment of foreigners] (February 1990).

Coalition against Racism (Minzoku Sabetsu to Tatakau Renraku Kyogikai), *Zainichi kankoku/chosenjin no hosho jinkenho* [A law for compensating and respecting the rights of resident Koreans] (Shinkansha 1989).

Construction Industry Study Group on the Problem of Foreigners (Kensetsugyo Gaikokujin Mondai Kenkyukai), ed., *Kensetsugyo ni okeru gaikokujin rodosha mondai to gaikokujin kenshusei no ukeire* [The problem of foreign workers in the construction industry and the acceptance of foreign trainees] (Taisei Shuppansha 1991).

Council for Public Policy (Kokyo Seisaku Chosakai), *Rainichi gaikokujin no shakai futekio jokyo ni kansuru chosa* [Study on the situation of social non-adaptation of foreigners in Japan] (March 1991).

Daido Mutual Life Insurance Co., 'Dai–2-kai keieisha 1000-nin enquete' [Second questionnaire survey of 1,000 managers], (No date).

Defence Lawyers Group in the Zhang Zhenhai Incident, *Zhang Zhenhai hijack jiken* [The Zhang Zhenhai hijacking incident] (Nitchu Shuppan 1990).

Ebashi, Takashi, ed., *Gaikokujin rodosha to jinken* [Foreign workers and human rights] (Hosei University Shuppankyoku 1990).

Economic Planning Agency a: Economic Planning Agency, Social Policy Bureau, 'Wagakuni ni okeru gaikokujin koyo to kokumin seikatsu ni kansuru enquete chosa kekka ni tsuite (gaiyo)' [On the results of a questionnaire survey on the employment of foreign workers and national life in our country] (March 1988).

Economic Planning Agency b: Economic Planning Agency, ed., *Sekai to tomo ni ikiru nihon – keizai unei gokanen keikaku* [Japan and the world – the five year economic plan] (Ministry of Finance Printing Bureau May 1988).

Economic Planning Agency c: Economic Planning Agency, Planning Bureau, *Rodoryoku no kokusaikan ido no kokunai rodo shijoto ni ataeru eikyo ni kansuru chosa hokokusho* [Report on survey on the effects of the international movements of labor on the domestic labor market], (April 1989).

Employment Advance Research Center (Koyo Kaihatsu Center), *Kigyo no kokusaika to gaikokujin ryugakusei kenshusei* [The internationalization of enterprises and foreign students and trainees] (1989).

Federation of Economic Organizations (Keidanren), *Jizokuteki na antei seicho to rodoryoku no kakuho wo mezashite* [Aiming for sustainable stable growth and a maintenance of labor power] (May 1992).

Fishing Industry Problems Study Group (Gyogyo Mondai Kenkyukai),

Gyogyo mondai kenkyukai hokokusho [Report of the Fishery Problem Study Group] (September 1988).
Forum on Asian Migrant Workers a: Forum on Asian Migrant Workers (Ajikon), ed., Shinpan asia jin dekasegi rodosha techo [Revised Asian workers handbook] (Akashi Shoten 1990).
Forum on Asian Migrant Workers b: Forum on Asian Migrant Workers (Ajikon), ed., *Okasareru jinken – gaikokujin rodosha* [Violated human rights – foreign workers] (Daisan Shokan 1992).
Fujisaki, Yasuo, *Dekasegi Nikkei gaikokujin rodosha* [Migrant Nikkeijin foreign workers] (Akashi Shoten 1991).
Fukamachi, Hiroki, 'Pakistan,' in *Ajiken News*, September 1989 (Institute of Developing Economies).
Fuke, Yosuke, 'Tonan Asia no rodoyroku ido' [Movements of labor power in Southeast Asia], in *Shinchihei*, September 1986.
Fukihara, Tadamasa, *Nanmin* [Refugees] (Nihon Kyoiku Shimbunsha 1989).
Gonoi, Hiroaki, *Dekasegi gaikokujin zankoku monogatari* [A tale of cruelty toward migrant foreigners] (Yale Shuppansha 1989).
Group Akakabu, ed., *Abunai nihongo gakko* [Dangerous Japanese-language schools] (Shinsensha 1989).
Hachiya, Takashi, *Soredemo gaikokujin rodosha wa yatte kuru* [In spite of it all the foreign workers keep coming] (Nikkan Kogyo Shimbunsha 1991).
Hagio, Shinya, 'Anyaku suru chukai gyoshatachi' [The brokers in the shadows], in *Gaikokujin rodosha to jinken* (Nihon Hyoronsha 1988).
Hanabusa, Masao, 'Kankoku no kigyo senshi' [South Korea's Corporate Warriors], in *Ajiken News*, September 1989 (Institute of Developing Economies).
Hanada a: Hanada, Masanori, 'Imin Senshinkoku France kara manabu mono' [Things to learn from France as an advanced migration nation], in *Economist*, 14 November 1989.
Hanada b: Hanada, Masanori, 'France hen' [France section], in Kanagawa Prefecture c.
Hanami, Tadashi, 'Gaikokujin rodosha – America kara nani wo manabu ka' [Foreign workers – what we can learn from America], in *Nihon Rodo Kenkyu Zasshi*, No. 375, January 1991.
Hanami, Tadashi and Kuwabara, Yasuo, eds, *Ashita no rinjin gaikokujin rodosha* [Foreign workers, tomorrow's neighbors] (Toyo Keizai Shimbunsha 1989).
Hatada, Kunio, 'Okubo Dori ni "taminzoku kokka Nihon" no ashita ga aru!?' [Does 'Japan the multiracial state' have a future along Okubo Avenue!?], in *Bessatsu Takarajima*, No. 106, 1990.
Hayashi a: Hayashi, Mizue, *France no nihojin* [France's foreigners] (Chuo Koronsha 1984).
Hayashi b: Hayashi, Mizue, 'EC shokoku ni shoku wo motomete – France no Magreb shusshinsha no genjo' [Looking for work in the EC countries – the situation of people from the Magreb in France], in Nakaoka.

Hinako a: Hinako, Satoru, 'Japayuki-san no keizaigaku' [The economics of Japayuki],' in Ishii.
Hinako b: Hinako, Satoru, *Kei, nen, kokuseki fumon – gaikokujin rodosha ga 100 mannin ni naru hi* [History, age, nationality unquestioned – the day the number of foreign workers reaches 1 million] (Diamondsha 1992).
Hirakawa, Hitoshi, 'Kankoku no yushutsu shiko-gata seicho to boeki' [South Korea's export-led directed growth and trade], in *Kankoku Keizai no Bunseki* (Nihon Hyoronsha 1988).
Hirowatari a: Hirowatari, Shingo, 'Nishi deutsche no gaikokujin seisaku tairitsu no kozu' [A map of policy disputes in West Germany concerning foreign workers], in *Gaikokujin rodosha to jinken* (Hogaku seminar Zokan) (Nihon Hyoronsha 1988).
Hirowatari b: Hirowatari, Shingo, 'Gaikokujin "togo" seisaku wo osou ooki na yuragi' [The distortions that attack policies to 'integrate' foreigners], in *Bessatsu Takarajima*, No. 106, 1990.
Hirowatari c: Hirowatari, Shingo, 'Deutsche no gaikokujin mondai to kokuseki' [Nationality and the problem of foreigners in Germany], in Momose and Ogura.
Hirowatari d: Hirowatari, Shingo, 'Gaikokujin ukeire no hoteki ronri' [Legal arguments on the acceptance of foreigners], in Iyotani and Kajita.
Honma, Hiroshi, *Nanmin mondai to wa nani ka* [What is the refugee problem?] (Iwanami Shoten 1990).
Hosomi, Taku, ed., *Gaikokujin rodosha – Nihon to Deutche* [Foreign workers – Japan and Germany] (Kawai Shuppan 1992).
Ibaraki Prefecture Department of Commerce and Labor, *Gaikokujin rodosha koyo jittai chosa kekka hokokusho* [Report on survey of the employment situation of foreign laborers], March 1992.
Iida, Noriko, 'Nikkeijin no machi – gravure "Little Brazil" ni yosete,' [Nikkeijin town – written for the photo series 'Little Brazil'], in *Sekai*, July 1992.
Iinuma, Jiro, *Zainichi Kankoku/Chosen jin* [Resident Koreans] (Kaifusha 1988).
Inakami, Tsuyoshi, Kuwabara, Yasuo, et al., *Gaikokujin rodosha wo senryokuka suru chusho kigyo* [Making foreign workers into weapons for small and medium-sized enterprises] (Chusho Kigyo Research Center 1992).
Institute for Social Affairs in Asia (Asia Shakai Mondai Kenkyujo), *Ajiajin kinrosha mondai ni kansuru chosa kenkyu* [Survey on the problem of Asian laborers] (Sangyo Kenkyujo June 1990).
Institute of Social and Education Affairs of Korean Residents of Japan (Zainichi Chosenjin Shakai-Kyoiku Kenkyujo), ed., *Kika*, [Naturalization] (Banseisha 1989).
International Federation of Chemical, Energy, and General Workers' Unions, Japanese Affiliates Federation (ICEF-JAF), *Kagaku energy sangyo ni miru rodosha ishiki 1987* [1987 attitudes of workers in the chemical and energy industries] (1988).
International Industry and Labor Research Center (Kokusai Sangyo-

Rodo Kenkyu Center), *Wagakuni kigyo ni okeru gaikokujin rodosha kenshusei no ukeire jittaito kongo no needs* [Situation and future needs for the acceptance of foreign worker trainees in Japanese companies] (1990).

Ishihara, Takumi, *Gaikokujin koyo no honne to tatemae – rodoryoku sakoku no ura de nani ga okite iru ka* [Real and professed intentions for employing foreign workers – what is going on behind the scenes in this closed-to-labor country?] (Shodensha 1992).

Ishii, Shinji, ed., *Japayuki-san monogatari* [Japayuki Story] (JICC Shuppankyoku 1986).

Ishikawa, Yoshimi, *Hito no kaikoku ka hito no sakoku ka* [Opening or closing the country to people] (Pan Research 1988).

Ishiyama, Eiichiro, *Philippines dekasegi rodosha* [Filipino migrant workers] (Tsuge Shobo 1989).

Ito, Kazuo, 'Nanmin nintei no seido/unyo minaose' [Review the system and administration of refugee recognition], in *Asahi Shimbun*, 16 October 1989.

Ito, Kiyoshi, ' "Nanmin tengoku Nippon" no genso wo ataeta no wa dare da' [Who created the illusion that Japan is a heaven for refugees?], in *Shokun*, November 1989.

Ito Ruri a: Ito, Ruri, ' "Doka naki togo" no sodai na jikken' [The grand experment of 'integration without assimilation'], in *Bessatsu Takarajima*, No. 106, 1990.

Ito Ruri b: Ito, Ruri, 'France ni okeru Islam-kei jumin no doka to hennyu – "doka ideology no sotaika" to iu bunmyaku no nakade' [The assimilation and incorporation of residents of Islamic descent – in the context of 'relativization of assimilationist ideology'] in Momose and Ogura.

Iyotani, Toshio and Kajita, Takamichi, eds, *Gaikokujin rodosha ron*, [Theories on foreign workers] (Kobundo 1992).

Iyotani, Toshio and Naito, Toshio, 'Tokyo no kokusaika de tenkan semarareru chusho kigyo' [Small and medium-sized enterprises being forced to change by Tokyo's internationalization], in *Economist*, 5 September 1989.

Japan Association of Corporate Executives a: Japan Association of Corporate Executives (Keizai Doyukai), 'Kore kara no gaikokujin koyo no arikata ni tsuite – "jisshu program" ni yoru chitsujo aru gaikokujin rodosha no ukeire' [On the future employment of foreigners – using a 'training program' to accept foreign workers systematically], March 1989.

Japan Association of Corporate Executives b: Japan Association of Corporate Executives (Keizai Doyukai), 'Gaikokujin to no kyosei wo mezashite' [Aiming for cohabitation with foreigners] (July 1989).

Japan Association of Corporate Executives c: Japan Association of Corporate Executives (Keizai Doyukai), 'Wagakuni no gaikokujin koyo no susumu beki hoko ni tsuite' [On the proper path for our country to take concerning the employment of foreigners] (June 1992).

Japan Building Maintenance Association (Zenkoku Building Maintenance Kyokai), 'Gaikokujin gakusei koyo no tame no tetsuzuki/jitsumu

manual' [Manual of procedures and applications for employing foreign students], (1989).
Japan-Brazil Cultural Study Center a: Japan-Brazil Cultural Study Center, 'Brazil ni okeru nikkei jinko chosa hokoku - 1987/1988 - bassui' [1987–1988 report from survey on the Nikkei population in Brazil - selections].
Japan-Brazil Cultural Study Center b: Japan-Brazil Cultural Study Center, *Brazil nikkeijin no ishiki chosa* [Attitude survey of Brazil Nikkeijin] (February 1992).
Japan Federation of Bar Associations (Nihon Bengoshi Rengokai), *Jinken no kokusaiteki hosho* [The international guarantee of human rights] (1988).
Japan Food Service Association (Nihon Food Service Kyokai), 'Gaikokujin koyo ni kansuru gaishoku sangyo kara no teigen' [Proposal from the food service industry on the employment of foreigners] (May 1990).
Japan General Research Institute (Nihon Sogo Kenkyujo), *Gaikokujin rodosha no juyo to kyosei ni kansuru kenkyu* [Research on the reception and coexistence with foreign workers] (1990).
Japan Institute of Labor (Nihon Rodo Kyokai), *Kaigai rodo jiho* [Overseas Labor News] (September 1987).
Japan Institute of Labor (Nihon Rodo Kenkyu Kiko), *Gaikokujin rodosha mondai no seisakuteki kento* [Discussions on policy toward the problem of foreign workers] (March 1991).
Japan Occupational Safety and Health Resource Center a: Japan Occupational Safety and Health Resource Center (Zenkoku Rodo Anzen Eisei Center), *Anzen center joho* [Safety Center News] (March 1991).
Japan Occupational Safety and Health Resource Center b: Japan Occupational Safety and Health Resource Center (Zenkoku Rodo Anzen Eisei Center), *Anzen center joho* [Safety Center News] (May 1992).
Japan Occupational Safety and Health Resource Center c: Japan Occupational Safety and Health Resource Center (Zenkoku Rodo Anzen Eisei Center), *Gaikokujin rodosha no rosai hakusho 92-nen ban* [1992 white paper on workplace accidents among foreign workers] (Kaifu Shobo 1992).
Japanese Trade Union Confederation (JTUC-RENGO), *Heisei 2-nen 3-nendo seisaku seido yokyu to teigen*, [Demands and proposals for policies and systems, 1990–1991] (1990).
JICA (Japan International Cooperation Agency), *Nikkeijin honpo shuro jittai chosa hokokusho* [Field survey on the employment situation of Nikkeijin in Japan] (February 1992).
Joho Center, Planning Division, 'Gaikokujin no hiseishain koyo ni kansuru koyo kanri no jittai chosa' [Field survey on employment management for the employment of irregular foreign workers], in *E' STIME* (special edition, 1991).
Kajita a: Kajita, Takamichi, *Ethnicity to shakai hendo* [Ethnicity and social change] (Yushindo 1988).

Kajita b: Kajita, Takamichi, 'EC togo to teiju gaikokujin no shorai – EC shokokumin to hi-EC shokokumin to no sai ni chakumoku shite' [The unification of EC and the future of settled foreigners – observations on the gaps between EC citizens and non-EC citizens], in Social Security Research Institute.

Kajita c: Kajita, Takamichi, 'Doka/togo/hennyu – France no imin e no taio wo meguru ronso' [Assimilation, integration, incorporation – debates on responses to immigration in France], in Iyotani and Kajita.

Kalabaw no Kai a: Kalabaw no Kai, 'Gaikokujin dekasegi rodosha no gohoka ni mukete' [Toward the legalization of foreign migrant workers] (July 1988).

Kalabaw no Kai b: Kalabaw no Kai, *Nakama janaika gaikokujin rodosha* [Aren't foreign workers our colleagues?] (Akashi Shoten 1990).

Kanagawa Prefecture a: Kanagawa Prefecture Bureau of Labor Affairs, Labor Administration Department, *Kigyo ni okeru gaikokujin rodosha koyo no iko/jittai chosa* [Survey on the will and situation of employment of foreign workers in companies] (March 1991).

Kanagawa Prefecture b: Kanagawa Prefecture Bureau of Labor Affairs, Labor Administration Department, *Rodokumiai yakuin no gaikokujin rodosha ni taisuru ishiki chosa* [Survey on attitudes of labor union executives concerning foreign workers] (March 1991).

Kanagawa Prefecture c: Kanagawa Prefecture Self-Government Research Center, *Oshuni okeru gaikokujin mondai ni kansuru chosa* [Survey on the problem of foreign workers in Western countries] (March 1991).

Kano, Hirokatsu, 'Chuto chi' iki no kokusai rodoryoku ido to imin taisaku' [International labor movement and immigration policies in the Middle East], in Momose and Ogura.

Kansai Association of Corporate Executives (Kansai Keizai Doyukai), Habahiroi gaikokujin koyo no sokushin wo [Toward the large-scale hiring of foreigners] (March 1989).

Kansai Economic Federation (Kansai Keizai Rengokai), 'Gaikokujin rodosha ukeire mondai ni tsuite' [On the issue of accepting foreign workers] (April 1990).

Kansai Employers' Association a: Kansai Employers' Association (Kansai Keieisha Kyokai), 'Gaikokujin rodosha no ukeire mondai ni tsuite' [On the acceptance of foreign workers] (No date).

Kansai Employers' Association b: Kansai Employers' Association (Kansai Keieisha Kyokai), *Kokusaika e no kigyo no taio* [Enterprises' responses to internationalization] (September 1989).

Kanto Federation of Bar Associations, *Gaikokujin rodosha no shuro to jinken* [The work and human rights of foreign workers] (Akashi Shoten 1990).

Kashiwagi, Hiroshi, *America no gaikokujin rodosha* [The United States' foreign workers] (Akashi Shoten 1991).

Kataoka, Yoshihiro, 'Kowasareta "kyozon kyoei" – Mie Kankokujin ama tekihatsu no hamon' [The end of 'coexistence and coprosperity' – the ripples of the disclosure of Korean ama working in Mie Prefecture], in *Migrant*, No. 4, 15 July 1988.

Kawahara, Ken' ichi, *America iminho* [The U.S. Immigration Law] (Yuhikaku Shuppan Service 1990).
Kawasaki City, Citizens Bureau, Department for Working Citizens, 'Showa 63-nendoban koyo rodo chosa kekka hokokusho' [Report on the 1988 survey on employment and labor], December 1988.
Keio University, Law Department, Miyazawa Koichi Study Group, *Gaikokujin rodosha mondai* [The foreign worker issue] (Higaishashagaku Kenkyujo 1989).
Kikuchi, Kyoko, 'Gaikokujin rodosha okuridashi koku no shakaiteki mechanism' [Social mechanisms in countries that dispatch foreign workers], in Iyotani and Kajita.
Kim Chandong, *Ihojin wa kimigayo-maru ni notte* [Aliens on board the vessel Kimigayo] (Iwanami Shoten 1985).
Kim Donghoon a: Kim, Donghoon, *Kaisetsu: jinshu sabetsu teppai joyaku* [Comments: The Treaty on Eliminating All Forms of Discrimination] (Kaiho Shuppansha 1990).
Kim Donghoon b: Kim Donghoon, *Kokuren/Iju rodosha kenri joyaku to Nihon* [Japan and the U.N. Treaty on the Rights of Migrant Workers] (Kaiho Shuppansha 1992).
Kim Dongmyung, 'Zainichi chosenjin no "daisan no michi" ' [The 'third path' for resident Koreans of Japan], in *Chosenjin*, No. 17, 1979.
Kim Sukbun, *'Zainichi' no shiso* [The idea of 'resident Koreanism'] (Chikuma Shobo 1981).
Kinbara, Samon, Ishida, Reiko et al., *Nihon no naka no Kankoku/ Chosenjin, Chugokujin* [The Koreans and Chinese inside Japan] (Akashi Shoten 1986).
Koido, Akihiro, 'Mexico-kei "higoho" imin rodosha to America kokka – rekishiteki dotai to 1986-nen iminho kaikaku' [Mexican 'illegal' immigrant workers and the U.S. state – historical changes and the 1986 revision of the Immigration Act], in Momose and Ogura.
Koido, Yuji, ed., *Gaikokujin rodosha, seisaku to kadai* [Policies and issues concerning foreign workers] (Zeimu Keiri Kyokai 1990).
Kojima, Reito, 'Chugoku no jinko ido' [Population movements in China], in Nakaoka.
Kojima, Tomoyuki, 'Umi wo koeta "minko moryu" ' [The 'blind rush' across the sea], in *Seiron*, November 1989.
Kojima, Yoko, 'Gaikokujin rodosha e no fukushiteki taio – kokusai hikaku no shiten kara' [Welfare responses to foreign workers – from an international comparisons perspective], in Susumu Sato.
Kokusai Jinryu, 'Tokei ni miru nihonjin no kaigai iju' [Looking at migrations of Japanese abroad through statistics], in *Kokusai Jinryu*, July 1990.
Komai a: Komai, Hiroshi, 'Nihonjin no Asia-kan' [Japanese views of Asia], in *Toyo Daigaku Shakaigakubu Kiyo*, November-December 1975.
Komai b: Komai, Hiroshi, *Gaikokujin rodosha wo miru me* [The Policy Implications of Immigrant Workers in Japan] (Akashi Shoten 1990).
Komai c: Komai, Hiroshi, *Gaikokujin rodosha no rodo oyobi seikatsu jittai ni kansuru kenkyu – kenshusei no bunseki* [Field research on the

working and living of foreign workers – analysis of trainees] (Tsukuba Daigaku Shakaikagaku-kei, March 1991).
Konno, Koichiro and Sato, Hiroki, eds, *Gaikokujin kenshusei* [Foreign trainees] (Toyo Keizai Shimposha 1991).
KSD (Chusho Kigyo Keieisha Saigai Hosho Jigyodan), 'Gaikokujin rodosha ni kansuru chosa hokoku' [Report from survey on foreign workers] (May 1990).
Kuwabara, Yasuo, *Kokkyo wo koeru rodosha* [Foreign workers crossing borders] (Iwanami Shoten 1992).
Liu Wenfu, 'Shonenba wo mukaeta Taiwan no gaikokujin rodosha mondai' [A crucial moment in Taiwan's foreign worker problem], in *Ajiken News*, September 1989 (Institute for Developing Economies).
Machida, Sachio, 'Fuho shuro gaikokujin no jittai' [The situation of illegal foreign workers], in *Jurist*, 1 June 1988.
Maeyama a: Maeyama, Takashi, 'Nikkei gaikokujin rodosha ni tsuite' [On foreign workers of Japanese ancestry], in *Kokusai Jinryu* (October 1988).
Maeyama b: Maeyama, Takashi, 'Nikkei gaikokujin rodosha no sono go' [Follow-up on foreign workers of Japanese ancestry], in *Kokusai Jinryu*, July 1990.
Mainichi Shimbun a: Mainichi Shimbun, ed., *Jipangu* [Japan], New and rebound edition (Mainichi Shimbunsha 1990).
Mainichi Shimbun b: Mainichi Shimbun, ed., *Daisan no kaikoku* [The third opening of the country] (Asahi Sonorama 1990).
Management and Coordination Agency, Administrative Inspection Bureau, *Gaikokujin no shuro ni kansuru jittai chosa kekka hokokusho* [Report on field survey on the labor of foreigners] (January 1992).
Marukawa, Tomoo, 'Chugoku kara Nihon e no "shugakusei" kyuzo' [The sudden increase in 'shugakusei' from China to Japan], in *Ajiken News*, September 1989 (Institute of Developing Economies).
Matsui, Kazuhisa, 'Malaysia e mukau Indonesia-jin rodosha' [Indonesian workers going to Malaysia], in *Ajiken News*, September 1989 (Institute of Developing Economies).
Ministry of Agriculture, Forestry and Fisheries, 'Gaikokujin kenshusei rodosha ni kansuru chosa kekka' [Results of survey on foreign trainee workers] (November 1989).
Ministry of Construction, Chief of Economic Affairs Bureau, *Kensetsu-gyo ni okeru gaikokujin no fuho shuro no boshi ni kansuru kyoryoku irai ni tsuite* [On requests for cooperation in preventing illegal foreign workers in the construction industry] (November 1988).
Ministry of Education a: Ministry of Education, Science and International Affairs Bureau, Student Exchange Department, 'Wagakuni no ryugakusei seido no gaiyo' [Overview of our country's exchange students system] (January 1991).
Ministry of Education b: Ministry of Education, 'Nihongo kyoiku ga hitsuyo na gaikokujin jido seito no ukeire shido no jokyo ni tsuite' [On the acceptance and guidance of foreign children and pupils who require Japanese language education] (April 1992).
Ministry of Foreign Affairs a: Ministry of Foreign Affairs, Minister's

Secretariat, Consular and Emigration Affairs Department, ed., *Kaigai zairyu hojinsu chosa tokei* [Statistics from reports on Japanese living abroad] (1990).
Ministry of Foreign Affairs b: Ministry of Foreign Affairs, Director General for Public Information and Cultural Affairs and Economic Cooperation Bureau Aid Policy Division, ed., *Keizai kyoryoku Q&A* [Q&A on economic cooperation] (Sekai no Ugokisha March 1992).
Ministry of Justice a: Ministry of Justice, Minister's Secretariat, Judicial System and Research Department, *Shutsunyukoku kanri tokei nenpo* [Yearly statistics on immigration and emigration control] (all years).
Ministry of Justice b: Ministry of Justice, Immigration Bureau, 'Fuho shuro gaikokujin ni kakawaru assen brokers no jittai ni tsuite' [On the reality of employment brokers assisting illegal foreign workers] (March 1987).
Ministry of Justice c: Ministry of Justice, Osaka Regional Immigration Bureau, 'Kinki bengoshi rengokai to no kondankai ni okeru setsumei yoshi' [Essentials of explanation at debate with the Kinki Bar Association] (1988).
Ministry of Justice d: Ministry of Justice, Immigration Bureau, Security Department, 'Fuho shuro gaikokujin no jittai' [The reality of illegal foreign workers], in *Kokusai Jinryu*, March 1988.
Ministry of Justice e: Ministry of Justice, Immigration Bureau, Refugee Recognition Department, 'Wagakuni ni okeru Indochina nanmin no genjo' [The situation of Indochinese refugees in our country], in *Kokusai Jinryu*, September 1988.
Ministry of Justice f: Ministry of Justice, Immigration Bureau, 'Tayoka bunsanka suru fuho shuro gaikokujin' [The diversification and spreading of illegal foreign labors], in *Kokusai Jinryu*, February 1989.
Ministry of Justice g: Ministry of Justice Immigration Bureau, 'Gaikokujin no shuro ni kansuru enquete chosa' [Questionnaire survey on the work of foreign workers], in *Kokusai Jinryu*, February 1989.
Ministry of Justice h: Ministry of Justice, Deliberative Council for the Immigration of Foreign Laborers, *Hokokusho* [Report] (Japan Immigration Association March 1989).
Ministry of Justice i: Ministry of Justice, Immigration Bureau, 'Tokei ni miru fuho shuro gaikokujin no jittai' [Looking at the situation of illegal foreign workers through statistics], in *Kokusai Jinryu*, April 1989.
Ministry of Justice j: Ministry of Justice, Immigration Bureau, 'Nihongo kyoiku shinko kyokai setsuritsu' [The foundation of the Association for the Promotion of Japanese Language Education], in *Kokusai Jinryu*, July 1989.
Ministry of Justice k: Ministry of Justice, Immigration Bureau, 'Kenshu jisshi kigyo ni kansuru jittai chosa kekka ni tsuite' [Concerning field survey on enterprises carrying out training] (August 1989).
Ministry of Justice l: Ministry of Justice, Immigration Bureau, 'Daitoshiken ni okeru fuho shuro tekihatsu doryoku kikan no jisshi kekka ni tsuite' [On the results of efforts carried out by organizations to apprehend illegal workers in the capital region], in *Kokusai Jinryu*, September 1989.

Ministry of Justice m: Ministry of Justice, Immigration Bureau, 'Showa 63-nen kamihanki ni okeru joriku kyohisha oyobi nyukanho ihan jikenno gaikyou nitsuite' [On the general situation of people denied entrance and incidents of violations of the Immigration Act in 1988], in *Kokusai Jinryu*, September 1988.

Ministry of Justice n: Ministry of Justice Immigration Bureau, 'Showa 63-nen joriku kyohisha oyobi nyukanho ihan jiken gaiyo' [General situation of people denied entrance and incidents of violations of the Immigration Act in 1988] (Japan Immigration Association 1989).

Ministry of Justice o: Ministry of Justice, Immigration Bureau, 'Zairyu nikkei Brazil-jin nado no kado jokyo nado ni kansuru jittai chosa no jisshi ni tsuite' [On the implementation of field survey on the work and situation of Nikkei Brazilians living in Japan] (April 1990).

Ministry of Justice p: Ministry of Justice, Immigration Bureau, 'Ugokida-shita kaisei nyukanho' [The start of the revised Immigration Act], in *Kokusai Jinryu*, June 1990.

Ministry of Justice q: Ministry of Justice, Immigration Bureau, 'Joriku kyohisha oyobi nyukanho ihan jiken no gaikyo' [Overview of entry refusals and incidents of violations of the Immigration Act], in *Heisei gan-nen shutsunyukoku kanri kankei tokei gaiyo* (Japan Immigration Association 1990).

Ministry of Justice r: Ministry of Justice, Immigration Bureau, 'Heisei gan-nen gaikokujin oyobi nihonjin shutsunyukokusha tokei' [Statistics on immigration and emigration by foreigners and Japanese in 1988], in *Heisei gan-nen shutsunyukoku kanri kankei tokei gaiyo* (Japan Immigration Association 1990).

Ministry of Justice s: Ministry of Justice, Immigration Bureau, 'Gaikoku-jin torokusha (heisei gan-nen 12-gatsu matsu genzai) no kokuseki shusshinchi betsu zairyu shikaku (zairyu mokuteki) betsu tokei ni tsuite' [On the statistics by country or area of origin and by residence category for registered foreigners as of December 1989] (September 1990).

Ministry of Justice t: Ministry of Justice, Immigration Bureau, 'Ugokida-shita kaisei nyukanho' [The start of the revised Immigration Act], in *Kokusai Jinryu*, November 1990.

Ministry of Justice u: Ministry of Justice, Immigration Bureau, *Heisei 2-nen shutsunyukoku kanri kankei tokei gaiyo* [Overview of statistics on the control of immigration and emigration in 1990] (July 1991).

Ministry of Justice v: Ministry of Justice, Immigration Bureau, 'Nyu-kanho ihan gaikokujin no shuchu tekihatsu no jisshi ni tsuite' [On the implementation of mass apprehensions of foreigners violating the Immigration Act] (November 1991).

Ministry of Justice w: Ministry of Justice, Immigration Bureau, Regis-tration Department, 'Nihon de kurasu gaikokujin – heisei 2-nen 12-gatsu matsu genzai ni okeru zairyu gaikokujin tokei' [Foreigners living in Japan – Statistics on resident foreigners as of December 1990] (November 1991).

Ministry of Justice x: Ministry of Justice, Immigration Bureau, 'Heisei

3-nen kamihanki ni okeru fuho shuro jiken ni tsuite' [On incidents of illegal work in the first half of 1991] (November 1991).
Ministry of Justice y: Ministry of Justice, Immigration Bureau, 'Fuho shuro gaikokujin ni taisuru joriku shinsa kyoka kikan jisshi kekka ni tsuite' [On the results of operations by organizations carrying out screenings upon entry of illegal foreign workers] (January 1992).
Ministry of Justice z: Ministry of Justice, Immigration Bureau, 'Honpo ni okeru fuho zanryusha su ni tsuite' [On the number of illegal foreigners in the country] (February 1992).
Ministry of Justice A: Ministry of Justice, Immigration Bureau, 'Honpo ni okeru fuho zanryusha no su ni tsuite' [On the number of illegal foreigners in the country] (June 1992).
Ministry of Justice B: Ministry of Justice, Immigration Bureau, 'Honpo ni okeru fuho zanryusha no su ni tsuite' [On the number of illegal foreigners in the country] (August 1992).
Ministry of Justice C: Ministry of Justice, Immigration Bureau, *Heisei 3-nen shutsunyukokoku kanri kankei tokei gaiyo* [Overview of statistics for the control of immigration and emigration in 1991] (Japan Immigration Association August 1992).
Ministry of International Trade and Industry a: Ministry of International Trade and Industry, Industrial Policy Bureau, ed., *Kyozonteki kyoso e no michi – globalization report* [The road to competition within coexistence – globalization report] (Survey Committee for International Trade and Industry July 1989).
Ministry of International Trade and Industry b: Ministry of International Trade and Industry, Conference for Labor Problems, Gaikokujin rodosha mondai e no taio ni tsuite [On responses to the problem of foreign workers] (May 1990).
Ministry of Labor a: Ministry of Labor, 'Gaikokujin rodosha no shuro no jittai nado ni tsuite' [On such matters as the reality of the work of foreign workers] (March 1988).
Ministry of Labor b: Ministry of Labor, 'Gaikokujin rodosha no shuro jittai ni tsuite' [On the reality of the work of foreign workers] (No date).
Ministry of Labor c: Ministry of Labor, Employment Security Bureau, ed., *Kongo ni okeru gaikokujin rodosha ukeire no hoko – gaikokujin rodosha mondai kenkyu hokoku* [Future directions for accepting foreign workers – report on research on the problem of foreign workers] (Labor Administration Research Institute March 1988).
Ministry of Labor d: Ministry of Labor, Employment Security Bureau ed., *Koyo taisaku kihon keikaku (dai 6 ji)* [Sixth fundamental employment policy] (Ministry of Finance Publishing Bureau July 1988).
Ministry of Labor e: Conference for Research on Foreign Workers' Affairs, *Gaikokujin rodosha mondai e no taio no arikata ni tsuite* [On ways to deal with the problems of foreign workers] (December 1988).
Ministry of Labor f: Ministry of Labor, Minister's Secretariat, International Labor Afairs Division, ed., *Kaigai rodo hakusho Showa 63-nen ban* [1988 white paper on foreign labor] (Japan Institute of Labor 1988).

Ministry of Labor g: Ministry of Labor, Labor Standards Bureau, 'Fuho shuro gaikokujin ni taisuru saigai hosho no jokyo ni tsuite' [On the situation of workers' accident compensation for illegal foreign workers] (June 1989).

Ministry of Labor h: Ministry of Labor, Employment Security Bureau, Employment Promotion Agency, General Institute of Employment, ed., *Gaikokujin rodosha no ukeire seisaku* [Policy on accepting foreign workers] (Koyo Mondai Kenkyu Kai 1989).

Ministry of Labor i: Ministry of Labor, Minister's Secretariat, Policy Planning and Research Department, ed., *Kensetsu/kowan unso kankei jigyo no chingin jittai – Heisei 2-nen ban* [1990 situation of wages in construction, ports, and transportation-affiliated enterprises] (Ministry of Finance Publishing Bureau 1990).

Ministry of Labor j: Ministry of Labor, Employment Development Bureau, Overseas Cooperation Department, ed., ' "Gaikokujin kenshusei no ukeire ni kansuru chosa" kekka no gaiyo' [Overview of results of a survey on the acceptance of foreign trainees] (October 1990).

Ministry of Labor k: Study Committee on the Effects of Foreign Workers on the Labor Market, *Hokokusho* [Report] (January 1991).

Ministry of Labor l: Ministry of Labor, Employment Security Bureau, ed., *Gaikokujin rodosha mondai no doko to shiten* [Directions and perspectives on the problem of foreign workers] (Labor and Administration Research Institute November 1991).

Ministry of Labor m: Minister of Labor's Secretariat, International Labor Affairs Division, *Kaigai rodo hakusho Heisei 4-nen ban* [1992 white paper on overseas labor] (Japan Labor Research Organization 1992).

Ministry of Labor n: Study Committee on the Effects of Foreign Workers on the Labor Market, Expert Group, *Hokokusho* [Report] (June 1992).

Miyajima, Takashi, Kajita,Takamichi, et al., *Senshin shakai no dilemma* [Dilemmas of developed societies] (Yuhikaku 1985).

Mizumachi, Ryosuke, *Okasareta Asia* [Asia raped] (Brain Center 1988).

Momose, Hiroshi and Ogura, Mitsuo, eds, *Gendai kokka to imin rodosha* [Modern states and immigrant workers] (Yushindo Kobunsha 1992).

Mori, Hiromasa, *Gendai shihonshugi to gaikokujin rodosha* [Modern capitalism and foreign workers] (Otsuki Shoten 1986).

Morita, Kirio, ed., *Kokusai rodoryoku ido* [International movements of labor power] (Tokyo University Shuppankai 1987).

Nagano Prefectural Employers' Association, 'Gaikokujin tanjun rodosha no ukeire ni kansuru enquete kekka hokoku' [Report of questionnaire survey on the acceptance of unskilled foreign workers] (July 1990).

Nagoya Chamber of Commerce and Industry, *Gaikokujin rodosha mondai ni kansuru ikensho* [Opinion paper on the issue of foreign workers] (July 1990).

Naito, Masanori, ed., *Deutche saitoitsu to Toruko-jin imin rodosha*

[German reunification and Turkish immigrant workers] (Akashi Shoten 1991).

Nakagiri, Shingo and Takayama, Okumasa, ed., *Subete no gaikokujin ni iryo hogo wo* [Medical protection for all foreigners] (Kaifu Shobo 1992).

Nakai, Kiyomi, *Teiju gaikokujin to komu shuninken* [Settled foreigners and the right to public service] (Tsuge Shobo 1989).

Nakaoka, Mitsumasa, ed., *Nanmin, Imin, Degasegi* [Refugees, Immigrants, Migrants] (Toyo Keizai Shimposha 1991).

National Association of Shinkin Banks, 'Gaikokujin rodosha no mondai ni tsuite' [On the problem of foreign workers] (October 1991).

National Committee for Developing Economic Foundations for the 21st Century (21-Seiki Keizai Kiban Kaihatsu Kokumin Kaigi), 'Gaikokujin rodosha ukeire no teigen' [Proposal on the acceptance of foreign workers] (December 1988).

National Federation of Construction Workers' Unions (Zenken Roren) Kanto Region Committee, *63-nen 10-gatsu 12/13-nichi kensetsu/jyutaku kigyo kosho – hokokusho* [Report of negotiations of construction and housing firms on 12, 13 October, 1988].

National Federation of Shipbuilding and Heavy Machinery Workers' Unions (Zenkoku Zosen Jukikai Rodo Kumiai Rengokai), 'Gaikokujin rodosha no ukeire handan kijun' [Standards for decisions on the acceptance of foreign workers] (February 1989).

National Institute for Research Advancement (Sogo Kenkyu Kaihatsu Kiko), *Gaikokujin rodosha no shakaiteki juyo system ni kansuru kenkyu* [Research on social demand systems to accept foreign workers] (1990).

National Police Agency a: National Police Agency, *Keisatsu hakusho, Heisei 2-nen ban* [1990 white paper on police] (Ministry of Finance Printing Bureau 1990).

National Police Agency b: National Police Agency, Criminal Investigation Bureau, 'Heisei 3-nen no hanzai jyosei' [Crime in 1991] (December 1991).

National Police Agency c: National Police Agency, International Criminal Affairs Division, 'Heisei 3-nen no rainichi gaikokujin ni yoru keihouhan no kenkyo jokyo ni tsuite' [On the situation concerning controlling criminal offenses committed by foreigners in 1991] (February 1992).

National Police Agency d: National Police Agency, Criminal Investigation Bureau, 'Heisei 4-nen kamihanki no hanzai josei' [The crime situation during the first half of 1992] (July 1992).

National Police Agency e: National Police Agency, *Keisatsu hakusho, Heisei 4-nen ban* [1992 white paper on police] (Ministry of Finance Printing Bureau 1992).

Nihon Hoso Kyokai (Japan Broadcasting Corporation) Reporting Group, *Hitobusoku shakai – dare ga nihon wo sasaeru no ka* [The labor shortage – who will support Japan?] (Japan Broadcasting Publishing Corporation 1991).

Nishio, Kanji, *Senryakuteki 'sakoku-ron'* [Strategic 'closed door' argument] (Kodansha 1988).
Ochiai, Hideaki, *Asia-jin rodoryoku yunyu* [Imports of Asian workers], (Gendai Hyoronsha 1974).
Ogawa, Yuhei, 'Chuto no Keizai Kaihatsu to Kokusai Rodoryoku Ido' [Economic development in the Middle East and international movements of labor], in Morita.
Okabe, Kazuaki, *Taminzoku shakai no torai* [The arrival of a multi-ethnic society] (Ochanomizu Shobo 1991).
Okazawa, Norio, 'Sweden ni okeru gaikokujin ukeire seisaku – chikyu shiminken no kokoromi' [Sweden's policy on admitting foreigners – an experiment in global citizenship], in Social Security Research Institute.
Okinawa International Foundation (Okinawa-ken Kokusai Koryu Zaidan), *Nanbei ijusha shitei no 'dekasegi mondai' ni kansuru jittai chosa hokokusho* [Report on field survey of the 'migrant labor' problem among offspring of people who migrated to South America], (November 1990).
Okuda and Tajima a: Okuda, Michihiro and Tajima, Junko, *Ikebukuro no Asia-kei gaikokujin* [The Asian foreigners of Ikebukuro] (Mekon 1991).
Okuda and Tajima b: Okuda, Michihiro and Tajima, Junko, ed, *Shinjuku no Asia-kei gaikokujin – shakaigakuteki jittai hokoku* [The Asian foreigners of Shinjuku – report on sociological situation] (Rikkyo Daigaku Shakaigakubu May 1992).
Onishi, Masatomo, *Keizai kankyo no henka to chusho kogyo* [Changes in the economic environment and small- and medium-sized factories] (Kansai Daigaku Keizai/Seiji Kenkyojo 1987).
Onuki, Kensuke, 'Fubyodo na gaikokujin hanzai no toriatsukai' [Unfair treatment of foreigners crime], in *Sekai*, January 1990.
Oonuma, Yasuaki, *Tan'itsu minzoku shakai no shinwa wo koete* [Overcoming the myth of a monoracial society] (Toshindo 1986).
Osada, Mitsue, 'Dekasegi ni kibo wo takusu Bangladesh no seinentachi' [Bangladeshi youth have put their hopes into becoming migrant workers], in *Ajiken News*, September 1989 (Institute for Developing Economies).
Osaka Chamber of Commerce a: Osaka Chamber of Commerce (Osaka Shoko Kaigisho), *Gaikokujin rodosha ukeire ni kansuru chosa hokoku* [Report on survey concerning the acceptance of foreign workers] (October 1988).
Osaka Chamber of Commerce b: Osaka Chamber of Commerce (Osaka Shoko Kaigisho), *Gaikokujin rodosha nado no saiyo ni kansuru chosa hokoku* [Report on survey concerning the employment of foreign workers] (May 1990).
Oshima, Shizuko and Francis, Carolyn, *HELP kara mita Nihon* [Seeing Japan from HELP] (Asahi Shimbunsha 1988).
Pacific Asia Resource Center a: Pacific Asia Resource Center, 'Rodoryoku yushutsu taikoku Philippines' [The Philippines: a labor export superpower], in *Sekai Kara* No.30, 1987.
Pacific Asia Resource Center b: Pacific Asia Resource Center, 'Philip-

pine-jin to kaigaidekasegi' [Filipinos and migrant labor], in *Shinchihei*, September 1987.
Park a: Park, Kyongshuku, *Chosenjin kyosei renko no kiroku* [Records of Korean forced laborers] (Miraisha 1965).
Park b: Park, Kyongshuku, ed., *Zainichi chosenjin kankei shiryo shusei* [Compilation of documents on resident Koreans in Japan] (San'ichi Shobo 1975).
Park c: Park, Kyongshuku, *Kaiho-go zainichi chosenjin undo shi* [A history of post-liberation resident Korean of Japan movements] (San'ichi Shobo 1989).
People's Finance Corporation a: People's Finance Corporation (Kokumin Kinyu Koko) 'Chushokigyo ni okeru gaikokujin rodosha no koyo' [The employment of foreign workers in small and medium-sized enterprises], in *Kokumin Kinyu Koko Chosa Geppo* (December 1991).
People's Finance Corporation b: People's Finance Corporation General Research Institute (Kokumin Kinyu Koko Sogo Kenkyujo), ' "Hito" no Kokusaika jidai ni ikiru chusho kigyo' [Small and medium-sized enterprises in the era of the internationalization of 'people'], in *Chosa Kiho*, No.20, February 1992.
Prime Minister's Office a: Prime Minister's Office, Prime Minister's Secretariat, Public Relations Office, 'Gaikokujinno nyukokuto zairyuni kansuru seron chosa' [Public opinion survey on the entry and residence in Japan of foreigners] (Survey conducted February 1988).
Prime Minister's Office b: Prime Minister's Office, Prime Minister's Secretariat, Public relations Office, 'Gaikokujin rodosha mondai ni kansuru seron chosa' [Public opinion survey on the problem of foreign workers] (Survey conducted November 1990).
Provisional Council for the Promotion of Administrative Reform (Rinji Gyosei Kaikaku Tsuishin Shingikai), 'Kokusaika taio kokumin seikatsu jushi no gyosei kaikaku ni kansuru dai niji toshin' [Second report on administrative reform, promoting internationalization and improving quality life] (December 1991).
RENGO's Research Institute for Advancement of Living Standards (RIALS), *Ningen yusen no keizai shakai system no sozo e* [Creating a socio-economic system to put people first] (Daiichi Shorin 1990).
Saitama Prefecture, Bureau of Labor Affairs, Labor Administration and Welfare Department, *Gaikokujin rodosha shuro jokyo chosa kekka hokokusho* [Report on a study on the working situation of foreign workers] (March 1991).
Sanwa General Research Institute, Research and Development Section, *Uchinaru kokusaika no tame no jinzai katsuyo* [Making use of personnel for internationalization within the firm] (May 1989).
Sanya, Tetsuo, *Japayuki-san* (Joho Center Shuppankyoku 1985).
Sasaki, Shoko, *Asia kara fuku kaze* [The wind blowing from Asia] (Asahi Shimbunsha 1991).
Sato, Susumu, ed., *Gaikokujin rodosha no fukushi to jinken* [The welfare and human rights of foreign workers] (Horitsu Bunkasha 1992).
Sato, Tatsuya, ' "Kokusaku" to natta dekasegi' [Migrant labor made into national policy], in *Sohyo Shimbun*, 17 June 1988.

Sato, Yasuo, 'Italia hen' [Italy section], in Kanagawa Prefecture c.
Sazaki, Shoji, *Kensetsu rodo to gaikokujin rodosha* [Construction labor and foreign workers] (Taisei Shuppansha 1991).
Schoneck, Masako, 'Deutche hen' [Section on Germany], in Kanagawa Prefecture c.
Shahedo Soam and Sekiguchi Chie, *Zairyu tokubetsu kyoka* [Special residency permit] (Akashi Shoten 1992).
Shimoda, Hirotsugu, 'Shudatsu sareru Asia no chiteki rodo' [Asia's intellectual labor is being plundered', in *Asahi Journal*, 11 April 1988.
Shimohira, Yoshihiro, 'Holland no imin rodosha to shakaiteki togo seisaku' [Holland's immigrant workers and social integration policy], in Social Welfare Research Institute.
Shinano Mainichi Shimbun a: Shinano Mainichi Shimbun ed., Sekai *shimin e no michi* [The road to global citizenship] (Akashi Shoten 1989).
Shinano Mainichi Shimbun b: Shinano Mainichi Shimbun ed., *Tobirawo akete* [Open the gate] (Akashi Shoten 1992).
Small and Medium Enterprise Agency a: Small and Medium Enterprise Agency, ed., *Chusho kigyo hakusho Showa 63-nen ban* [1988 white paper on small and medium enterprises] (Ministry of Finance Publishing Bureau 1989).
Small and Medium Enterprise Agency b: Small and Medium Enterprise Agency, ed., *Chushokigyo hakusho Heisei gan-nen ban* [1989 white paper on small and medium enterprises] (Ministry of Finance Publishing Bureau 1990).
Social and Economic Congress of Japan (Shakai Keizai Kokumin Kaigi), *Heisei 2-nen ban kokumin kaigi hakusho* [1990 white paper of the Social and Economic Congress of Japan] (1990).
Social Security Research Institute, *Gaikokujin rodoshato shakai hosho* [Foreign workers and social security] (Tokyo Daigaku Shuppankai 1991).
Sugata, Sho, 'Fuho shuro konzetsu wo mezasu Singapore' [Singapore aims for the eradication of illegal labor]' in *Ajiken News*, September 1989 (Institute of Developing Economies).
Sugiura, Akimichi, 'Kotoba, saiban, Thai-jin – Nagoya no case' [Language, trial, Thais – the Nagoya case], in Ebashi.
Suh, Kengsuku, *Kominka seisaku kara shimon onatsu made* [From the policy of making Koreans into subjects of the Emperor to fingerprinting] (Iwanami Shoten 1989).
Sumi Kazuo, *ODA enjo no genjitsu* [The reality of ODA] (Iwanami Shoten 1989).
Tabata, Shigejiro, *Kokusaika jidai no jinken mondai* [Human rights in the age of internationalization] (Iwanami Shoten 1988).
Takahashi, Hidemi, *TOKYO gaikokujin saiban* [Tokyo trials for foreigners] (Heibonsha 1992).
Tanaka a: Tanaka, Hiroshi, 'Shugakusei mondai no kozu' [Map of the shugakusei problem], in *Asia no Tomo* April 1989 (Asian Students Cultural Association).

Tanaka b: Tanaka, Hiroshi, *Zainichi gaikokujin* [Foreigners in Japan] (Iwanami Shoten 1991).
Tanaka, Hiroshi and Miyoshi, Ayako, eds, *Gendai no Esprit 249, Japayuki-san no genzai* [Today's Esprit 249 – the situation of Japayuki] (Shibundo 1988).
Tenmei, Yoshiomi, *Gaikokujin rodosha to rodo saigai – sono genjo to jitsumu Q&A* [Foreign workers and workplace accidents – reality and practical questions and answers] (Kaifu Shobo 1991).
Tezuka a: Tezuka, Kazuaki, *Gaikokujin rodosha* [Foreign workers] (Nihon Keizai Shimbunsha 1989).
Tezuka b: Tezuka, Kazuaki, *Rodoryoku ido no jidai* [The age of labor power mobility] (Chuo Koronsha 1990).
Tezuka c: Tezuka, Kazuaki, 'Suisse ni okeru gaikokujin rodosha no ukeire' [The acceptance of foreign workers in Switzerland], in *Nihon Rodo Kenkyu Zasshi*, July 1990.
Tezuka d: Tezuka, Kazuaki, *Zoku: gaikokujin rodosha* [Foreign workers (continued)] (Nihon Keizai Shimbunsha 1991).
Tezuka, Kazuaki, Watanabe Hisashi et al., eds, *Symposium Nihon to Deutche no gaikokujin rodosha* [Symposium: foreign workers in Japan and Germany] (Akashi Shoten 1991).
Tezuka, Kazuaki, Miyajima, Takashi et al., eds, *Gaikokujin rodosha to jichitai* [Foreign workers and local governments] (Akashi Shoten 1992).
Tezuka, Kazuaki, Komai, Hiroshi et al., eds, *Gaikokujin rodosha no shuro jittai – sogoteki jittai chosa hokokushu* [The working situation of foreign workers – comprehensive field survey report] (Akashi Shoten 1992).
Tochigi Prefecture Association of Corporate Executives (Tochigi-ken Keizai Doyukai), 'Gaikokujin rodosha no ukeire ni tsuite (teigen)' [(Proposal) on the acceptance of foreign workers] (November 1989).
Tokyo Association of Shinkin Banks Research Center (Tokyo-to Shinyo Kinko Kyokai Kenkyu Center), *Kokusaika no shinten ni tomonau chusho kigyo e no eikyo* [The effect of the development of internationalization on small and medium-sized enterprises] (October 1990).
Tokyo Chamber of Commerce and Industry a: Tokyo Chamber of Commerce and Industry (Tokyo Shoko Kaigisho), 'Gaikokujin rodosha no ukeire mondai ni kansuru chukan iken ni tsuite' [Intermediate opinion on the problem of accepting foreign workers] (September 1988).
Tokyo Chamber of Commerce and Industry b: Tokyo Chamber of Commerce and Industry (Tokyo Shoko Kaigisho), 'Gaikokujin no ukeire ni kansuru chosa (gaiyo)' [Survey on the acceptance of foreign workers (summary)] (No date).
Tokyo Chamber of Commerce and Industry c: Tokyo Chamber of Commerce and Industry (Tokyo Shoko Kaigisho), 'Gaikokujin rodosha jukuren keisei seido no sosetsu nado ni kansuru teigen' [Proposal on such matters as instituting a system for training foreign workers] (December 1989).
Tokyo Chamber of Commerce and Industry d: Tokyo Chamber of Com-

merce and Industry (Tokyo Shoko Kaigisho), 'Rodo seisaku ni kansuru yobo' [Demands on labor policies] (July 1990).
Tokyo Federation of Corporate Taxpayers Associations (Tokyo Hojinkai Rengokai), *Chusho kigyo no jugyoin no koyo jittai ni tsuite* [On the employment situation of employees in small and medium-sized enterprises] (November 1988).
Tokyo Metropolitan Government a: Tokyo Minato-ku Cultural and International Exchange Planning Division, *Minatoku zaiju gaikokujin no ishiki chosa* [Attitude survey of foreigners living in Minato-ku] (January 1989).
Tokyo Metropolitan Government b: Tokyo, Shinjuku Ward Municipal Government Survey (No title, No date).
Tokyo Metropolitan Government c: Tokyo, Toshima Ward Municipal Government, *Toshimaku no kokusaika ni kansuru gyosei juyo chosa* [Survey on administrative requests concerning the internationalization of Toshima Ward] (February 1989).
Tokyo Metropolitan Government d: The Tokyo Metropolitan Government, Bureau of Public Health, 'Nihongo gakko shugakusei ni taisuru kekkaku kenshin kekka (saishu shukei) ni tsuite' [Final results on examinations for tuberculosis among foreign *shugakusei* studying in Japanese language schools] (October 1989).
Tokyo Metropolitan Government e: Tokyo Metropolitan Government, Bureau of Citizens and Cultural Affairs, *Tokyo-to ku-shi-cho-son ni okeru kokusai koryu jigyo nado ni kansuru chosa kekka* [Results of survey on such matters as international exchange in local government in Tokyo-to] (December 1989).
Tokyo Metropolitan Government f: Tokyo Metropolitan Government, Office of Information, *Joho renraku (shiryohen)*, No 14 [Information & Communications (Documentation), No. 14] (December 1989).
Tokyo Metropolitan Government g: Tokyo Metropolitan Government, Bureau of Citizens and Cultural Affairs, *Ryugakusei shugakusei no seikatsu ni kansuru jittai chosa hokokusho* [Report of survey on the lifestyles of foreign students and *shugakusei*] (1989).
Tokyo Metropolitan Government h: Shinagawa Ward Labor Administration Office, *Gaikokujin no koyo ni kansuru ishiki/jittai chosa* [Attitude and situation survey of the employment of foreign workers] (1989).
Tokyo Metropolitan Government i: Council on the Problem of Foreign Labor, *Tokyo-to ni okeru gaikokujin rodosha no genjo to kadai* [The reality and issues concerning foreign workers in the Tokyo metropolis] (June 1990).
Tokyo Metropolitan Government j: Tokyo Metropolitan Government, Toshima Ward Municipal Government, *Gaikokujin sodan ni miru Toshima-ku no kokusaika* [The internationalization of Toshima Ward seen through consultations by foreigners] (September 1990).
Tokyo Metropolitan Government k: Tokyo Metropolitan Institute for Labor, *Tokyo-to ni okeru gaikokujin rodosha no shuro jittai*, [The reality of foreign workers in the Tokyo metropolis] (1991).
Tokyo Metropolitan Government l: Tokyo Metropolitan Government,

Bureau of Citizens and Cultural Affairs, *Ryugakusei shugakusei ni kansuru jittai chosa hokokusho* [Report from survey on the situation of foreign students and *shugakusei*] (March 1992).
Tokyo Metropolitan Government m: Tokyo Metropolitan Government, Office of Information, 'Toshi seikatsu ni kansuru seron chosa' [Opinion poll on city life] (May 1992).
Tokyo Metropolitan Government n: Tokyo Metropolitan Government, Office of Information, 'Kokusaika ni kansuru seron chosa' [Opinion poll on internationalization] (June 1992).
Tokyo Tomin Bank, Ltd., ' "Rodoryoku busoku" to gaikokujin rodosha no koyo ni tsuite' [On the labor shortage and the employment of foreign workers] (July 1989).
Tomioka a: Tomioka, Jiro, *Gendai Inglez no imin rodosha* [Recent immigrant workers in England] (Akashi Shoten 1988).
Tomioka b: Tomioka, Jiro, *Inglez ni okeru imin rodosha no jutaku mondai* [Housing problems of immigrant workers in England] (Akashi Shoten 1992).
Tomonaga, Kenzo, *Jinken to wa? kokusai jinken kiyaku to Nihon* [Human rights? the Universal Declaration of Human Rights and Japan] (Kaiho Shuppansha 1989).
Tsuzuki, Kurumi, 'Nikkei Brazil-jin no seikatsu jittai chosa yori – chukan hokoku' [Mid-term report on field survey of the living conditions of Nikkei Brazilian], in *Nagoya Daigaku Shakaigaku Ronshu*, No. 13, 1992.
Uchida, Susumu, 'Hong Kong no imin ryushutsu to gaikokujin yunyu' [Hong Kong's outflow of immigrants and imports of foreign workers], in *Ajiken News*, September 1989 (Institute of Developing Economies).
Uchino, Masayuki, *Sabetsuteki hyogen* [Discriminatory expressions] (Yuhikaku 1990).
United Nations University and Soka University, Asian Studies Institute, *Nanmin mondai no gakusaiteki kenkyu* [Scholarly research on the refugee issue] (Ochanomizu Shobo 1986).
University of Tsukuba a: University of Tsukuba, Institute of Social Sciences, *Okinawa kara chikyu e*, [From Okinawa to the world], (1987).
University of Tsukuba b: University of Tsukuba, Institute of Social Sciences, *Chikyu/kokka/chiiki shakai – Hokkaido kara no shikaku* [Earth/state/local society – a view from Hokkaido] (1988).
University of Tsukuba c: University of Tsukuba, Institute of Social Sciences, *Tokyo kara TOKYO e* [From Tokyo to TOKYO] (1990).
University of Tsukuba d: University of Tsukuba, Institute of Social Sciences, *Kokkyo wo koete – gaikokujin rodosha no genkyo* [Crossing borders – the reality of foreign workers] (1991).
Utsumi, Aiko and Matsui, Yayori, *Asia kara kita dekasegi rodoshatachi* [The migrant workers from Asia] (Akashi Shoten 1988).
Wakabayashi, Keiko, 'Chugoku ni okeru jinko "moryu" ' ['The blind flow' of population in China], in *Jinko Mondai Kenkyu*, Vol. 46, No. 1 (Ministry of Health and Welfare, Institute of Population Problems April 1990).

Washio, Hiroaki, 'Thai wo meguru kokusai rodo ido' [Thai-related international movements of labor], in *Ajiken News*, September 1989 (Institute of Developing Economies).

Watado, Ichiro, 'Sekai toshika no naka no gaikokujin mondai' [The problem of foreign workers in the context of global urbanization], in *Toshi Mondai*, September 1988.

Watanabe, Masako, 'Brazil kara no Nikkei dekasegi rodosha to "Nihon" to no deai' [Brazilian Nikkei migrant workers' encounters with 'Japan'], in *Shakai Chosa Jisshu Hokokusho*, vol. 8 (Meiji Gakuin Daigaku Shakaigaku-bu March 1992).

Watanabe, Masako and Mitsuyama, Shizue, 'Brazil kara no Nikkei dekasegi rodosha no jittai to Nihon shakai no taio' [The situation of Nikkei migrant workers from Brazil and the response of Japanese society], in *Shakaigaku/Shakai Fukushigaku Kenkyu*, No. 89, March 1992.

Watanabe, Masako, Yuge, Harumi et al., 'Nikkei dekasegi rodosha no kyuzo ni tomonau Nihon shakai no taio to mosaku' [Grasping for responses in Japanese society to the sudden increase in Nikkei migrant workers], in *Meiji Gakuin Daigaku Shakaigaku-bu Fuzoku Kenkyujo Nenpo*, No. 22, March 1992.

Yamagami a: Yamagami, Susumu, 'Nihongo gakko ni kansuru guideline sakutei sareru' [Making guidelines for Japanese language schools], in *Kokusai Jinryu*, March 1989.

Yamagami b: Yamagami, Susumu, 'Kenshusei ni kansuru nyukoku jizen shinsa kijun no meikakuka ni mukete' [Toward building clear standards for pre-entry screenings for trainees], in *Kokusai Jinryu*, June 1989.

Yamagami c: Yamagami, Susumu, 'Tokei kara mita gaikokujin shugakusei no nyukoku jokyo' [Looking through statistics at the situation of foreign 'shugakusei' entering the country, in *Kokusai Jinryu*, July 1989.

Yamagami d: Yamagami, Susumu, 'Boat people wo meguru genkyo to kadai' [Situation and issues surrounding boat people], in *Kokusai Jinryu*, October 1989.

Yamagami e: Yamagami, Susumu, *Wagakuni wo meguru kokusai jinryu no hensen* [Changes in international population flows relating to our country] (Japan Immigration Association 1989).

Yamagami f: Yamagami, Susumu, *Nanmin mondai no genjo to kadai* [Situation and issues surrounding the refugee problem] (Nihon Kajo Shuppan 1990).

Yamaguchi a: Yamaguchi, Reiko, 'Kane ni tsukareta Chugokujin "ryugaku" sei' [Chinese 'foreign students' lured by money], in *Bungei Shunju*, September 1988.

Yamaguchi b: Yamaguchi, Reiko, 'Shubun fukidasu Nihongo gakko' [Scandalous Japanese language schools] in *Bungei Shunju*, December 1988.

Yamamoto, Kazumi, 'Philippines' in *Ajiken News*, September 1989 (Institute of Developing Economies).

Yamanaka, Ichiro, 'Pakistan ni okeru kaigai iju rodo' [Overseas immigrant labor from Pakistan], in *Asia Keizai*, March 1984.

Yamashita, Kesao, *Hito no kokusaika ni kansuru sogoteki kenkyu – tokuni gaikokujin rodosha ni kansuru chosa kenkyu wo chushin ni* [Comprehensive research on the internationalization of people – with a central focus on surveys and research on foreign workers] (Toyo Daigaku Shakaigaku-bu 1992).

Yamazaki, Tetsuo, 'Nyukanho no kaisei/gaikokujin rodosha mondai e no taio' [The Immigration Act revision/responding to the problem of foreign workers], in *Kokusai Jinryu*, June 1989.

Yamazaki, Yoshihiko, Wakabayashi, Chihiro, et al., 'Ueno no machi to Iran-jin – masatsu to kyosei' [The town of Ueno and the Iranians – coexistence with friction] (Todai Igakubu Hoken Shakaigaku Kyoshitsu July 1992).

Yanobe, Hiroyasu, 'Komyo na Singapore no gaikokujin rodosha taisaku' [Singapore's cunning policies toward foreign workers], *Economist*, 3 October 1989.

Yokohama Chamber of Commerce (Yokohama Shoko Kaigisho), 'Gaikokujin rodosha ukeire ni kansuru chosa kekka gaiyo' [Overview of a survey on the acceptance of foreign workers] (January 1990).

Yun, Koencha, ' "sainyukoku Kyokasho" to toko no jiyu' ['Re-entry permits' and the freedom of travel], in *Sekai*, January 1990.

E References in other languages

Asia-Pacific Mission for Migrant Filipinos, *Proceedings of the First Regional Conference of Overseas Filipinos* (Asia and the Pacific), Hong Kong, 1988.

Briggs, V.M.jr., *Immigration Policy and the American Labor Force*, Baltimore: Johns Hopkins University Press, 1984.

Castles, S. and Kosack, G., *Immigrant Workers and Class Structure in Western Europe*, Oxford: Oxford University Press, second edition, 1985.

Catholic Institute for International Relations, *The Labour Trade: Filipino Migrant Workers around the World*, Manila, 1987.

Cohen, R., *The New Helots*, England: Gower, 1987.

(U.S.) Council of Economic Advisors, *Economic Report of the President*, 1986.

Dickson, M. and Jonas, S., eds, *The New Nomad*, San Francisco: Synthesis Publications, 1982.

Documentation for Action Groups in Asia, *Migrant Labour for Sale?*, Hong Kong, 1986.

Gasparde, F. and Servan-Schreiber, C., *La Fin des immigrés*, Editions du Seuil, 1984.

Glazer and Moynihan a: Glazer, N. and Moynihan, D. P., *Beyond the Melting Pot*, Mass: Massachusetts Institute of Technology, 1963.

Glazer and Moynihan b: Glazer, N. and Moynihan, D. P., eds, *Ethnicity:*

Theory and Experience, Cambridge, Mass: Harvard University Press, 1975.

Gordon, M., *Assimilation in American Life*, New York: Oxford University Press, 1964.

Kim and Choi: Kim Sugon and Choi Dongil, *Hae il-lyeong jin-chul eu gyeong-je jeok hyo-ggwa bun-seog*, (Han-gug Gae-bal Yeon-gu-won 1985).

Komai d: Komai, Hiroshi, 'Are Foreign Trainees in Japan Disguised Cheap Laborers', in *Migration World*, Vol. 20, No. 1, Winter 1992.

Piore, M. J., *Birds of Passage*, Cambridge: Cambridge University Press, 1979.

Sassen, S., *The Mobility of Labor and Capital*, Cambridge: Cambridge University Press, 1988.

Wallraff, G., *Ganz Unten*, Koln: Kiepenheuer and Witch, 1985.

World Bank, *World Development Report*, New York: Oxford University Press, 1990.

Index

For Product Safety Concerns and Information please contact our EU representative GPSR@taylorandfrancis.com
Taylor & Francis Verlag GmbH, Kaufingerstraße 24, 80331 München, Germany

www.ingramcontent.com/pod-product-compliance
Ingram Content Group UK Ltd.
Pitfield, Milton Keynes, MK11 3LW, UK
UKHW020018200926
475702UK00014B/1951
9781138981065